# THE SOVIET POLITICAL AGENDA

*Problems and Priorities,*
*1950–1970*

## DANIEL TARSCHYS

*First published 1979 by*
THE MACMILLAN PRESS LTD
*London and Basingstoke*
*Associated companies in Delhi*
*Dublin Hong Kong Johannesburg Lagos*
*Melbourne New York Singapore Tokyo*

---

British Library Cataloguing in Publication Data

---

Tarschys, Daniel
  The Soviet political agenda
  1. Russia – Politics and government,
  1953–
  I. Title
  354'.47'03      JN6524

ISBN 978-1-349-03866-4     ISBN 978-1-349-03864-0 (eBook)
DOI 10.1007/978-1-349-03864-0

---

# Contents

# Acknowledgements

This study was carried out at the Department of Political Science of the University of Stockholm, with financial support from the Swedish Council for Social Science Research. I am much indebted to the three research assistants who took part in the project, Michal Drzewiecki, Leonid Kantor and Bertil Nygren, and to Charles Rougle who translated the Swedish manuscript into English. Chapter 2 of this book has previously been published in the *European Journal of Political Research* vol. v (1977) as 'The Soviet Political System: Three Models'.

DANIEL TARSCHYS
May 1978

# 1 Problems in Soviet Politics

'Politics', writes Spiro, 'is the process by which a community deals with its problems'.[1] This book is a study of the problems which the leaders of the Soviet Union attempted to induce their society to resolve during three different years after the Second World War: 1950, 1960, and 1970. It is therefore a study of political content. It defines the shortcomings observed by the leadership, the people and the organisations they tried to mobilise, and shows the measures they decided to take to remedy these. It also considers the leaders' values and views of man and the world, and it deals with political change during a period extending from Stalin to Brezhnev and from relative poverty to relative prosperity.

The subject is a vast one. Many scholars choose to employ all available sources to settle just one question. Here the approach is the opposite: a single source has been used to elucidate several questions. Both research strategies are based on the assumption that science is a collective and cumulative undertaking. The old German titles were often introduced by a *Beitrag zur Kenntnis* . . . The present study should be regarded as just that: a contribution to our knowledge of Soviet politics, socialist politics, and perhaps to some degree politics in general.

The source that is exhaustively exploited in the study consists of the editorials in the daily newspaper *Pravda*, the official organ of the Central Committee of the Communist Party of the Soviet Union. These texts are studied carefully by everyone desiring to keep abreast of the reactions and ambitions of the Soviet Party leadership, including East European governments, diplomats and journalists in Moscow, and millions of career-conscious Soviet citizens. *Pravda* has often been used in research on Soviet politics, but has never been subjected to a methodical and comparative study, apart from a few quantitative content analyses of sharply restricted problems. What is undertaken here is a systematic and multidimensional ransacking of the informational content of the *Pravda* editorials, with the aim of establishing the 'agenda' determined by the apex of the Soviet social pyramid for political and administrative work at all lower levels. The source materials have been prepared with the help of information retrieval, a technique that has been widely employed in bibliographical work, but seldom for analytical research purposes. The

1

technique is based upon the programmed retrieval of selected information from a textual mass stored on magnetic tapes. Strategic passages from numerous *Pravda* editorials have been extracted, punched, recorded, and then sorted according to a great many different retrieval procedures. The primary advantage of the method is that hypotheses can be formulated and revised accordingly during the course of the work. Whereas conventional quantitative content analysis is based on a very sharp reduction of informational content by coding, which forces the researcher to restrict his questions at an early stage, information retrieval allows him to make an 'open' analysis.

The editorials in *Pravda* are orders of the day to officials at all levels of the Soviet system. Their purpose is to channel energy toward stated objectives. The materials employed in the present study consist of the concrete instructions in these orders, and 5523 such instructions have been examined. Taken together they provide a picture of the priorities of the Soviet Party leadership and the shifts that have occurred in those priorities in the course of time. They indicate which political problems the leaders have tried to tackle.

Political problems may be said to be the key point of the study. Following an initial provisional definition of the concept in the section immediately below, the next chapter will return to the question of how political problems are registered in Soviet society, and in the chapter after that will be discussed the sort of problems reflected in the *Pravda* sources.

## 1.1 WHAT IS A POLITICAL PROBLEM?

The Greek *problema* originally meant 'something cast forward' or 'something posed'; a question, a riddle, or a scientific assignment. It represented an intellectual challenge, and that sense is still present in modern usage. A problem may be difficult to solve, but it is at any rate something solvable. If the difficulties cannot be overcome we no longer have a problem, but rather a fact of life to which we must reconcile ourselves. Any state of things or course of events that cannot be influenced or modified is not so much a problem but a predicament. The notion that our physical, social, economic and intellectual surroundings confront us with problems is inseparably bound to the faith in progress inherent in both Marxism and liberalism. When the world around us is defined as problematic, this is not an expression of a resigned view of society, but rather of a constructive and optimistic attitude. 'Problem' is a word in the vocabulary of social engineering.

But a problem is also something that demands energy. If a goal can be attained easily there is no problem. 'A person may be said to have a problem if he is motivated toward a goal and his first goal-directed response is unrewarding', writes the psychologist Johnson.[2] The emphasis according to him must lie on 'first' and 'unrewarding'. Problem-solving is a series of activities through which a subject attempts to attain something that he has failed to achieve on the first try. A problem, then, must hover somewhere between the possible and the impossible; the obstacles must be neither easy to overcome nor insurmountable. 'Problems are obstacles perceived on the road toward goals', notes Spiro.[3] Together with Johnson he stresses that problems are always associated with goal-rational behaviour. An object does not become problematic until it blocks a striving to attain a goal. The Alps, for example, do not in themselves constitute an obstacle, but when Hannibal tried to force his way into Italy with his elephants and soldiers they obviously became one. The perception of a problem presupposes motivation and frustration. Only when someone wants to cross the mountains and believes it possible do they then present a problem.

Thus, problems have no independent objective existence.[4] The mere fact that certain people are living in destitution, for example, does not mean that they regard their poverty as a problem. For that to be so they need to believe that a better life is possible and have a desire to better their lot. 'Problemisation' does not occur until insights have been deepened and ambitions raised. From this point of view, poverty can appear as a greater problem in a relatively rich society than in a relatively poor one. As the definition is treated in the present study, a problem is not a reliable measure of objective conditions, but rather a combination of objective circumstances and subjective judgements of what is possible and desirable.

It follows that problems can arise in different ways. Johnson's definition presupposes that motivation is a constant, and that the problem is not generated until the subject's first attempt to attain his goal fails to succeed. This is undoubtedly quite correct in the short term, but in a longer perspective it is also possible to influence motivation. Without changing the objective circumstances, the subject can be impressed with new conceptions as to what is possible and desirable, so that previously accepted conditions are seen as problematic. Consequently, that something is 'problemised' may be due either to the fact that:

(1) the subject notes an insufficient measure of goal-achievement in his first attempt to attain a desired goal (Johnson); or that
(2) the subject has acquired new notions as to what is possible; or to the fact that
(3) the subject has acquired new conceptions as to what is desirable.

'Problemisation' introduces a process which might be divided up schematically as follows:

(1) *Registration* – the subject observes a discrepancy between the desired and obtained results of an action or event;

(2) *Diagnosis* – the subject localises and examines the disturbance thought to be the cause of the discrepancy;

(3) *Analysis* – the subject traces the disturbance to independent variables;

(4) *Solution* – the subject determines how the disturbance is to be corrected or eliminated;

(5) *Action* – the subject takes measures to implement the solution;

(6) *Evaluation* – if the result proves unsatisfactory, the subject returns to (1).

As the final point above suggests, problem-solving is usually an iterative process. If the first effort fails, new methods are tried; a new diagnosis, a new analysis, a new solution, or a new action. Success is one way out of this circle, giving up is another. One common reason for giving up is the acquisition of new knowledge: the subject's experience of the problem-solving process upsets his original idea of what he can achieve. Another conceivable reason why attempts are abandoned is because the subject's preferences change and the goal no longer appears to be so desirable. It is often possible to observe an interaction between these two courses of events – the subject's view of reality and values are greatly dependent upon one another in both 'problemisation' and 'de-problemisation'.

The decisions at various stages in the problem-solving process may be either individual or collective. For Johnson, who has an individual in mind, it is natural to see problem-solving as a psychological activity. Spiro, on the other hand, speaks of how a community deals with its problems, and from that point the process may be interpreted as political. In the latter case the subject is split – a community contains many different views as to which problems ought to be considered, which diagnoses ought to be made, which causes ought to be established, which solutions ought to be selected, and which measures ought to be taken. The politically organised society, however, also has instruments for aggregating these views, reducing the number of problems to be treated, producing authoritative decisions, taking measures to implement those decisions, and processing information received about the results. The 'problemisation' of a question thus becomes equivalent to its being 'politicised' or brought up for consideration by the political authorities. Analogously, the question is politically 'de-problemised' or 'de-politicised' when it no longer attracts political attention. To put it simply, then, the political problems of a society are what the political institutions of that society are occupied with.

## 1.2 THE STUDY OF POLITICAL PROBLEMS

Several trends in modern political science place political content in the foreground. Most of these fall under the broad umbrella of *public policy research*. A rapid expansion of policy studies has led to a shift in interest from the forms of decision-making to its results and effects. Researchers no longer restrict themselves to investigating the operation of political institutions, but also want to know what such bodies accomplish. This brings them to the question of the sort of problems considered in the political system. The following represent pertinent approaches to that question:

(1) A series of studies on the *political problemisation* process start from Bachrach and Baratz's thesis that political power cannot only be traced through the decisions that are made in a society, but must also be sought in 'non-decisions', i.e. in decisions by the authorities to stifle political demands or prevent them from being translated into authoritative decisions.[5] This perspective has been taken in discussions of the prerequisites for the transformation of social conditions into political issues. In *The Un-politics of Air Pollution*, for example, Crenson has studied how air pollution became a political problem in East Chicago but not in the neighbouring city of Gary, in spite of the fact that the objective circumstances were comparable.[6] Another environmental study has proposed ten different indicators of 'issueness' that can be used to measure 'the transformation of a fact of life into a political issue'.[7] A third book takes a broader grip on the subject, and attempts to explain the construction of 'the political agenda' in American society.[8] Expressions such as 'agenda-setting' or 'agenda-building' have become common concepts in the literature on political problemisation.[9]

(2) The question of just which problems are included on the political agenda and thereby become central *national goals* constitutes the theme of another group of studies. The goal-catalogue compiled in America by the President's Commission on National Goals in 1960, for example, has been used as the starting-point for an attempt to reconstruct the values and questions given highest priority in American politics since 1776. Through a content analysis of State of the Union Addresses the author found that the 'democratic process' was the primary topic during the first century of the republic, 'economic growth' and 'the individual' had the highest frequencies during the first half of the twentieth century, and 'economic growth' together with 'arts and sciences' received particular attention in the period 1954–64.[10] A German scholar has made a similar study of the shifts in American presidential priorities during the 1960s (see Figure

1.2.1.)[11]. An attempt to understand the changes in Soviet politics up to 1943 has been made by Yakobson and Lasswell, who analysed the content of the slogans propagated by the Communist Party for the May Day demonstration.[12] Their graph illustrating the decline in slogans urging world revolution and the combating of counter-revolution, and the increase in those oriented toward domestic reconstruction, is presented as Figure 1.2.2.

(3) A third content-oriented trend consists of comparative research on *state activities*, including a number of studies on public expenditures, which attempt to chart and explain differences in the level of activities through the course of time and between various political units.[13] The temporal perspective in certain such investigations is very long; Crowley, for example, tries to show fluctuations between state interventionism and *laissez-faire* ever since the eleventh century.[14] In most cases, however, the subject has been the modern expansion of the state. Basing his investigation on the changes that have occurred during the past century in the organisation of ministries in thirty-two states of the European type, Rose examines the shifts that have taken place in public activities. He distinguishes between three main activities ('defining', 'mobilising physical resources', and 'social services') and establishes that they replace each other successively as expansive and central state functions.[15] The studies on state activities also include a number of works in the area of political development and modernisation which advance hypotheses on the functions of the state at various stages of the historical process.[16]

All the categories above deal with the content of politics, but the three are oriented toward various phases of political problem-processing. Research centred around 'issueness' and 'political agenda-setting' deals primarily with the transformation of social conditions into political questions and with the selection of political issues. The studies which attempt to interpret 'national goals' are based on indicators reflecting the priorities of the political decision-makers. Here we no longer consider the early stages of problem-solving because we are in the middle of the process or even near its end – the leaders have already taken a position and present a hierarchical list of their preferences in order to gain support from certain groups in society. In the third category – attempts to chart changes in state activities – the focus is moved another step forward. That a given public activity is undertaken is no certain indication that there is a political problem as defined here, but the activity does testify to the fact that the question has at least been political. What government actually does constitutes a kind of résumé of concluded and not-yet-concluded problem-solving processes.

These three categories indicate that political problems may be regarded at different stages of their life-cycle – *in statu nascendi, in vita,*

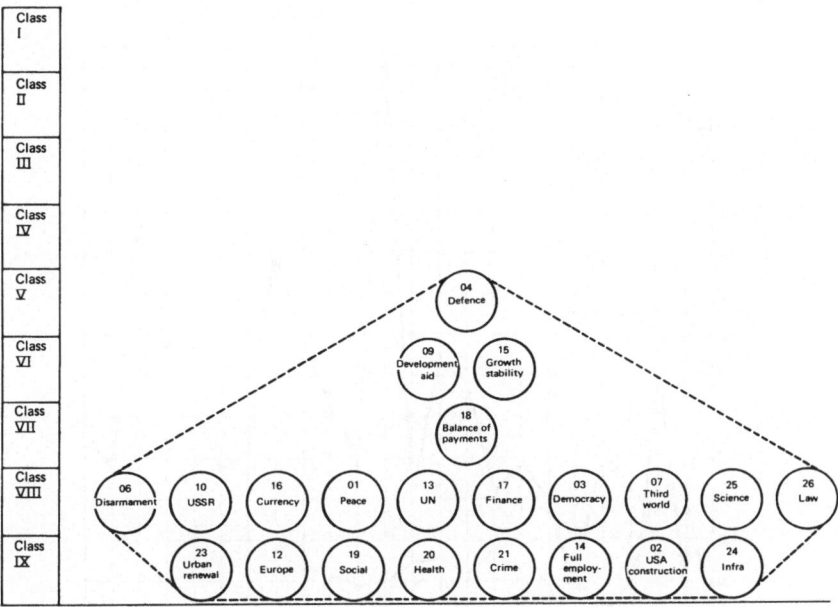

The goal hierarchy of the Kennedy administration 1961

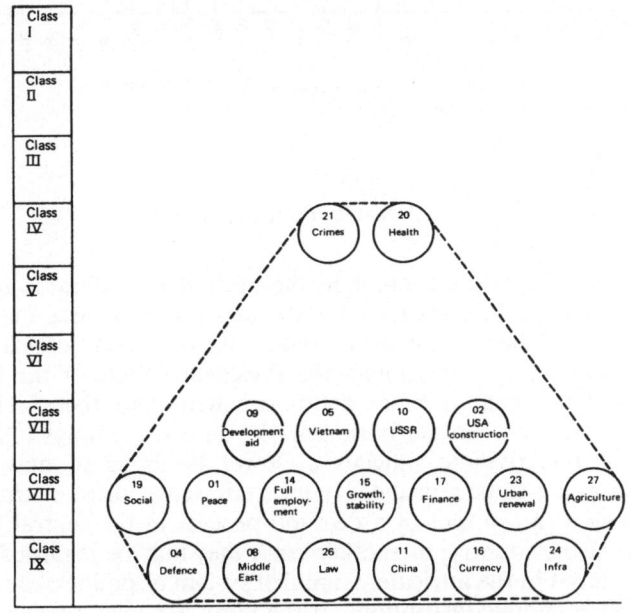

The goal hierarchy of the Johnson administration 1968

Fig. 1.2.1 American goal hierarchies

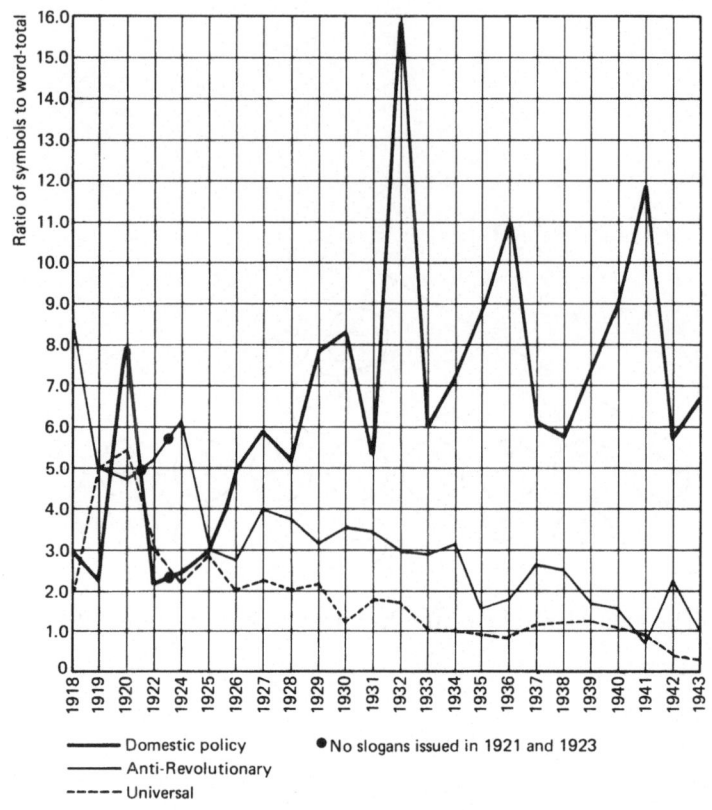

FIG. 1.2.2  Soviet goal hierarchies

or *post mortem*. At which point in the cycle it is preferable for the
observer to cut in depends to a great extent on the source materials
at his disposal. The present study makes use of a body of materials
which, to some degree, resembles the President's State of the Union
Addresses, but which is more action-oriented than these. The instructions examined contain both remarks on shortcomings in Soviet
society and directives to officials at lower levels as to how these
shortcomings are to be remedied. In a certain sense, these instructions
may be seen as an output of a decision process in the central power
apparatus of the country; in another sense they may be regarded as an
important input in the intricately ramified system of political, administrative, and economic institutions. If the term 'agenda' is reserved for

questions that are considered by political institutions, the instructions in *Pravda* provide only posthumous evidence of the issues, but in a broader sense these instructions may be said to constitute an agenda for all levels under the Politburo in the Soviet power pyramid. For the content of the *Pravda* editorial is an agenda in the most literal sense of the word, a daily answer to Bolshevism's classic question 'chto delat?' ('What is to be done?').

When Lenin and Chernyshevsky before him posed that question they addressed themselves to a movement that functioned outside and against the established system. Now the same question is raised and answered by the rulers of the system, and the measures prescribed are aimed at the system's development and consolidation. Before tackling the problems that occupy the leaders, we shall take a closer look at some different approaches to the political system of the Soviet Union – the totalitarian model, the pluralist model, and the bureaucratic model. In this discussion three alternative interpretations of how problem-solving processes are initiated in Soviet politics will be presented.

# 2 The Soviet Political System: Three Models

'Politics begins where there are millions,' Lenin once said.[1] That embraces the vast scope of the political process, but it also says something about the difficulties involved in the study of politics. Social interplay among a few people – in a family, a club, a business enterprise – is something one can observe and survey in an overall perspective, in even the physical sense. Social interplay among millions is much more difficult to grasp. The political life of a society is so comprehensive and many-sided that it can never be encompassed by the observations of a single researcher. What we see are but parts of a greater whole – fragments which we piece together to form patterns that become comprehensible only through the identities that can be glimpsed between new and old observations.

Political theory and rhetoric abound in such analogous figures of speech. During the course of history the state has often been described as a ship, a school, a body, or a machine; and its rulers have been likened to fathers, teachers, shepherds, or servants. In international politics we speak of balance and imbalance, tensions and explosions. Struggling classes and estates have often sought vindication in social contracts and natural rights. Metaphors borrowed from nature, from the world of everyday experience, and from neighbouring social sciences have always flowed through political science and served as instruments of interpretation in political analyses.

When we speak of the 'political system' of a country, we must not forget that this is also an instrument of interpretation. The systems theory (or cybernetic) vocabulary that has invaded the modern social sciences is free of many of the narrow premises with which older political models were burdened, but it is none the less based on a comparison that is anything but proven – namely a similarity between politics and the automatic control circuit. As a synthesis (at a higher level) between organicism and mechanicism, two time-honoured traditions in the social sciences, systems theory may certainly be said to be better equipped than any of its predecessors to provide a neutral language of analysis, and the relativisation of its key notions achieved by Bertalanffy, Boulding, and others has made it more unbiased and thus more useful. But the idea of a political 'system' still contains certain notions of

10

normal properties and processes (integration, equilibrium tendency, feedback, entropy, the dichotomy of control subject – control object, etc.) which easily harden into axioms, although they deserve only the rank of working hypotheses. When we speak of the 'Soviet political system' in the present study, this risk should be kept in mind: the term 'system' will be used in its vaguest and least pretentious meaning.

Interpretative instruments fetter ideas, but they are nevertheless indispensable in political analyses. Without certain fundamental assumptions on the structure of society and the nature of politics, observations of individual events and actions cannot be meaningfully interpreted; our observation fragments remain but fragments. A speech by a Party secretary, the appointment of a minister of defence, or a decision relating to the economic plan in the Soviet Union tell us nothing unless we have some idea of the usual procedures in connection with such speeches, appointments and decisions, of the roles and functions of the actors involved, of the forms and effects of the measures. Such ideas, which are often influenced by more or less abstracted comparisons with patterns from other societies or other disciplines, are often encountered in the form of stylised pictures of the political system's construction and operation. In the study of Soviet politics there exists an abundant assortment of such models and fragments of models which have guided analysts in compiling and interpreting their data. Paying what has become the customary obeisance to Kuhn, we could speak of different paradigms in the study of Soviet politics, but since that would require us to stretch Kuhn's ambiguous notion – one observer has noted twenty-one different meanings of the term in the work in which it was coined – it may be more suitable to restrict ourselves to a better established usage and simply call the various ways of regarding the Soviet body politic different models of its political system.[2] In order to introduce and at the same time trace the origins of the alternative interpretations that will be used in the present study, we shall in this chapter describe two classical models in research on Soviet politics, the *totalitarian* and the *pluralist*, and the as yet incomplete synthesis of these two views which will here be known as the *bureaucratic* model.

## 2.1 SOME TENDENCIES IN RESEARCH ON THE SOVIET UNION

Sweden, together with a handful or so of other states, functions in many countries as an archetype in the discussion of social systems. As one of several reform models, Sweden is often viewed in the light of domestic considerations. Supporters paint a bright picture of the Swedish welfare system, whereas sceptics are drawn to its darker sides. Different criteria produce different results. The controversial social pattern of Sweden forces all engaged observers to take a stand: is it *that* good, or is it not *that* good? Even a reporter who has no definite notions as to the relevance of Swedish solutions to the problems of his own country can sense the presence of the questions. In analysing a controversial social system it is difficult to avoid thinking about the side-effects one's presentation may have. The subject itself seems to be electrically charged.

Other archetypes confirm this pattern. The United States, the United Kingdom, and France have all functioned as paragons for social and political reforms. Yugoslavia became a disputed model in the debate among radicals after the Second World War, as did Cuba and China later. Whenever a positive view of a foreign society has become widespread, a 'counter-literature' has arisen pointing to the other side of the coin. The power of example is so significant in politics that aggressively attractive ideals must be neutralised. How an archetype is to be presented and evaluated can in such a way become an important issue in the political competition among people and ideas.

Motives such as these have played an important role in the study of Soviet politics. With the October Revolution of 1917 Russia became a central archetype throughout the developed world. The new Soviet society aroused both hopes and apprehensions, and polemical purposes commonly slanted the accounts that reached other countries. As the greatest social innovation of the age, the Russian experiment was observed with both curiosity and strong feelings. The power struggle within the country also left its mark upon the ideas that outsiders formed about the new system. The heat generated by the Revolution never cooled in the literature on Russia of the inter-war period. As long as White, Socialist Revolutionary, Menshevik Bolshevik, and eventually even ex-Bolshevik versions competed with one another, practically all analyses were coloured by strong convictions.

The emotional feelings generated by the Soviet Union were perhaps no less intense during the first short-lived détente after the war and during the years of the Cold War, and they continued to leave their mark on Western analyses. But accompanying the increasing distance in time from the great upheavals, there followed all the same a kind of restraint which made possible a more scientific study of the Soviet experience. It was still impossible for many observers and researchers to regard Soviet society *sine ira et studio,* but there arose none the less an interest in its distinctiveness that was more empirical than normative. If the Soviet Union continued to a certain degree to be an archetype in political debates, it also became such an archetype in scientific discussions. At the same time, the conditions for methodical studies of the operation of the system were variously improved. Area studies in Soviet politics began to take form.

As we view the short history of this field, it seems obvious that conceptions of the Soviet social model are still strongly influenced by the international political atmosphere.[3] The Western image of Soviet politics still serves offensive and defensive purposes, and even if scholars themselves may not wish to contribute to the moulding of public opinion (seeing themselves instead as objective seekers of truth), they have hardly succeeded in escaping the ideological tensions of the surrounding world. The same is true, to an incomparably greater extent, of the research being done in the Soviet Union on Western politics. One indication of the influence big-power politics has indirectly exerted on scientific developments can be seen in the shifts that have taken place in the Western image of the Soviet Union during the last few decades. Thus there was an apparent ambition in the research of the sixties to find other tools for understanding the socialist societies than the instruments designed during the days of the Cold War. One natural explanation of this reversal is that the Soviet archetype began to be perceived as less threatening and the West could therefore lower its guard. International détente affected the intellectual community as well, paving the way for a more refined view of planned economies.

Another important factor in this development was the moderation that took place in East European politics. After Stalin's death there appeared – to quote Karl Deutsch – 'cracks in the monolith', and it became increasingly obvious that a more complex political pattern was beginning to develop. This process stimulated the search for new instruments and objects of observation, undermining at the same time the concepts held by many scholars as to the stability and invariableness of the Soviet governmental system. There evidently existed, within the framework of the social formation that emerged out of the Russian revolution, several variant systems, and certain elements that were regarded earlier as being permanent no longer appeared vital to the continued existence of the system. De-Stalinisation in the Soviet Union and the emergence of a more differentiated political structure in the Eastern Bloc encouraged new interpretations of the operation of the socialist state.

A third reason for the revision of the Western image of Soviet society during the past twenty years is to be found in the internal development of the social sciences. During the early post-war period there arose a number of centres for area studies, which were intended to provide an interdisciplinary informational base for research in various fields. These institutions effectively stimulated education and research in such fields as Latin American studies, African studies and Soviet studies. One recognised drawback in the area orientation, however, was its isolation from the theory of the various subjects. The reaction against this state of affairs coincided with a general expansion in comparative research. There was increasing interest during the sixties in integrating research on Soviet government with comparative political science, and a number of new instruments of analysis and new theoretical frameworks began to be used in the study of socialist countries. A growing interest in development and modernisation also resulted in a partial shift of perspective – where certain observers of the fifties had seen a stagnated dictatorial society, many of those of the sixties perceived a model for development through effective mobilisation.

The three developments described above – the successive devaluation of the Soviet archetype in Western political debates, de-Stalinisation, and the new currents within the social sciences – have all contributed to renewing the Western image of Soviet politics. While conceptions in the fifties were to a great extent based on a comparison between different types of dictatorship, later analysts have tried to find more varied and differentiated theories. The totalitarian model, which long reigned in solitary majesty, has been called into question today, and a majority of sovietologists probably prefer some other viewpoint. No generally accepted model can be distinguished, however, and the field is open to many different interpretations of Soviet society. If there are more and more cracks in the Soviet 'monolith', the cracks in sovietology itself are no less numerous – the variety of opinions there has if anything increased during recent years. The three schools discerned here are consequently characterised by both breadth and diversity. The purpose of the following survey is not to provide an exhaustive description of the development of the study of Soviet politics, but only to elucidate certain central points and attitudes in the research of the past few decades.

## 2.2    THE SOVIET UNION AS A TOTALITARIAN SYSTEM

The totalitarian model may be said to be rooted irf Bolshevik ideology. A strong organisation was from the outset a key point in Lenin's political theory. In the party doctrine he developed in *What Is to Be Done?* (1902) the notion of a firmly united, disciplined and ideologically conscious vanguard was a fundamental element, and when the Bolshevik faction seized power it was natural that the principles that had guided the revolutionary struggle should also guide the effort to consolidate achieved victories. The politico-administrative philosophy asserted by the new government after the October Revolution was closely related to the Bolshevik Party's doctrine. Hierarchically authoritative chains of command, insistence on the meticulous execution of assigned missions, strict control, and severe penalties became at an early stage essential components in the normative theory of the Soviet state. At what tempo and to what extent this programme was realised is a difficult empirical question, but there can be no doubt that the Bolsheviks had far-reaching ambitions. They proceeded from the view that the new society ought to be governed from a single power centre, in accordance with a single firm Party will.

'The dictatorship of the proletariat' was the term used to characterise this system. The expression contained a reference both to the classical notion of dictatorship – the form of government in the Roman Empire in times of danger – and to contemporary recollections of dictatorial rulers. The power that was to be established was forceful and uncompromising. Its function was to liquidate feudal and capitalist social patterns, and erect a new social order. The subjugation of the old ruling classes and the disintegration of the institutions that had upheld their economic exploitation of the people were to Lenin mechanical and military operations. The state was an 'instrument', an 'apparatus', or even a 'bludgeon' to be used against the class enemy. Obviously, it was the proletariat and its leadership that were to wield the club and amass all power in the society. From this point of view, all theories advocating a division of power or restrictions in the jurisdiction of the state were bourgeois or petty bourgeois aberrations. The Bolsheviks defined the political arena in military terms: it was a field on which two forces confronted one another, where only the utmost discipline and unity could guarantee victory. The new Soviet state was an army, and it had to be ruled like an army if it was to survive.

With the successive stabilisation after the end of the Civil War, the programmatic demands in the Bolsheviks' doctrine acquired an increasingly firmer foothold in reality. The Soviet Union began to appear as a system guided with tight reins from a single centre. Opposition was suppressed, first outside the Party and then within it. A number of organisations – trade unions, co-operative societies, etc – which for a time after the Revolution had been allowed to operate relatively freely, were bound more tightly to the Party and state leadership, and in official doctrine they began to be defined as 'transmission belts' between Party and masses. At the end of the NEP period there was a further expansion of the state-directed sector of the economy. The government's control of society was both deepened and broadened. In ideology as well as in practical policies, the Soviet state approached the ideal model of the dictatorship.

The fact that this process took place in parallel with the consolidation of Fascism in Italy and the decomposition of democracy in Germany invited comparison. Different parts of Europe saw the establishment of systems supported by mass political movements, aspiring to a mono-polist control of society. There were also a number of structural similarities among these movements, such as the concentration of power within them, their leader cults, their intensive agitation, and their mobilisation of paramilitary groups for the suppression of all popular opposition. The ideological differences were of course considerable, but there were also points where views converged, as in their criticism of liberal democracy and the reformism which Popper later described as 'piecemeal social engineering'. To many observers, the communist and fascist states appeared as distinct variants of a single governmental model.

The term 'totalitarian' was one of several labels that came to be associated with this model. The expression is of Italian origin. In a speech before Parliament on 22 June 1925 Mussolini spoke of the Fascists' strong totalitarian will – 'la nostra feroce volontà totalitaria' – and he often used the word in the following years. The new Italy was designated in official usage by such terms as 'lo stato totalitario'. The German Nazis also used the expression but never made it a leading slogan. Schmitt attempted to formulate a Nazi theory of the 'totalitarian state', but Hitler himself did not use the term especially often, tending when he did to add 'so-called' before 'totalitarian'. His own favourite word was 'authoritarian', which became an attribute for both the new German order and a great many elements of Nazi culture. The term was never adopted in the Soviet Union as a designation for the Soviet system, but it was used after 1940 as a negatively charged label for the fascist systems of government.[4] Outside the dictatorships, totalitarian became during the latter part of the inter-war period a fairly common attribute for either the fascist states or for these and the communist states together. Sabine used it in his article on the state in the first edition of the *Encyclopedia of the Social Sciences* (1934) as a label for one-party systems. It was some time, however, before the structural similarities in the fascist and communist social orders began to generate comparative research and general theorising, and only after the war did the totalitarian model enter into the debate at the scholarly level. As usual, Minerva's owls did not appear until twilight.

The scientific atmosphere in which the totalitarian view of Soviet politics assumed form was deeply marked by post-war militant liberalism. A number of writers who had personally experienced Nazism, Fascism, or Communism contributed to a growing body of literature on the nature of dictatorial systems. Could those dreadful years provide mankind with insights into tyranny's mechanisms and structures, into political violence, and into the power and dynamics of hate in oppressed societies? Such questions were treated in many different disciplines, and researchers often traced the root of evil directly to their own field of study. Adorno and others attempted in *The Authoritarian Personality* (1950) to show the socio-psychological prerequisites of Fascism and Nazism. In *The End of Economic Man* (1939), Drucker analysed the subjection of individual rationality by the totalitarian system, and Hayek warned in his influential *The Road to Serfdom* (1944) of the moral degeneration and individual lack of freedom that inevitably resulted from a centrally planned economy. To these theoretical works were added a number of artistic portrayals of the dictatorial system and autobiographical accounts of its effects on the human plane. Koestler, Orwell, and Huxley expressed the disillusionment of the inter-war generation in widely discussed novels. A subtle but less noted work on the same theme was Milosz's *The Captive Mind* (1953), which analysed the influence of the totalitarian environment on the intellectual and his creation.

The philosophers and historians chose other approaches. Popper's *The Open Society and Its Enemies* (1945) attempted to link together the modern dictatorship and its predecessors. It aimed a general attack on intellectual systems which, in seeking to block out objectionable views, stagnated in their own fallacies. Popper drew a line from Plato to Hegel, Marx and the theoreticians of Fascism, classifying them all as enemies of the Open Society. Talmon performed a similar operation in a study, *The Origins of Totalitarian Democracy* (1960), which attempted to trace the fundamental ideas of dictatorship to their sources in the thought of the eighteenth and nineteenth centuries. But historical derivation – whether it was, as in Popper, conducted on the level of epistemology and social theory or was anchored in the theory of an unbroken national continuity or 'Caesarist' tradition, as in the works of certain experts on Russian and German culture – also had its adversaries. Arendt maintained in *The Origins of Totalitarianism* (1951) that it was incorrect to regard the totalitarian dictatorship simply as a variant of the old authoritarian police state, a Leviathan in modern guise. It was instead a system of an entirely new type that had never before occurred in history – a society in which lawlessness appeared in a constitutional mask, ideology was consciously used by a ruling élite for purposes of manipulation, and political control was rendered especially effective through the isolation of the individual. One of many means of achieving this isolation was organised terror, which dislodged the individual from his environment, dissolving his organic ties with such units as his family, his circle of friends, his fellow-workers or colleagues.

The literature described above focused on the pathology of the totalitarian society. These works dealt with diseased systems that exhibited a number of unpleasant symptoms, and the object of this diagnosis was to expose the root of evil. Various infected societies were compared with one another and with the ideal model of a healthy society, but it was always a matter of 'deviant' rather than 'normal' countries. To the extent that the democratic states appeared to be ailing, this was taken as a sign that the germs had spread or that the freedoms enjoyed in modern industrial society were constantly threatened by extermination. As in the case of conservative liberals such as Lippmann and Ortega y Gasset, observations of Communism's and Nazism's popular mobilisations occasionally resulted in pessimistic warnings against the potentially destructive influence of the masses on Western democracy. Knowing where the currents of totalitarianism led was for them a necessary vaccine against a development that had by no means yet been averted.

Militant liberalism, more or less successfully sublimated by social scientists who were also influenced by demands for unbiased scholarship, constituted the natural background to the study of the Soviet Union that emerged after the Second World War. The Soviet system appeared first of all as a *controlled society*, and the questions that attracted political scientists centred to a great degree around the forms of that total control. What power did the leader exercise? What instruments did the political élite have at its disposal to maintain its supremacy? How was public opinion manipulated? How did the leaders manage to master unruly forces such as religious and national minorities which resisted incorporation into the new patterns? Such problems attracted a great deal of attention in the research devoted to the democratic system's antithesis, the totalitarian dictatorship. Early postwar sovietology became the study of an autocracy, a one-party tyranny, and a conformist culture. To the extent it rose above the 'area' level and attempted to establish a comparative perspective on Soviet developments, it became a science of 'totalitarianism'.

The components of this concept were for a long time only faintly outlined. The leader, discipline, and the lack of political freedom were given keystones in all theoretical structures, but there were also other features of the totalitarian society which struck the eye. Friedrich and Brzezinski formulated a six-point definition according to which the totalitarian dictatorship was characterised by (1) an official ideology directed toward an ultimate historical goal and meant to be instilled into the entire population; (2) a single mass party, hierarchically organised, either superior to or integrated with the governmental administration and usually led by a single man; (3) a secret police with extensive authority and resources; (4) monopoly control of the mass media; (5) a monopoly of weapons and means of coercion; and (6) central control of the entire economy.[5] This 'six-point syndrome' gained considerable currency and soon figured in writings on the subject as a standard definition of the totalitarian social order. It failed to satisfy all observers, however, and the question of the fundamental properties of the dictatorial system prompted a discussion that was at times rather heated.[6] Again one could easily note a tendency towards 'professional cleavage' – economists were primarily interested in the organisation of trade and industry, sociologists studied human relations and group formations, and psychologists discussed the processes of socialisation and influence.

One characteristic noted within several distinct disciplines was the atomism of Soviet society. In the totalitarian state, spontaneous associations and autonomous groupings had been eliminated, and all organisations had been brought under the leadership of the Party. The boundaries between state and society had been erased, as had those between state and individual. Kornhauser developed this theory in *The*

*Politics of Mass Society* (1959), where he contrasted the 'mass society' with the pluralist society, which contained an independent social infrastructure. Local élites in the 'mass society' were dependent for their position upon the central leadership, and they therefore contributed to unifying the system. According to Kornhauser, totalitarian movements were not based on classes, but rather on socially isolated individuals from all classes. Only a society that possessed considerable autonomy, offered its élites extensive opportunities for formulating collective demands, and allowed individuals to belong to a variety of independent groups was capable of resisting the enslavement of the 'mass society'. Kornhauser's analysis resembled Arendt's in vital respects.

With their strong emphasis on the conformism and comprehensive central control of the dictatorial system, researchers subscribing to the totalitarian model tended to interpret the institutions of Soviet society in instrumental terms. Soviets, economic councils, trade unions, etc., were tools of the political leadership. An intricate network of institutions made it possible for the rulers to control and administer society effectively. The Party apparatus was the real muscle in this system, while the functions of state institutions were interpreted in various ways. For a constitutionalist current of thought one important task of these institutions was to provide a false front – the soviets were powerless legislative and executive organs which masked and legitimised the dictatorship of the Party. Other observers tended toward a dualistic view of the Soviet power structure – the Party and governmental apparatus were rival hierarchies which split the political élite at all levels into two blocs. This interpretation attained particular popularity in the years following Stalin's death, when the highest offices within the two hierarchies were held by different persons. According to one hypothesis, the economic and technical experts in the governmental administration functioned as the initiators of a liberalising, reformist process, whereas Party officials assumed a more conservative position.[7]

In Soviet society conceived as a controlled system, the political leadership constituted the most interesting object of study. To obtain knowledge of social developments and forecast the future of the society, it was above all necessary to investigate the men who ruled the country – their backgrounds, their views, and their part in the power struggle. The psychological profiles of the leaders were the focal point; if (as Friedrich and Brzezinski suggested in the second point of their 'syndrome') the dictator's will moulded society, it was obviously important to study the processes that had formed his will. Beside producing biographies of individuals, this approach also led to investigations of the collective characteristics of the Party élite such as Leites's study of the 'operational code' of the Politburo.[8]

The totalitarian model reached its prime in the fifties. De-Stalinisation, a relative liberalisation, economic reforms, and the dissolution of the one-man dictatorship into a collective leadership upset certain objective foundations of the model. At the same time a more conciliatory and optimistic view of Soviet society's developmental potential resulted in a re-examination of its inherent value judgements. The view that the model 'had served its purpose' became increasingly common; it had been accurate with respect to its analysis of Stalin's Soviet Union, but no longer provided a reliable picture of the system that emerged under his successors. A more radical wing went further, maintaining that the 'totalitarian' theory had from the outset been inseparably connected with cold war ideology and had never been a serviceable intellectual instrument.

One consequence of this criticism was that many scholars chose to work on a 'softer' variant of the totalitarian model. Criteria already outstripped by the course of events – primarily that of one-man dictatorship – were laid aside or supplied with the reservation that they were typical but not obligatory. The thesis, so strongly emphasised in earlier analyses, that the secret police and permanent purges were indispensable to the survival of the system retreated into the background. According to one sociologist, the political system that emerged out of de-Stalinisation could be described as 'totalitarianism without terror' – it was no longer an iron-handed autocracy, but a society ruled with more flexible methods, i.e. an 'administered society'.[9] Another approach lowered the limelight from the dictator to the political movement that held the totalitarian state together. Tucker pleaded for a comparative study of 'movement regimes', retaining the assumption that the revolutionary movement built up a machinery that made possible the realisation of its political goals.[10]

A further revision of the older model involved a reinterpretation of the leadership's aspirations. A number of researchers looked upon the post-Stalin political order primarily as a totalitarian system in which the ruling élite had lost its teeth. The revolutionary *élan* in the reconstruction of the twenties and thirties was contrasted with the increasing satiation of the consumer society of the sixties and seventies. The development did not consist in a change in the structure of the command organisation, but rather in the fact that the purpose of the commands now being issued was increasingly to maintain the prosperity already achieved. The totalitarian system appeared in this version as a 'petrified oligarchy', in which the Party retained its grip on society but did not use it to innovative ends.[11] In this light, ideology functioned as a set of radical symbols legitimising a conservative policy. The concept of oligarchic petrification was above all an answer to the theories popular in the first decade after Stalin's death, which predicted that convergence and liberalisation would develop concurrently with increasing well-being.

Another significant factor in the development of the totalitarian model was the shift at this time within the social sciences toward an interest in the Third World. The classic objects of comparison in earlier Soviet studies had been Fascist Italy and Nazi Germany. The totalitarian state was regarded from a predominantly static, liberal viewpoint: 'the controlled society' was above all an attack on the individual, a form of oppression aspiring to the despotic control of all human thoughts and actions. Through the perspective provided by modernisation theory, this control acquired a broader significance. It was a means of mobilising human resources, an instrument of social transformation. Now it became possible to fit the Soviet system into other patterns as well. Bolshevik strategy became one of several possible alternatives for the modernisation of a society. The Soviet system was compared in studies of the sixties with Nkrumah's Ghana and Nyerere's Tanzania. The totalitarian model also found a niche in such general theories of development as Rostow's *The Stages of Economic Growth* (1960) and Organski's *The Stages of Political Development* (1966), not as a necessary transitional stage, but as one of several conceivable political systems for the phase of accumulation and industrialisation through which any backward society must pass on its road to economic affluence.

These various interpretations shared the fundamental assumptions of homogeneity and control from the top, which constituted one of the cardinal points in the totalitarian model. Whether the Soviet Union was regarded as a dictatorship among other dictatorships or an underdeveloped country among other underdeveloped countries, its political system was specifically distinct from those of the Western democracies. The 'pluralism' of the capitalist or mixed-economy states contrasted with the 'monism' of the totalitarian society. Constitutionally, of course, the Soviet Union was a faithful reflection of the institutional system of liberal democracy, but its representative institutions and independent social organisations had different functions; the impulses they conducted travelled for the most part from the top down, not from the bottom up as in the Western democracies.

As the 'totalitarian' tradition within Soviet studies came under fire, however, this thesis also threatened to topple. The partisans of a global comparative approach in political science criticised the simple dichotomies which lowered an iron curtain between socialist and non-socialist industrial states. The supporters of the convergence theory detected a growing similarity in the social structure of the two political blocs, and in this connection there were also noted certain tendencies toward group autonomy in the socialist society. Was there not a 'pluralism' here, albeit of a different nature from that in the Western democracies? Interest in the influence of formal and informal groups on political decisions in Eastern Europe pointed toward new paths of research. A new perspective took form – Soviet society was no longer merely 'controlled', it also embraced rival strata and groupings which strove to influence its development in different directions. Nor was the Soviet polity unique, but contained elements and processes present in all political systems. Out of such comparisons sprouted the notions that laid the foundation for a new outlook on the socialist societies of Eastern Europe.

## 2.3   THE SOVIET UNION AS A PLURALIST SYSTEM

Just as the totalitarian model was rooted in a specific ideological soil – the sharp polarisation between democratic and dictatorial social orders of the early post-war period – the pluralist model was conditioned by the new atmosphere created during the years of international détente. Western scholars attempted to detach themselves from Cold-War phraseology and adopt a more understanding attitude toward the political systems of the Eastern Bloc. They began to discern familiar features behind the monolithic façade – in Soviet society as well as elsewhere were to be found strata and groups competing for power and a certain measure of freedom of movement for ideas and interests. The earlier notions of an iron-handed Party dictatorship contrasted with new observations of conflicts and controversies. True, socialist society provided its various groups and élites with fewer opportunities to participate in politics, but it did not exclude a political process of approximately the same model as in other countries. Comparative political studies afforded analysts new conceptual patterns and new objects of comparison: sovietology was no longer confined within the Moscow–Berlin–Rome triangle, but was now able to operate over broader fields.

The pluralist model directed attention to the inputs of the Soviet political system. If earlier scholars had been interested almost exclusively in political manoeuvres within the top leadership and the efforts of that leadership to translate its decisions into actions, interest was now focused on the process by which individual desires and aspirations were asserted. Professional and organisational groups were no longer only objects of influence – they were also potential political agents. Interests were articulated and aggregated through various channels. Institutions, structures and methods, of course, differed to a significant degree from those which supported the democratic societies of the West, but a socialist society still contained a political process of basically the same nature as that of other states. It was not purely and simply a dictatorship, but a system in which diverse collectives could voice their interests. If the cardinal points in the totalitarian model were control and command, the pluralist model emphasised above all dynamic competition and political process. The Soviet Union, to put it briefly, was a society much like ours, though a little different.

Like the totalitarian interpretation, this new outlook was rooted in a number of intellectual traditions and schools of thought. Political science in the fifties devoted a great deal of attention to groups in politics. One rediscovered classic was Bentley's *The Process of Government* (1908) – an elegant and European-inspired muck-raking attack on the idealistic democratic doctrines of the time. According to Bentley, concepts such as 'national interest' and 'our common best' were nothing but 'spooks' meant to conceal the selfish and corporative interests which were the real decisive forces in politics. The political process was governed not by lofty ideals, but rather by wilful groups which had to be identified and seen through if one were to understand the real workings of public life. By groups Bentley meant not only formal organisations, but 'any mass of human activity tending in a common direction'.

Truman, whose *The Governmental Process* (1951) breathed new life into this approach, operated with a narrower notion of the group. When correspondence in attitudes, actions, or social structure was not reflected in a formal organisation or a high degree of interaction, he preferred to speak of latent groups, and this category was decidedly less significant in his analysis than the well-organised groups. The pluralist renaissance of the fifties implied above all that attention was focused on interest groups. In opposition to the still dominant study of constitutional theory and practice, a new generation of political scientists turned to the investigation of the extra-constitutional components of the political system.

These impulses were first absorbed into Soviet studies through the vitalised Kremlinology that emerged after Stalin's death. Attention was turned to factions and power groupings in the political leadership. Methodologically, these analyses were close to the early studies of Soviet politics by men who had for the most part participated in the Russian revolutionary movement or had at least observed it at close quarters. They had the same awareness as the Bolshevik leaders themselves of the group competition present within the leadership. The idea that politics at the highest level was dominated by group conflicts (*gruppovshchina*) was borrowed directly from the Soviet leaders, and it became an essential instrument for the analysis of Soviet events in the works of writers such as the Menshevik Nikolaevsky and the former Comintern official Borkenau.[12] The former maintained contact with members of the Bolshevik leadership for some time, and was able as late as 1934 to compile a well-informed and detailed report on the group conflicts in the Party élite, based on a famous interview with Bukharin. The latter formulated a theory as to how the phenomenon of *shefstvo* (patronage) influenced the circulation of élites and the balance of power in the Party. According to Borkenau, it was important to note that leading politicians surrounded themselves with cohorts of auxiliary functionaries who often accompanied them throughout their careers, both up through the apparatus and back and forth across the country. By identifying and watching the Khrushchev men, the Malenkov men, etc., the researcher could draw conclusions and make predictions as to the changes recurring in Soviet politics.

The Soviet politics of the de-Stalinisation era offered an exciting field of application for such speculative theories. Journalistic reports and scholarly publications alike abounded in theories about the divisions and factional groupings within the Soviet leadership. At times groups formed on a purely personal basis were distinguished; at other times these formations were considered to be more distinctively ideological or strategic in nature. Certain observers perceived a significant gap between the governmental apparatus and the Party or between the managers and experts on the one hand and the political officials on the other. According to others, such alliances were surpassed in importance by sectoral loyalties – heavy industry had its advocates, light industry had others. Liberal and conservative sympathies were observed in cultural questions, orthodox Stalinist and modern technocratic tendencies were noted in Party matters. The majority of these analyses shared a marked orientation toward splits within the Kremlin itself. Antagonisms there attracted attention because they could provide information about the power struggle going on at the summit of the Soviet leadership. This power struggle then provided a basis for prognoses – a victory for the liberal faction or for the agriculture partisans laid the foundation for predictions of future developments. [13]

Analysis of the participation of different groups and organisations in the political process was deepened at about this time within the comparative study of political science from observations of individual cases to theoretical constructions aspiring to the level of generalisations. Dahl, Riesman, and others launched a 'pluralist' theory in the study of community power in Western democracies. According to these scholars it was wrong to regard American society, locally or nationally, as dominated by homogeneous and closely knit élites. The characteristic feature of the democratic system was rather a split between various power groups which, by controlling the decision process in different areas (Dahl) or by acting as negative power centres ('veto blocs') were able to effect a considerable dispersal of influence within the society (Riesman). The pluralist model of analysis, further developed by Dahl in his works on the 'polyarchical' system, stimulated a number of studies of politics within the industrialised countries.

At the same time new ground was being broken in the study of government in the Third World. Easton's general model of the political system and Almond's scheme of the political functions required in any political process – socialisation and recruitment, articulation, aggregation, communication, rule-making, rule implementation, rule adjudication – provided notions that could be employed as instruments in a comparison of widely differing forms of government as well as in a political study of non-governmental organisations.[14] Although system analysis and structural-functionalism were not based directly on a pluralist social theory, the broadening of perspective to which they led implied nevertheless the breakthrough of that outlook. After Easton and Almond, political science wrenched itself once and for all out of its constitutional framework and turned its attention to political behaviour at all levels of society and at all distances from the centre of power.

The effects of this breakthrough appeared clearly in the research on the Soviet Union that followed Almond's patterns. Barghoorn, who in his *Politics in the USSR* (1966) made the first structural-functional presentation of the Soviet system, devoted considerably more than half his book to the functions on Almond's input side. Even if the emphasis of previous analyses on the strict social control of the Soviet system was not completely abandoned, this shift of interest toward the genesis, articulation and aggregation of demands still marked a new departure. Competing groups gained significance in the Western image of the socialist polity, and the study of individual institutions emphasised the many nuances in their functions. In a more limited study using the same approach, Gehlen (1969) showed how the Soviet Communist Party fulfilled a variety of functions connected with the survival and efficiency of the system.[15] It was not merely an instrument of control for the leadership, but also a structure which participated in political socialisation, political recruitment, and in the choice, specification, and attainment of political goals.

The social analysis that grew out of this new orientation operated with a notion of the group which was broader than that used in Kremlinology. The focus of attention no longer rested exclusively on rival cliques, but also included competing élites or interest groups. The view that the socialist system contained a mosaic of groups which were in some measure able to behave like autonomous actors (or at least strove to do so) paved the way for a new interpretation of the political process. As a result of this, the dynamics of the Soviet system were not only perceived to result from the efforts exerted by a monistic regime of mobilisation, but could also be derived from the organisations and professional and national groups which in various ways sought to assert themselves politically. The idea also spread to East European thought, both in underground social criticism and in some accepted sociological research in Poland and Czechoslovakia.[16]

The most distinct formulation of the pluralist model was made in a widely noted article by Skilling (1966), who summarised the accumulated criticism of the totalitarian notional apparatus. Skilling showed that various types of group analyses had become increasingly common in the study of Soviet politics, and he suggested certain useful terminological refinements, distinguishing between three types of group:

To put it another way, three levels of 'groupness' may be distinguished. A group may be marked by certain distinctive characteristics, for instance, that all members are Ukrainian, or peasants, lawyers, or writers, *obkom* secretaries or managers. Such a 'categoric' group may or may not possess similar attitudes on matters relating to their group or on public issues in general. Certain common attitudes *may* be present, held either by all or the overwhelming majority of the group, or by a distinct section. The members of such an 'attitudinal' group may not, however, have an opportunity to express their views collectively, except in the most informal way, still less to make a specific claim on the public authorities for action corresponding to their attitude. Therefore, it does not constitute a political interest group in our meaning of the term. It is only when a common attitude, associated with, but not identical to, a common characteristic, leads to an expressed common claim that a 'political interest group' may be said to exist. [17]

The real political interest group, then, was a group not only *an sich* but also *für sich*. According to Skilling, it could be considered to perform several functions in the Soviet system. On the one hand, it expressed its own interests and functioned as an independent political subject. On the other, it was also a mediator between state and society, a filter that reduced the flood of demands, and a watchful eye on the lookout for social and economic problems that served to direct the supreme leaders' attention to areas calling for public action.

In 1971 Skilling and Griffiths returned with a collection entitled *Interest Groups in Soviet Politics,* which contained studies by a number of experts on various political interest groups in Soviet society: Hough treated Party officials, Barghoorn the secret police, Kolkowicz the armed forces, Hardt and Frankel the managerial élite, Judy economists, Simmons writers, and Barry and Berman the legal profession. Several of these analyses, however, violated the stated definitional framework of the book, since it could scarcely be shown that the 'categorical' groups considered were also held together by a subjective group identification. The 'three Cs' – consciousness, cohesion, and conspiracy – which Meisel had defined as appropriate characteristics of a self-conscious élite could not be discovered in any group. [18]

The question of the identity of the interest groups, however, was of great significance for the tenability of the pluralist model. A self-evident premise in the conception of a rivalry between professional, national or sectoral élites was that the various groups really strove to assert themselves in Soviet politics. The study of the self-consciousness and power aspirations of diverse groups presented in Lodge's book *Soviet Elite Attitudes Since Stalin* (1969) was therefore a potentially significant test of the theses assumed by the pluralist school. Lodge proceeded from a distinction in Brzezinski and Huntington's *Political Power: USA/USSR* (1964) between ideological and instrumental systems. The relationship between state and society in the former category was characterised by 'control and manipulation' on the part of the leadership of the ruling party, whereas the latter type of system was distinguished by 'access and interaction', i.e. various social groups were able to participate in politics and assert their interests. Like Brzezinski, Lodge maintained that the Soviet Union after Stalin had moved from the ideological pole toward the instrumental one, and he attempted in his study to determine the extent to which specialised élites had developed group identities and were demanding the right to participate alongside the Party in the political decision-making process.

Lodge selected as the foundation of his study signed articles in a number of professional newspapers and journals — *Kommunist* and *Partiinaya Zhizn'* for the Party apparatus, *Voprosy Ekonomiki* and *Ekonomicheskaya Gazeta* for the managerial élite, *Krasnaya Zvezda* for the armed forces, *Sovetskoe Gosudarstvo i Pravo* and *Sovetskaya yustitsiya* for the jurists and *Oktyabr, Literaturnaya Gazeta* and *Novyi Mir* for the writers. A selection of 600 texts per élite and year were coded for the eight years between 1952 and 1965, making a total of 24,000 texts. On the basis of these Lodge attempted to detect a tendency in attitudes toward the question of which groups ought to take part in making decisions. The number of times a text in a given publication mentioned its 'own' professional group was interpreted as indicative of the collective consciousness of that group, descriptions of the Party's contributions were used to evaluate its political role, etc. Despite small absolute figures, the author contended he could show a clear trend within the different Soviet élites toward a growing interest in political participation, stronger objections to the Party's power monopoly, a firmer group identification and consequently an increasing regard for the instrumental model.

Lodge's method of quantitative content analysis and his treatment of the data have been criticised.[19] Of greater interest here, however, is the circular argumentation inherent in his investigation. His observation of an increasing group articulation and a growing collective consciousness within the various specialised élites is based, as noted above, on the premise that the professional publications may be regarded as the mouthpieces of the various groups. This premise, however, is tenable only if we postulate that the groups already have considerable influence in Soviet society or at least control the specialised newspapers and magazines. Since the totalitarian model (or, to use Brzezinski and Huntington's terminology, the ideological system) presupposes that the lower and intermediate levels of the political pyramid are tightly controlled by the central leadership and that all specialised hierarchies are integrated into the Party's control of society, such a viewpoint is hardly undisputed. The pluralist hypothesis can scarcely be confirmed by presuming that which was to be proven, namely that newspapers such as *Krasnaya Zvezda* and *Literaturnaya Gazeta* really are the mouthpieces of the Soviet military and literary élites.

If the opposite view is correct – that is, if the specialised newspapers and magazines are rather channels through which the Party exerts influence on various collectives – a different interpretation of Lodge's data would seem reasonable. As Ionescu has noted, the Party uses appeals to professional pride as an important instrument of group mobilisation.[20] 'The Soviet physician', 'the Soviet writer', etc., are idealised figures constantly used in political preaching; the Party seeks to exert a moral influence on the various target groups by inculcating upon them the properties which characterise the conscientious professional. From this point of view, a rising frequency in references to diverse occupational categories is more than anything else indicative of an intensified effort on the part of the leadership to establish contact with the different sectors, and is by no means evidence of a professional group emancipation movement in conflict with the Party's aspirations to control.

A number of circumstances support the latter hypothesis. The Party watches over the Soviet press very closely and does not permit any major deviations from the established line. One efficient instrument of power is control over promotions: each Party organisation, except the very lowest, has among its functions the supervision of appointments within an allotted area, and for this purpose keeps special lists, so called *nomenklatura.* This surveillance embraces appointments within both the governmental apparatus and the public organisations – trade unions, the *Komsomol,* academic associations, etc. Hence, advancement within all types of institutions and hierarchies depends upon the good will of the Party organisations and no climbing is conceivable without the support of favourably disposed superiors.

Control of recruitment and promotion, of course, is an important instrument of government in all organisations (in the West as well as in the East) but the *nomenklatura* system lends the Soviet social structure certain distinctive features. Mosca, who in his *Elementi di scienza politica* (1896–1923) penetratingly analysed the significance of the promotional system in the exercise of political power, distinguished between the 'autocratic' principle (recruitment from above) and the 'liberal' principle (recruitment from below). In these terms, it is obvious that democracies of the Western model are characterised by a combination of both types – government officials are recruited for the most part autocratically, whereas politicians can to a certain extent advance according to the liberal principle by building up a local base of their own. Within the interest groups or special élites which constitute the framework of the pluralist society there is often a mixture of the two principles. Many careers, of course, are the result of autocratic recruitment, but a liberal element is present none the less; and the ability, in the event of a conflict, to appeal downward in the hierarchy to the members of the organisation or to their representatives encourages officials to pay greater attention to these lower strata. And to the extent that autocratically promoted officials are subordinated to liberally controlled politicians, there are also certain prospects that the liberal atmosphere will permeate administrative ideology.

The great insistence on discipline and loyalty accompanying the postulate of Party leadership over the whole of Soviet society creates a cultural complement to the autocratic promotional model of that society. The Soviet official is not only aware that his future career will be determined by the Party, he is also convinced that the Party line must be followed. If his ambition is to be accepted and respected by his colleagues, he is at the same time aware that such an attitude is not just one of several alternatives, but is rather an obligatory means of acquiring a good reputation in the Party. Local or sectoral ties can in the Soviet system never be a substitute for a foothold in the organisations in the charge of *nomenklatura*.

The distinction between these recruitment patterns has important implications for the pluralist model of Soviet society. It seems obvious that the Soviet system is at any rate not pluralist in the same sense as Western polyarchies. Even if interest groups in both types of polity may be thought of as functioning as two-way channels of communication for influence on the political leadership, on the one hand, and control by it, on the other, it is unlikely that the former function can ever develop fully in an autocratic society. The social atomisation of such a system cannot be overcome; given the organisational structure of the society, it will never become possible to rally together an interest group and express the special interests of a professional élite to the political leaders. The prerequisites for effective interest-group politics simply do not exist.

Thus, while the totalitarian model exaggerates the structural differences between the Western and socialist social orders, the pluralist model exaggerates their functional similarities. The partial insights afforded by the two perspectives are of course of lasting value; the analyses both of Freidrich and Brzezinski and of Skilling, to designate them as outstanding representatives of their respective schools, have contributed considerably to our understanding of the Soviet system. But neither the model based on contrasts nor that constructed on an extended comparison seems to do the subject justice. To regard Soviet society only as a controlled system is to ignore important aspects of its political order, but an interpretation that attempts to trace important decisions to the activities of interest groups also seems inadequate, because potential professional, ethnic, and religious groups have but negligible possibilities to lend force to the views advanced by individual representatives. The organisational model to be discussed immediately below may be regarded as an attempt to synthesise the two previous ones and neutralise the reasoning in analogies that detracts from their relevance to the study of the mature Soviet polity.

## 2.4   THE SOVIET UNION AS A BUREAUCRATIC SYSTEM

The fragmentation of society was an important theme in eighteenth and nineteenth-century political thought. Rousseau, Hegel and Marx all regarded individual wills as a threat to social solidarity and human morals. Marx saw an association of independent producers as a remedy for this division within 'bourgeois society'. Organised co-operation was considered to be an alternative to the market anarchy of the capitalist economy. Early organisational theory often presented the modern administrative apparatus in a similar way, as an ideal instrument for co-ordinating and uniformising social processes. Weber looked upon bureaucracy as the most splendid of all forms of organisation: 'Precision, speed, unambiguity, knowledge of files, continuity, discretion, unity, strict subordination, reduction of friction and of material and personal costs – these are raised to the optimum point in the strictly bureaucratic administration.'[21] A rationally controlled, disciplined governmental organisation appeared to be an answer to many of the problems posed by the extensive economic differentiation of modern society.

A developed governmental apparatus, however, also required its own differentiation. Classical organisational theory advanced a great many prescriptions for the administrative division of labour through the creation of bureaux, departments, divisions, etc., and these schemes received considerable practical application in administrative developments in various countries. But this expansion and specialisation was also accompanied by an increasing distance between different parts of the public sector, so that the organised and unorganised wholes gradually began to exhibit the same symptoms of disintegration. The fragmentation of the social system was reproduced in the governmental apparatus; large organisations appeared to contain approximately the same tendencies as large societies. Although the gaps were not as wide, quite obvious divergencies in outlook and ambitions also appeared *within* the administrative machinery. Added to this was kind of institutional obstinacy on the part of the various units that obstructed effective control by the higher levels. The notion of the bureaucracy as the perfect system of command began to crack.

Interest in such tendencies toward independence within the modern administration began to stir in the organisational research of the postwar period. In *Policy and Administration* (1949) Appleby criticised the established doctrine that reduced public administration to an exclusively executive function, ignoring its role in the shaping of political decisions. Simon, Smithburg and Thompson (1950) discussed the administration as a political subject in relation to its environment and superior authorities showing how organisations struggled to survive by mobilising external support.[22] Through his theory of limited rationality, Simon also contributed to deepening this perspective and demonstrating how the 'organisation man' determined his behaviour.[23] Studies on political economy devoted an increasing amount of attention to the sub-optimal solutions chosen by actors with limited areas of responsibility. Several works in political science and organisation theory established the administrative unit as an autonomous actor in the political system (Downs, 1967; Wildavsky, 1964; Niskanen, 1972; Rourke, 1969; Allison, 1971; and others).[24]

The notion of 'bureaucratic politics' became a fruitful point of departure for new interpretations of both domestic and foreign policy-making. It also brought out in relief the experience gained in the practical administrative reforms effected in the sixties and early seventies. A number of decision and control techniques (systems analysis, cost/benefit and cost/efficiency analysis, programme budgeting, etc.) were tested during this period in North America and Western Europe, but contrary to expectations they yielded relatively little. This contributed to undermining the premises relating to global rationality, synoptic decision-making and an identity of interests between administrative authorities on different levels, upon which the methods were based. These disappointed hopes gave rise to a number of 'disillusionist' writings which scrutinised the exaggerated claims and unrealistic presuppositions of modern rationalisation projects. They pointed to both the resistance generated by the narrow horizons and organisational self-interest of the authorities and to an unwillingness on the part of politicians to live up to the theoretical ideal of the decision-maker (Merewitz and Sosnick, 1971; Levine, 1972; Hoos, 1972; Thoenig, 1974; and others).[25] 'L'état c'est aussi une société', wrote a group of French observers in a book with the expressive title *Pour nationaliser l'Etat* (1968).[26] Such was the general conclusion of these works.

Another French scholar, Jean-Pierre Worms, derived the fragmentation tendencies within the administration from the new contacts that arose through the expansion of the public sector. Through its even broader contacts with diverse client groups, the administration tended to 'colonise' society. At the same time, it was also affected by society's values and demands. In this way the government apparatus absorbed the antagonisms in society at large: '. . . l'Administration est ainsi conduite à intérioriser l'ensemble des conflits sociaux de la sociéte. Reproduisant ces conflits en son sein, elle les transforme en conflits "bureau-cratiques" . . . .'[27]

The fragmentation treated in the above studies was thus of a different nature from that upon which previous conflict analysts had concentrated their interest. Social division was for Marx an inevitable consequence of class-antagonisms rooted in the system of production; but it was difficult to trace division within the administration to a similar source. Institutional conflicts among various parts of the administration seemed to have a more complex background. In part, the organisations aggregated the individual ambitions of their members – the desire for security, development of the personality, advancement, freedom of movement ('organisational slack'), etc. In part it was a matter of attitudinal differences created by different educational backgrounds, contacts with client groups, and other work experiences.

The tendency to identify with a particular part of the system was often strengthened by the fact that an *esprit de corps* or local patriotism was found to facilitate control within the institution, and was therefore encouraged by those in charge of that part of the system. A number of factors, therefore, contributed to producing the 'positionally' conditioned splits in the administrative system which Rufus Miles, a high official in the U.S. Department of Health, Education and Welfare, described with the phrase 'Where you stand depends on where you sit'.[28] 'Miles's law' might be said to mean that the official in a vast system can never be guided only by the goals established by the highest administrative levels, but is also influenced by the flood of information passing through his 'node' in the network, and by the individual and collective aspirations germinating in the neighbourhood of this 'node'. In the official interplay, therefore, the official often functions as a spokesman for a part of the system – a department, an institution, a level, a sector of the organisation, a segment of the population, or a certain complex of problems which he has dealt with.

Interest in the centrifugal forces in large organisations was accompanied by growing sympathy for the predicament of centralised government. The organisational studies of the fifties and sixties illuminated the decision-maker's sequential attention to goals, his limited capacity for assimilating information, his difficulties in obtaining neutral feedback from the activities under his control, and his dependence on the selective information furnished by various institutional or sectoral interests. Systems theory considered the phenomena of inertia and entropy which reduced the manageability of large organisations. These currents in the study of corporations and public agencies helped lay the foundation of a new approach to administrative systems. Alongside the traditional perspective of 'from the top down' there emerged a tendency to view organisations 'from the bottom up'. The boundaries between control subjects and control objects became increasingly hazy.

The absorption of these new viewpoints into research on Soviet government was favoured by several factors. For one thing, here were good natural prerequisites in the form of an extensively developed administration that seemed to contain many examples of bureaucratic politics and administrative fragmentation. For another, there had existed since even before the Revolution an organisationally oriented tradition in the study of socialist societies. The European Social-Democratic followers of Marx often pictured the socialist (or communist) land of the future as an association or cartel. As late as September 1917, Lenin described the socialist state apparatus as a huge bank with branch offices in all districts and factories.[29] The organisational model also occupied a prominent position in the political debate of the first two decades after the Revolution. Trotsky's dispute with Stalinism's bureaucratisation in *The Revolution Betrayed* (1937) and elsewhere included criticism of the fragmentation of the state machinery, and the ex-Trotskyist James Burnham adopted a similar outlook when he maintained in *The Managerial Revolution* (1941) that socialist and capitalist societies were both increasingly governed by a caste of hired officials.

In *Terror and Progress USSR* (1954), Moore based his bureaucratic model of the Soviet system on Weberian premises. Other students (Berliner, Granick, Armstrong) looked at the economic élite at the middle level, which created a better empirical basis for comparisons between the Soviet and Western bureaucracies and 'technostructures'.[30] Such similarities were noted in the 'convergence debate' which became especially heated in the late fifties and early sixties. Proceeding from his communicational model, Deutsch contended that the overloaded Soviet informational channels could easily burst the totalitarian system. The result would be 'a steady drift to peripheralisation and pluralisation of the centres of decision' and the decomposition of the centralised structure of the system.[31] But it was not until the appearance of some works by Meyer that the image of the Soviet system as 'a bureaucracy writ large' assumed distinct form. Meyer launched this idea in an article entitled 'USSR, Incorporated' (1961), where the Soviet Union was described as a bureacratic command structure with all the features familiar to students of bureaucracy, and he later developed his thesis in a larger work on the Soviet system which he dedicated to 'a type of personality that is becoming increasingly dominant in modern societies in both the American and Soviet variants, and therefore increasingly merits our careful attention and study . . . the bureaucrat'.[32] Meyer formulated the gist of *The Soviet Political System: An Interpretation* (1965) as follows:

The main theme of the preceding chapters has been that the USSR is best understood as a large, complex bureaucracy comparable in its structure and functioning to giant corporations, armies, government agencies, and similar institutions – some people might wish to add various churches – in the West. It shares with such bureaucracies many principles of organization and patterns of management. It is similar to them also in its typical successes and inefficiencies, in the gratifications and frustrations it offers its constitutents, in its socialization and recruitment policies, communications problems, and many other features. The Soviet Union shares with giant organizations everywhere the urge to organize all human activities rationally, from professional life to consumption patterns and leisure activities. It has in common with them a thoroughly authoritarian political structure, in which the élite is independent of control by the lower-ranking members of the organization, even though all or most giant bureaucracies in the modern world insist that their rank-and-file constituents participate in the organization's public life. Both in the USSR and in the large organizations elsewhere, the individual finds himself thrown into a situation in which unseen and uncontrollable authorities ceaselessly impose social change unwanted by the constituents. All human beings must live in a world they themselves did not make; but in modern bureaucracies they live in worlds someone is constantly seeking to remake. [33]

Daniels offered a similar interpretation of the characteristics of the system in an essay on the Soviet political development after Khrushchev. He maintained that a new kind of politics was beginning to manifest itself in the Soviet Union, a 'participatory bureaucracy' in which information and influences flowed in many directions. Daniels as well as Meyer traced this tendency to factors inherent in the nature of the bureaucratic system:

In any complex bureaucratic organization, it is impossible to function purely from the top down: all manner of influence – information, advice, recommendations, problems, complaints – must flow upwards . . . [34]

The upward flow of information within the Soviet administrative system was further elucidated in a number of studies on regional and local politics. [35] Hough demonstrated in *The Soviet Prefects* (1969) that the regional leaders, the first secretaries of the Party *oblast* committees, functioned to a considerable extent as a kind of 'broker politicians' between the decision-makers in their regions and Moscow. In another investigation centred on the same strategic power élite, Stewart attempted to survey the demands articulated by the *obkom* secretaries in their speeches and articles. In *Governing Soviet Cities* (1973) Taubman described local Soviet political life as 'bureaucratic politics'. [36] Focusing on power centres other than the Kremlin provided broader information on the conflicts between agencies on different levels and within various organisational hierarchies. It was not always possible here to define the different camps in terms of professional or attitudinal groups, because the tensions rather appeared to be connected with institutional ties and aspirations. As a suggestive alternative to the command society of the totalitarian model and the ideological and professional competitive society of the pluralist model, the Soviet system now stood out as a swarming bureaucracy with all the characteristic paraphernalia – jurisdictional disputes, tug-of-wars over funds, buck-passing, limited rationality, excessive formalisation, goal displacement, etc. In this literature, Soviet politics came to be regarded as politics among bureaux.

Even such a model may with some stretching of the term be said to be pluralist. Hough has suggested a distinction between 'classical pluralism', which implies that citizens can choose among the programmes of rival élites and freely organise to advance their own interests, and 'institutional pluralism', which instead presumes that all efforts to attain political goals take place within 'the official institutional framework'.[37] But if one reduces the political arena in such a manner, it seems doubtful whether it is worth while to speak of a social order based on competition and co-operation among vying groups. The concept of pluralism in the conventional sense of political science seems to be inseparably connected with the principle of promotion which Mosca defined as liberal, that is, 'promotion from below'.[38] The opposite phenomenon of autocratic recruitment occurs, to be sure, in all social systems, but a distinctive feature of the Soviet system is that this 'promotion from above' is totally dominant and that the political actors have no possibility whatsoever of challenging their superiors by appealing to a constituency. The interaction between different units within the Soviet system – whether these be enterprises, Party organisations or government agencies – therefore resembles that between different units in an administrative organisation rather than the relations among their counterparts in a Western pluralist society. To the extent that social interests are articulated and aggregated by such Soviet institutions, this happens in a manner more strongly reminiscent of the activities of, say, Swedish or American agencies than of the operation of independent public organisations. It is therefore not especially apt to characterise such manifoldness as pluralism (or, to use Hough's term, institutional pluralism). We choose instead to speak of a *bureaucratic* model.

Such a model does not deny the existence of totalitarian or pluralist features in the Soviet system, but it attaches greater importance to other properties. By defining the system as a giant organisation, it emphasises both its closed and compact character and the element of internal politics noted in large organisations by the modern social sciences. It does not restrict itself to tracing elements of control and supervision or elements of group competition within the administrative network, but also stresses the connection between these elements and the distinctiveness of the conflicts within the closed system. For it is precisely in the interdependence of different units that we find the source of constant antagonisms within the organisation and the origin of the specific structures through which these antagonisms are reconciled. The extensive integration of the system creates a relationship of mutual dependence among its various parts which stimulates actors on different levels to summon central intervention. The achievement of 'success indicators' by one sector or institution within an integrated system is greatly dependent upon the activities of other sectors or institutions, and failures in the latter also threaten the goals of the former. The political activity that evolves in order to assert such sectoral or institutional interests then assumes characteristics of the maneuvering that occurs within large organisations in connection with reorganisation, policy development, and the distribution of resources, etc. A distinctive feature of such intra-organisational tug-of-wars is that the goals established by the top leadership are generally accepted as a matter of course, and discussions centre round various ways of attaining these objectives. The typical strategy of the sub-system is to present its own aspirations as a means of accomplishing the goals toward which the entire organisation is presumed to be striving. [39] Conflicts of interest between sub-systems are to a considerable extent camouflaged by the harmony presumed to exist throughout the system.

## 2.5 THE MODELS AND THE POLITICAL AGENDA

The three models presented above offer us three alternative views of the Soviet political system and, among other things, three different hypotheses on the emergence of political problems – the process that has been called 'agenda-building' 'agenda-setting' or 'the transformation of a fact of life into a political issue'.

According to the *totalitarian* model, the Soviet Union is primarily a controlled system. The supreme political leadership has developed a collection of mutually complementary instruments for the penetration and supervision of society. Parallel informational networks have been constructed so that no one unit can gain autonomy or organise resistance. The power of promotion is purposefully employed to ensure the stability of hierarchically structured sub-systems. Discipline is maintained by means of penalties, which can at times be brutal. The cultural sphere is under close surveillance. The analogy to an automatic feedback loop is an apt one: the centre is definitely a control subject, while the rest of society appears as a conglomerate of control objects. Conscious control is exercised by the summit of society.

The model presupposes a strong will on the part of the Party leadership: political decisions are shaped by rulers who have considerable power over those around them and can themselves choose among various courses of action. The formulation of problems and the establishment of goals are controlled processes. The decision-makers function as rational actors in the sense that they themselves determine their objectives, acquire the necessary knowledge of alternative strategies, and decide which means will be used to attain set goals. Information about society is primarily something that is extracted, not something that flows toward the rulers from independent sources. The totalitarian model is based on the assumption that decision-initiative is for the most part the prerogative of the men in the Kremlin.

The *pluralist* model delineates a society split into categories with differing interests – professional, economic, national, religious, ideological etc. Each individual is theoretically ranged in many such categories, but his solidarity is in many cases dormant or latent, while in others it is activated or manifest. Which divisions acquire political significance in actual fact depends on the extent to which enterprising group leaders succeed in 'mobilising bias'. In the ideal type of pluralist system there is rivalry not only between opposing interest groups, but also between a variety of different 'cleavage projects' advanced by political entrepreneurs competing for the group loyalties of the citizens.

This competition makes possible the articulation of a great many demands and aspirations. The group leaders vie with each other in getting the problems of their particular categories on to the political agenda in order to gain the support of those in power. The latter for their part depend upon the support of the groups, and the political process thereby assumes the character of a social exchange. Information on shortcomings in society is pushed in toward the centre, and this responds by taking measures on the basis of that information. Decisions are to a great degree the result of the impulses transmitted by mobilised social groups toward the central power organisations.

Thus, while the totalitarian model emphasises the active element in the conduct of the political leadership, the pluralist model stresses the reactive and reflective ingredients. In the latter approach, the rulers' actions are regarded as responses to pressures exerted upon them or as efforts to tune to and provide for the interests of various groups. The *bureaucratic* model resembles the pluralist one in the respect that it also presupposes decentralised initiatives and a flow of information which to a significant extent can be controlled from below. There is an essential difference, however, in the view it takes of the group loyalties which govern the creation of the actors' opinions and the articulation of their demands. While the pluralist model emphasises the citizen's latent and manifest private interests, the bureaucratic model attaches great significance to his role as a member of a production unit. The individual is regarded as an organisation man, and the political antagonisms present in society are interpreted as tensions among different 'bureaux'.[40] In terms of systems theory, this means that input and output functions are for the most part performed by the same institutions. Bureaucratic agencies function not only as the executors of political decisions, but also articulate and aggregate the demands for these decisions. From this point of view, then, it is the formal institutions, rather than the top political leadership or the various interest catagories, that are assumed to be in control of the political agenda. Information on shortcomings in society is pushed in toward the centre from the institutions responsible for the various sectors of the Soviet national economy. A large part of this information consists of complaints about the imperfect attainment of goals by institutions other than those which are complaining. The most conspicuous political competition in such a society is a rivalry between organisations, and the result of that competition can be perceived in the decisions made by the rulers.

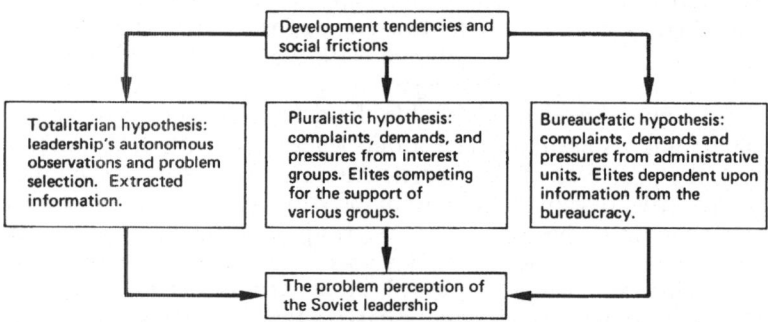

FIG. 2.5.1 Three hypotheses on the problem perception of the leadership

The three models are to be regarded as ideal types. They represent different ways of approaching the Soviet political system and thus different ways of interpreting political data. Such models can neither be confirmed nor refuted by individual empirical studies, but they can to some degree be tested on the basis of the relative plausibility of the interpretations to which they point. We cannot submit the models to the sort of rigorous test which would satisfy Popper, but can only make a cursory examination which may provide us with certain indications as to the functioning of the system. Proceeding from the decisions that comprise the data base of this study, we ought to be able to draw certain conclusions as to the components of Soviet society that have initiated or stimulated political problem-processing, and it should then be possible to compare such conclusions with what the three models lead us to expect. If the totalitarian model is accurate, we can expect to detect traces of a controlled amassing of information. If the pluralist model is more plausible, we should find in the instructions of the Party leadership examples of the demands and ambitions of various groups; and if the bureaucratic model is to be confirmed it must be possible to connect these demands to the goals pursued by different 'bureaux'.

It is impossible to attain a clear-cut picture of the nature of the Soviet political order from this examination, but we can at least obtain a somewhat better idea of the ratio of totalitarian, pluralist, and bureaucratic elements within the system.

# 3 Data and Research Design

The main source on which this study is based consists of the instructions issued by the Central Committee of the Soviet Communist Party to members and subordinate organisations through editorials in *Pravda*, the chief Party newspaper. These instructions fall into two parts – a diagnostic part which points out shortcomings in Soviet society and a prescriptive part urging that the necessary measures be taken to remedy those shortcomings. The instructions contain an explicit or implicit causal analysis of the faults noted; the factors considered to be responsible for such deficiencies usually become apparent in the way blame is dealt out or in the formulation of the strategy recommended to attain the desired results. The analysis often indicates both strategically important agents and strategically important constellations of conditions and instruments in the causal and corrective process. Taken together, these elements in the instructions provide a good picture of how the Central Committee interprets the social, economic and political relationships of Soviet society.

To facilitate a comparative study of different cross-sections of these materials, the data were transferred to magnetic tapes and a dictionary was compiled for use in information retrieval. The technique resembles that employed in certain content analytical research projects using *The General Inquirer* and other such dictionaries, but since our ambition was not to achieve a reliable automatic quantification but rather to use the computer to structure our materials for a conventional comparative analysis, system development and validation required less refinement.[1] Our dictionary may be of use for other politological research problems within the Russian language area, but it has not been our intention to pave the way for text analyses in other disciplines. On the other hand, the method applied here is less liable to result in erroneous conclusions or faulty precision than most content analytical methods, including *The General Inquirer*. Information retrieval, which is already widely used as a bibliographic and reference aid in areas with extensive but relatively uniformly structured texts (for example, law and patent processing), also has a significant but little exploited potential as a research instrument. One methodological purpose of the present study is to illustrate that potential.

Our intentional concentration on a single type of materials, the *Pravda* instructions, and the unusual procedure we have chosen to process these materials, warrant a fairly detailed presentation of our sources and method. The following section will describe *Pravda*'s role in the Soviet political system and the selection criteria that led us to base the study on a particular part of its contents. Other possible important sources in the study of Soviet domestic politics will also be considered, and that discussion will be followed by an account of the methods employed to retrieve information from the text.

## 3.1 THE DATA

### 3.1.1 The Soviet Press

All societies are influenced and shaped by the press, but in few societies is the press employed so consciously, for political socialisation and control, as in East Europe. The official function of the newspaper there – as Lenin put it – is to be a 'collective propagandist, collective agitator and collective organiser'. News distribution is subordinate to that purpose. No effort is made to distinguish between 'news' and 'views'. According to prevailing doctrine, the entire paper should function as a mouthpiece of the publishing organisation and participate in accomplishing the tasks set for that organisation. Official press ideology makes no secret of the fact that the primary job of the newspapers is to propagandise. Journalistic textbooks openly discuss how this function can be performed with maximum efficiency. A good press, according to established values, is one that strongly influences its readers. Since the populace is composed of groups with different interests and intellectual capacity, the mass media must be differentiated so that the Party line can reach all citizens.[2]

The Soviet press is therefore stratified both sectorally and territorially. There is a nationwide newspaper for each important sector of society (the Party, the governmental apparatus, the trade unions, the armed forces, the educational system, cultural life, industry, agriculture, the health services, commerce, the railroads, youth, children): the Central Committee of the Party publishes *Pravda*, the Council of Ministers *Izvestiya*, the trade unions *Trud*, the Party youth organization *Komsomolskaya Pravda*, the Ministry of Defence *Krasnaya Zvezda*, etc. At the republican level, two papers are usually published jointly by the republican Party organisation and its council of ministers, one in Russian and the other in the language of the republic. There are 38 republican dailies. At the regional level (including *oblasts, krais,* autonomous republics and autonomous *oblasts*) there are about 100 dailies and over 100 papers published five days a week. The district newspapers, over 3000 of them, usually appear three times a week. The base of the Soviet press pyramid is made up of the nearly 5000 local enterprise and *kolkhoz* papers.[3] There are in addition thousands of wall newspapers in plants, schools, etc.

Influence is exerted on these newspapers both by the organisations responsible for publication and by the Party's propaganda divisions at various levels. Overlapping instruments of control include a purposefully shaped journalistic training, periodical conferences and other forms of advanced education, a definite mass media ideology which is constantly reviewed and supplemented by resolutions of the Party leadership, careful surveillance by the Party agencies at the newspapers and a firm control of personnel policy through the so-called *nomenklatura* system, the significance of which is that important posts are included on a Party agency appointment list and cannot be occupied without the approval of that agency. Periodically recurring discussions with correspondents are another technique in the supervision of journalistic personnel.[4]

Everyday control and supervision of the press is effected primarily through directives from the Propaganda Section of the Central Committee. The central press in general and *Pravda* in particular are normative with respect to ranking and evaluting news material. As late as the 1950s the Soviet radio waited for *Pravda's* judgement before compiling its own news reports.[5] Beside these open signals, there are also sealed instructions. The latest and most detailed account of this control is Hollander's, which is based on oral communications from a previously high-ranking Soviet journalist. According to this report, an 'instructions conference' is held every other Tuesday in the Propaganda Section of the Central Committee. The conference is attended by the editors-in-chief of all union newspapers and magazines and by important radio and television officials; occasionally representatives of the local Moscow press also participate. The first part of the meeting takes up general political questions such as which of the latest economic successes should be treated on the front page. Changes in policy, such as a re-evaluation of a foreign politician, are sometimes announced. The policy directives communicated at these conferences are also sent in written form to the Party regional and district committees so that the corresponding divisions there can inform their own press. The next part of the conference is devoted to a review of mistakes made by the mass media during the last two weeks, and often includes an announcement of the penalities imposed. The discussion during this part of the meeting is not necessarily communicated to the lower levels. Finally, coming campaigns, events and directives are announced so that the mass media can prepare public opinion. The campaign against 'hooliganism', for example, was organised in this way; the subject was first discussed for some time in the press, after which the Supreme Soviet passed laws demanded by public opinion. Such announcements are passed on to journalists through accounts in the professional magazine *Zhurnalist*.[6]

The republican, regional and local press organisations maintain similar close contact with the corresponding Party agencies. The editors-in-chief are often members of the Party bureau.[7] Principal responsibility for the press, however, is borne by a special department of propaganda included in all republican and regional Party organisations. Other departments also keep in touch with the journalists. As one first secretary of a district Party committee has expressed it:

> We have very frequent contacts with the editorial staff. Most news items pass through our hands. Before anything is printed, the editor always brings it to our attention and we approve it. We are in a better position to know whether criticism or praise is needed . . .

This very interventionist line is criticised by the Soviet propaganda expert citing the statement, but the first secretary holds his ground:

> We know more about the situation in the company. We know who ought to be praised or scolded. Besides, the paper is our mouthpiece so why shouldn't we control it?[8]

It is difficult to say whether most of the local Soviet press is so strictly controlled by Party officials, but instructional works make it quite clear that careful supervision is desirable. In the Soviet scheme of things, the fact that a paper is the mouthpiece of a certain organisation implies that it is firmly bound to that organisation. There is no such thing as a doctrine of editorial independence from the owner.

### 3.1.2 *Pravda*

As the newspaper of the Central Committee of the Party, *Pravda* is the unchallenged leader among Soviet papers and magazines. Its viewpoints and judgements function as guideposts for the rest of the press, and its verdict in any debate is always conclusive. 'It is inconceivable', wrote one former Soviet journalist, 'that a district or regional newspaper should utter an opinion about *Pravda*; for only *Pravda* has the right to evaluate all other papers, itself being above all criticism. The rest of the press can only praise *Pravda* and print its articles, since criticism would result in the dismissal and perhaps arrest of the editor and in extensive sanctions on the editorial staff.'[9] This was written in 1955, but may still be considered valid. It is still quite common for *Pravda* to criticise other mass media, and if such criticism is formulated as a direct reprimand, the attacked paper customarily reprints *Pravda*'s opinions and publishes self-criticism admitting its mistake. Arkadii Gaev, a former correspondent for *Pravda* and *Izvestiya*, describes this as follows: '*Pravda*'s opinion is the law of the Soviet press. If *Pravda*'s view differs from that of another newspaper or magazine, the latter is obliged to mend its ways and publicly reject what it advocated a few days earlier.'[10]

*Pravda* also outranks other institutions. If the newspaper criticises a ministry, a civil service department, a regional Party committee or an enterprise, a self-critical response usually follows within a few days, often entitled 'After criticism', 'Measures taken', etc. Only extremely rarely do those under attack attempt to defend themselves.

*Pravda*'s unique authority is also apparent in its relationship to the censorship (the Chief Administration for the Guarding of State Secrets in the Press, or *Glavlit*). The paper, of course, is read by the censors, but the only object of this supervision is to eliminate information of possible military interest. Political control is exercised instead directly by the Central Committee, the Politburo and its Secretariat.

The newspaper is formally subordinate to the Central Committee's Agitation and Propaganda Section, which has been headed in various periods by such dignitaries as Zhdanov, Shepilov and Suslov. This agency is responsible for the entire *agitprop* machinery and is often described as a strategic power centre in the Soviet system. It is possible that other sections of the Politburo are also in touch with *Pravda*'s editors, but the extent of such direct links is not known. Prior to 1953 *Pravda* was controlled directly by a special press division in Stalin's personal secretariat that checked each issue of the paper before it was printed. Stalin's personal secretary, first Mekhlis and then Poskrebyshev, was regarded as the actual editor-in-chief. It was customary during that period for the editorial leadership to meet every day at noon to discuss the implementation of issued directives. Information from later years is less abundant, but it seems fairly certain that *Pravda* is still controlled very firmly and that the editors are in constant contact with the Politburo and its officials. *Pravda* journalists have access to the Kremlin's special internal telephone network, the so-called *vertushka*.[11]

*Pravda*'s internal structure resembles that of other Soviet dailies. There are about fourteen departments; the number keeps shifting. The editorial staff in charge of the paper consists of the department heads together with the editor-in-chief and two assistant editors-in-chief. There is no special leading article department; editorials are written by journalists from the various departments and in some measure by local correspondents. It has not been determined whether functionaries in the Central Committee write editorials as 'guest correspondents'. According to one *Pravda* department head, however, leaders in 1974 were written by as many as 87 persons on the editorial staff and 10–20 outside it.[12] Newspapers at a lower level sometimes have special editorial writers, so called *peredoviki*, but the task is also given to journalists who specialise in various professional fields.

Work at *Pravda* is slow and meticulous. The staff is large compared with those of other Soviet newspapers and includes many of the top journalists of the country. Assignments are distributed according to a monthly plan established by each department and approved by the editorial board, and the time allowed for their completion is generous, often ten to fifteen days or more. In certain parts of the paper and for certain tasks, of course, work must be done more rapidly, but even in such cases it is very carefully checked by several persons. Precision is always evaluated more highly than quick reporting, and considerable pains are taken to avoid oversights. Technical tolerances are also small.[13] Printing errors in *Pravda* are practically unknown.

The 'instructors' comprise an important group of *Pravda* employees. Their job is to organise contacts between the paper and the masses. They write nothing themselves, but work with various types of communication with the public, such as the investigation of reports of injustices and deficiencies, the organisation of reader initiative, the reception of letters to the editor, etc. Soviet sources state that *Pravda* receives over 400,000 letters a year, and even if the vast majority of them are probably spontaneous, it should be noted that the paper also actively tries to elicit opinions.[14] Empirical studies of letters to Soviet newspapers indicate that letter-writing increases with the age of the reader. A particularly large number of people write to the central papers, but the local press also receives a good deal of mail; it can be mentioned by way of comparison that all newspapers in the Sverdlovsk region (population 4,300,000) are reported to have received 250,000 letters in 1972.[15] According to one Soviet writer, the district press uses a majority of its letters, while another source maintains that *Trud* publishes only 2.1 per cent and *Izvestiya* only 1 per cent of theirs.[16] Even the large newspapers, however, process their mail, classifying it for study by the editors. *Pravda* sorts its letters into seventeen categories according to content.[17]

The average size of the newspaper was increased in 1967 from four to six pages. On special occasions such as Party congresses, however, it often expands to several times that volume to include the speeches, which are traditionally published *in extenso*. Official texts (declarations by the Party leadership, ukases from the Presidium of the Supreme Soviet, communications relating to certain diplomatic visits, appearances by the General Secretary or First Secretary of the Party, etc.) are given supreme priority and usually appear on the front page. When such materials are lacking or do not fill the entire page, this space is occupied by the editorial, news of production and sometimes short telegrams from abroad. Positive reports from various economic sectors and appeals for increased efforts are given a prominent place in the rest of the paper as well. The second and third pages are generally reserved for articles and reports dealing with such domestic topics, and these pages also carry discussion of theoretical and Party questions. Page 4 contains both Soviet and foreign matter, often including long articles. Page 5 is usually devoted to foreign news and page 6 to sport and short items.[18]

*Pravda*'s departments received a good deal of their material through an extensive network of permanent correspondents throughout the country. According to sources from the early 1950s, this network employed 1500–1600 persons, many of whom, however, worked at the same time on local papers or were TASS correspondents. Sixty permanent local editorial offices were reported to exist in 1975.[19] *Pravda* also has a number of correspondents abroad and thus uses partly its own material and partly news agency telegrams obtained primarily from TASS. Materials from other agencies, both socialist and non-socialist, are used to a limited extent.

The paper's connection with the Central Committee gives its correspondents a special position in Soviet society. They are regarded as employees of the highest political authority and are treated accordingly. As one Soviet journalist in exile describes the *Pravda* journalist's working conditions:

> The relation between any raion Party organisation and a *Pravda* correspondent are in no way comparable to those of the same organization with a representative of its own raion or even oblast newspaper. A correspondent of *Pravda* is admitted everywhere at all times. All economic, Party, trade union and public organizations open their doors wide to a member of that newspaper's staff. People talk to him with deference and at length, putting aside the most urgent work, conferences and consultations, as do ministers, directors of enterprises, secretaries of Party organizations on the oblast and Republic levels, scientists, artists, deputies of the Supreme Soviet and so forth. A *Pravda* correspondent is a representative of the highest organ in the country – the Central Committee of the CPSU(b).

A correspondent of *Izvestiya* has considerably less authority, but it is still fairly high. After that the authority decreases in proportion to the importance of the organization of which the newspaper is the organ. If the correspondent of the *Uchitel'skaya Gazeta* [Teachers' Newspaper] should venture, let us say, into a machine tool manufacturing plant, the Ministry of Defense, or to a lumber works, probably no one would condescend to talk to him, but the same man would receive a great deal of attention in a primary school or at the Institute of Communications.[20]

Some of the articles by *Pravda* journalists never reach the public. Certain reports on administrative and political deficiencies are instead delivered to the appropriate institutions, which are then expected to react as if the criticism had appeared in the newspaper. Yu. Boldyrev, a Party historian, relates in his doctoral dissertation how a 'brigade' from *Pravda* worked in the Northern Caucasus during collectivisation and reported errors to the territorial Party committee (*kraikom*). The brigade's report was sent to all districts as 'guiding instructions'.[21] On the basis of documents in the Kazakhstan Party Archives, another writer tells that in the late 1940s *Pravda* sent letters concerning unsatisfactory conditions in the republic to various ministries and local Party organisations. The Kazakh Central Committee was stigmatised on 12 October 1948 for failing to answer the communications promptly.[22]

### 3.1.3 *Pravda*'s readers

*Pravda*'s 10,000,000 copies make it the second largest newspaper in the Soviet Union – only the children's paper *Pionerskaya Pravda* has a wider circulation.[23] The enormous area of distribution involved necessitates decentralised production. The type is set in Moscow and transmitted by wire to other cities: Leningrad, Kuibyshev, Kiev, Lvov, Sverdlovsk, Omsk, Novosibirsk, Khabarovsk, Rostov-na-Donu, Kharkov, Tashkent, Baku, Tbilisi, Alma-Ata, Irkutsk, Odessa and others.[24] Distribution is increased in various ways. Like other Soviet newspapers, *Pravda* is pasted up on bulletin boards in many places. Articles and editorials are also commonly read over the radio. In addition, lower-level newspapers often reproduce *Pravda*'s materials, especially the editorials. The public reading of *Pravda* at plants, offices, farms, etc., has long been a traditional form of agitprop.

Soviet sociological press studies provide a certain amount of information about *Pravda*'s readers.[25] In one survey (1966), 12.7 per cent of the men interviewed and 11.3 per cent of the women in the city of Kamyshlov (Sverdlovsk region) stated that they read *Pravda*, which together with *Komsomolskaya Pravda* was the most widely circulated national newspaper there. The local paper *Za kommunizm* and the regional paper *Uralskii rabochii* were more widely read, by 22–31 per cent and 15–16 per cent respectively. In certain professional groups the central Party newspaper occupied a leading position. Thus 17.6 per cent of the men in the service sector and 16 per cent of male salaried employees and specialists stated that they read *Pravda*. Party members in Kamyshlov read the central and the regional Party organs to about the same extent, 26.1 per cent and 25.4 per cent respectively. Only 8.4 per cent of non-Party people declared that they read *Pravda*.[26]

In a comparable study in Leningrad (1967), no less than 40.5 per cent of the participants said that they read *Pravda*.[27] Even if each copy has several readers and many read the papers on the bulletin boards throughout the country, these figures are relatively high in relation to *Pravda*'s circulation. It is not impossible that the interviewees, considering that a good citizen is expected to read the chief Party organ, may have exaggerated their interest in the newspaper. That a certain social pressure is involved is shown by the Kamyshlov study, in which the participants were asked which factors determined their choice of newspaper. The most common answer was 'personal needs' (35 per cent), but other alternatives included 'entrance into the Party or Komsomol' (8.6 per cent) and 'required of Party, Komsomol or trade union activists' (8.1 per cent).[28]

According to another Soviet study (1968), the average *Pravda* reader was 42 years of age. Three-fourths of the readers were Party members. According to this study 40 per cent lived in regional capitals, while only 25 per cent lived in rural areas or small communities. The average *Pravda* reader had somewhat less education than the average reader of *Izvestiya* but was better educated than the *Trud* reader. Asked what they read in the paper, the respondents answered as follows:

|  | % |
| --- | --- |
| Official communications | 81 |
| Foreign events | 74 |
| Articles on international topics | 63 |
| Moral issues – upbringing and education | 57 |
| Satirical articles | 57 |
| Editorials | 45 |
| Party matters | 41 |
| Others | 40 |

In a similar study of *Izvestiya*, only 30 per cent stated that they read the editorial regularly, while 85 per cent said that they read parts of it or read it occasionally.[29]

Studies on the Soviet newspaper reader have also been made in other countries. Rogers conducted a series of interviews in the United States between 1965 and 1967 with persons who had formerly lived in the Soviet Union to investigate their selectional criteria and reading habits. In the first part of the experiment the participants were given six issues of *Pravda* and four issues of *Izvestiya*, after which they were asked to indicate which parts of the papers they would have read had they read them in the Soviet Union. The informants were then requested to read ten selected articles and mark the passages they had read carefully, those they had glanced through and those they had skipped, and finally, they were asked to state which parts of the articles they found especially important or interesting.

The subjects were classified in groups according to their position in the Soviet Union (high or low, 'leaders' or 'non-leaders'), and the latter group was divided into sub-groups according to education (high or low). Those who had occupied leading posts and/or had been Party members ranked the materials of the paper in the following order:

1. Editorials
2. Political speeches
3. Letters concerning domestic matters
4. Analyses of foreign events
5. Human interest items
6. Analyses of domestic events

For both of the lower social groups the list was headed by analyses of foreign events and human interest items. These readers gave editorials a low priority. The groups also differed with respect to how they read. The subjects who had occupied leading positions alternated for the most part between reading word for word and skimming. The uneducated category generally read word for word, while one-third of the intermediate group (educated 'non-leaders') read word for word and two-thirds skimmed. Skipping occurred seldom in the highest group and most often among the uneducated 'non-leaders'. Rogers also noted a tendency among these latter readers to skim the first and concluding paragraphs of the Soviet articles.[30]

What effect does *Pravda* have upon its readers? A great many self-critical contributions to the paper testify to specific reactions aroused by individual articles. Soviet sociology has also begun to study the role of the press in attitude formation and social processes.[31] One scholar in Sverdlovsk has used a combination of content analyses and questionnaires to investigate the reactions of enterprise executives (managers and department heads) to information received through the press. A majority of the subjects stated that the newspapers stimulated them to take concrete measures, but it is doubtful whether any great significance can be attached to such a finding.[32] No specialised study of *Pravda*'s role in the processes of political control and the moulding of public opinion is available.

Nor do we have any studies on what motivates the Soviet citizen's interest in *Pravda*, but here some assumptions present themselves. As has been suggested above, it seems likely that many Party members regard it as their moral obligation to follow the Party's paper and inform themselves of the views and directives of the leadership. For officials of various hierarchies and levels this is more or less a professional duty. Keen awareness of *Pravda*'s opinion was for a long time wise from the point of view of personal safety; the political arena was fraught with dangers, and it was important to anyone anxious to avoid errors to tune in on as many signals as possible. In addition, Party members who are more or less permanently assigned to instruct, organise or agitate others find fresh information in *Pravda*. Western observers have often noted that Soviet newspapers in general and *Pravda* in particular are studied very carefully by certain readers. As an exchange fellow in Leningrad in 1966, I often observed a doctoral student in Party history, who was an active Party member, reading *Pravda* pen in hand, and carefully underlining passages in important political articles.

There is an interesting first-hand report by a Soviet writer who spent some time during the 1930s at the CPSU Central Committee sanatorium together with a number of intermediate officials. He was struck by the fact that his fellow-patients — district Party secretaries, department heads in the Central Committee, editors-in-chief and prominent journalists, heads of regional executive organs, etc. — spent the entire morning assiduously reading the newspapers. Besides *Pravda* and *Izvestiya* they regularly read regional newspapers, district papers and specialised publications. Even small details were devoured with great interest. For example, in a report on organised voluntary labour (so-called *subbotniki*) in connection with the construction of the Moscow subway, it was carefully noted to what extent mobilisation included workers from factories that had failed to fill their quotas, students cramming for examinations, and housewives. The readers were looking for answers to practical questions — what should one do if priests volunteered for *subbotniki*? According to this observer, keeping up with the explicit and implicit communications in the most important newspapers was to these career-conscious men a vital necessity.[33]

Thus, one reason for the reader's interest in *Pravda* may be to broaden the knowledge on which he bases his own actions. Another closely related factor consists of a general curiosity as to future developments in society at large and happenings within the isolated and much gossiped-about section of Soviet society known as the *verkhushka* (top people). For millions of Soviet readers, for high-ranking officials in other Eastern European countries, for journalists and diplomats in Moscow, *Pravda* functions as a peephole into the Kremlin, a source of information on the leaders' reactions and intentions. A profuse tangle of rumours springs up out of speculative interpretations of diverse communications and announcements in *Pravda*. Both Moscow correspondents and diplomatic reporters base an important share of their accounts of the political situation on information in the Party mouthpiece. Countless observers have also used *Pravda* as a source in historical analyses. The undeniable point of departure common to all these reader categories is that the newspaper is closely associated with the Party leadership and entirely dependent upon its directives.[34] Since control of *Pravda* was tightened in the early 1930s that is a judgement few would care to doubt.

### 3.1.4 The *Pravda* Editorial

Since Soviet press ideology demands that a newspaper should function entirely as an instrument of the publishing organisation and therefore of the Party as well – the 'leading role' of which in Soviet society implies that it inspires and governs all state and non-state organisations – no political distinction can be drawn between the editorial and the content of the rest of the paper. Everything printed – news items as well as letters, personal contributions as well as *causeries* – must conform to the Party line. This does not exclude debates, but it means that they arise only on questions for which the Party finds discussion desirable and only within limits the Party establishes as reasonable. Press debates are carefully planned and employed in certain media, for example youth publications, as a more effective opinion-moulding instrument than openly didactic articles.[35] Strict *partiinost'* (roughly Party spirit) is demanded in the editing of any Soviet paper, and this necessitates a meticulous perusal and assimilation of all published materials.

Thus, it is not the opinion-forming function of the editorial that distinguishes it from the rest of the paper. The editorial is not the sole or necessarily even most important expression of the paper's political views. Official proclamations carry greater weight, and a new course is often marked in a long article in *Pravda* by a well-known correspondent. So called *podval* articles, feature items extending over several pages, are particularly authoritative. In most issues, however, the editorial may be said to be the most prominent political item, and its concentrated form and specific content almost always make it the most pregnant summary of the Party line.

Soviet editorials, especially *Pravda*'s, always have a semi-official character. Their function is not only to present a viewpoint, but also to indicate what action is to be taken by those to whom the articles are addressed. These include Party agencies at various levels and Party members and organs within other hierarches – ministries, soviets, enterprises, schools, etc. What the newspaper writes about such institutions are not idle opinions but rather a kind of order of the day that is expected to be acted upon. Party officials and members are presumed to know *Pravda*'s instructions and to strive to implement them. Articles often clearly indicate who is to be mobilised and what is to be accomplished. The special role of the editorial in the political and administrative system is defined by the fact that *partiinost'* is demanded not only of the journalist and the editors but also of the reader; Party members are under constant pressure to work toward the aims and objectives outlined by the Party's chief organ. Leonhard describes the function of *Pravda*'s editorials as follows:

The leading articles in Pravda are not leading articles in the sense of a newspaper in the non-Soviet world. Topical internal or international events are only dealt with in exceptional cases and then only when there is the opportunity of formulating a specific attitude of the Soviet leadership. The leading article puts forward the general party line for a specific area of public life on every occasion. This line remains valid until it is revised by a new leading article. The themes of the leading articles remain fixed. On average each month seven articles appear on external politics, seven on internal politics, five on industry, five on agitation, propaganda and party organisation, five on agriculture and one on cultural policy. The directives of the leading articles are binding for all USSR functionaries. For Western observers they are the most important material for the analysis of Soviet policy.[36]

This interpretation of the purpose of the editorial is reflected in the fact that such articles are often defined in Soviet literature on the press as *direktivnye stati* – directive articles. The designation can be traced to a resolution adopted by the Central Committee on 7 June 1922 entitled 'On the Plan for Local Newspapers'. It was emphasised in this document that the function of an editorial was to 'provide leadership, guidance, to explain the principal course of action. Editorials and sub-editorials are not conversations, not contributions to a discussion but political instructions, directives'.[37] The authoritative *Spravochnik zhurnalista* ('The Journalist's Handbook') states of this definition:

> This instruction, which has retained its significance to the present day, determines the distinctive characteristics of the directive article (editorial article), which is meant to explain and popularize the decisions of the Party and indicate the correct means for implementing them. Directive articles are regarded as direct decrees from the Party committee represented by the newspaper in question to local Party, soviet, trade union and Komsomol organizations.
>
> Such articles should be addressed specifically, appealing to the definite groups upon which the solution of a given problem depends; they should indicate the concrete measures necessary for the best solution of the task and provide a precise and generalized analysis of pertinent facts and statements.[38]

To achieve these purposes, Soviet editorials are often arranged according to a stereotyped pattern. If the topic concerns, say, sheep-breeding, the first part of the article is usually devoted to the successes of Soviet sheep-breeding, new production records, etc. This presentation, which usually takes up approximately half the article, generally also contains a specific account of positive results in the field, often including the mention of advanced enterprises, collectives or individual workers.

Then the positive part of the editorial is broken by an *odnako* ('however'), *no* ('but') or *vmeste s tem* ('at the same time'), which introduces a description of less successful production units and the faults in their work. This negative section often provides a brief diagnosis of the causes of the failures, and is followed by a third, constructive, part containing the actual directives. Here the old question of what is to be done is answered concretely – directives as to specific measures to be taken, often including the specific indication of instruments and methods, are addressed to specific organisations and/or persons. These orders are followed by a conclusion which often resumes the positive tone of the introduction, links the recommended course of action to some coming event (Lenin's birthday, a Party congress or plenary assembly, the anniversary of the Revolution, etc.) or incorporates it in a broader perspective such as the construction of communist society.

The stereotyped structure of practically all domestic editorials containing concrete directives is responsible for a certain inevitable monotony, a characteristic noted even by many Soviet critics. A *feuilleton* that appeared in the periodical of the Union of Soviet Journalists during the Khrushchev years was aimed at the superficial and repetitive nature of the genre. The summary below gives us some idea of how journalists regard editorial writing:

We are at the *letuchka* of a provincial newspaper [a meeting of the editorial board that critically discusses the issues of the past week]. The critic designated to lead the conference praises the two editorial writers Tochkin and Kochkin. A special correspondent recently returned from an assignment in the district, however, is of another opinion. He has met a reader who had learned most of the paper's editorials by heart and could predict their contents by merely reading the title. Well, that only shows that people read our articles, answer the editorial writers. But the editors find the situation somewhat troublesome and decide to help Tochkin and Kochkin to improve the genre. A number of suggestions are made as to how the editorials might be made more interesting – their topics ought to be more varied, arguments ought to be presented more forcefully, their style needs to be freshened up and new writers should be engaged on them. Two promising young candidates are elected, and the rest of the article describes how one of them, Samokhvalov, is trained to write editorials.

Full of enthusiasm, Samokhvalov turns to Kochkin to learn the difficult art. He finds his older colleague pacing back and forth with an old issue of the paper in his hand, dictating to a stenographer. The article is ready in a few minutes, and Samokhvalov is given his first assignment – to write an editorial on the repair of children's shoes.

He spends a sleepless night trying to structure and entitle the article. Should he call it 'Better and Quicker Repairs of Children's Shoes' or 'Quicker and Better Repairs of Children's Shoes'? The next morning he decides to study the problem out in the field and goes to a shoemaker. His attempt to interview the craftsmen over the counter fails, however, because angry customers think he is trying to crowd ahead of them in the line. Back at the paper Samokhvalov is scolded for wasting his time on such 'contacts with life', and Kochkin thoroughly revises the rough draft of his article. Finally, our young hero's more experienced colleague gives him a standard pattern, and he learns that an editorial should contain the following four points:

1. *The significance of the topic.* For example, the repair of children's shoes (or the planting of onions) is of great economic significance.
2. *What is good is good.* Refer to the best units (districts, kolkhozes), which have attained good results with the help of the people. Enumerate a great many public organisations.
3. *But not all units are as good as the best.* This statement is supported by examples that can be listed *ad infinitum,* but two or three are enough.
4. *Conclusion.* Let us mobilise everyone to eliminate the lags and deficiencies still existing, let us move onward to new victories!

This concludes Samokhvalov's training – now he knows how to write an editorial properly. He no longer needs to look for knowledge in actual life, but can gather all his information from official decrees. Now his wife takes all their children's shoes to the shoemaker, the editorial of the paper is once again above reproach, and the *letuchka* can turn to the mistakes and oversights of the other departments.[39]

Similar complaints about the sterile, stiff, and formalistic character of Soviet editorials are a frequent theme in specialised journalistic publications. In an article entitled 'The Flag of the Issue Must be Colourful', one critic, Gurenkov, exhorts editorial writers to strive for a fresher and more expressive style. Historical digressions and abstract viewpoints must not be allowed to crowd out concrete and topical subjects. Bombast must be replaced by everyday-ness, remoteness must yield to familiarity. It is quite permissible to write an editorial using the personal pronoun form in order to address the public directly. The important thing is 'to arouse a feeling of responsibility in the reader's heart and mind, to influence him through the use of imagery, emotionally charged arguments, a clear and expressive presentation of facts, through the whole discussion of the subject'.[40]

Stereotyped planning is sometimes mentioned as an explanation of the monotony of the editorial genre. Balbekov, a *Pravda* journalist, maintains in a critical survey of the editorials of fourteen republican and regional newspapers that the quality and active interest of writers seems to have declined in recent decades. The editorial plan indicates only which subjects are to be discussed, and the individual writer is not always able to present the topic with sufficient depth or clarity. [41] A third Soviet observer, Khlynov, complains that newspaper editorials are often too schematic. If the article is to achieve its purpose it must be concrete and cogent. Hollow arguments must not be allowed to replace facts. Analyses must provide real guidance and leave no doubt as to what must be done. [42]

Certain of Khlynov's views on the content of editorials deserve to be quoted as representative of the role assigned to the genre in Soviet press ideology. The purpose of an editorial, Khlynov declares, is 'to transmit the Party's directives to the masses and advise the reader specifically on their implementation'. [43] Further, an editorial is not a command or an official document — it is a directive in content rather than in form, and must therefore be topical and efficient. It should often summarise the material in the rest of the paper and draw general conclusions. Longer, signed articles sometimes also perform such a summarising function but this is generally assigned to the editorial, in which it is important to refer to other parts of the newspaper, popularise difficult material and point out its social and political significance.

Sometimes the paper prints a Party or government declaration instead of an editorial, but this does not obviate the need for one or more articles to explain and illustrate the declaration and mobilise readers to implement it. A more detailed treatment of the topic, however, can be presented in other parts of the paper. Khlynov concludes:

> The guiding ideas in a directive article are inseparably linked to an analysis of a given branch of the economy, of practical experience. The editorial indicates how a particular Party decision is to be interpreted, it shows which practical problems are the most important and it indicates the efforts needed to solve those problems satisfactorily. [44]

The programme described by Klinkov, Gurenkov and Khlynov has been realised to some extent in the past decade. A general rise in quality with respect to the points mentioned and a smaller degree of schematisation can be noted in both *Pravda* and other large newspapers. [45] To the Western reader, however, it is clear that the weaknesses discussed above have not been totally eliminated. Monotonous repetitions and hackneyed phrases still abound, and the use of stylistic variations and artistic devices appears to be restricted considerably by the functional norms imposed on the editorials by official press ideology.

The paradigm described by Klinkov is still fully recognisable in the vast majority of editorials in *Pravda* and other Soviet newspapers. Certain exceptions, however, deserve to be noted. Editorials dealing with foreign topics naturally contain very few directives to Party organs and Soviet communists. To the extent that they include such operative messages, they are addressed to foreign states, and the recipient is in these cases rarely mentioned explicitly. Another category of some quantitative significance consists of editorials on general topics such as 'Leninism—our Banner', 'The Soviet Union—Bulwark of Peace', 'Labor's Festival', etc. This group includes some of the yearly recurring editorials dedicated to surveys of the past or future published in connection with New Year's Day, Lenin's birthday, May Day, the anniversary of the Revolution, etc. A characteristic feature of this group is that the positive introduction typical of all editorials never ends: that is, the entire article deals with successes and victories. In addition, these editorials are general with respect to their subjects — they usually concern the entire Soviet people and their work, not the chemical industry and its production. This type is known among *Pravda*'s editorial staff as 'general political editorials', in contrast to the main category, which consists of 'problem editorials', 'specific editorials' or 'thematic editorials'.[46]

Thus, if we survey all the domestic materials published in editorials, we can distinguish three elements: (1) positive, general descriptions of a situation and positive examples; (2) negative examples; and (3) operational guidelines. This rhetorical model is not restricted to editorials. Speeches and debates often follow the same pattern — positive features are presented first, followed by a discussion of the problems, and more or less clear suggestions of possible solutions. In a study of articles written by *obkom* first secretaries, Stewart has found that the 'types of affect' in these texts consisted of 63 per cent 'praise', 21 per cent 'criticism' and 16 per cent 'demands'.[47]

This considerable proportion of 'praise' or positive description has been interpreted in various ways. Brzezinski suggests that a pronounced *penchant* for revolutionary rhetoric and symbolism results from bureaucratic sterility of thought.[48] Stewart contends that the positive tone in his material is rather a function of the *obkom* secretary's position and needs: 'Frequent expressions of praise may be designed to please his superiors by creating an atmosphere of achievement, and thus minimize pressures from the center.'[49] The long positive prologue often emphasises victories in areas with which the author himself is concerned. It also functions as a rhetorical instrument to mark loyalty to the system and a positive overall attitude; specific criticism never takes the form of grumbling. Emphasis on the progress being made makes it clear that mistakes and faults are marginal phenomena in socialist society.

The positive passages in the *Pravda* editorial can hardly be intended to placate superiors, since the directives there are aimed only downwards, to Party members and organisations at lower levels. But a eulogistic introduction can achieve a similar rhetorical purpose even in such communications. One function is to arouse the reader's interest and make him favourably disposed to the Party's communication; this is treated in classical rhetoric under the heading 'exordial topics', the study of introductions.[50] Another may be to reinforce the reader's feeling of belonging to the system. Leaders often emphasise victories to enhance their own prestige. In the study of American 'national goals' mentioned above, Biderman shows that over half of the content of the President's 'State of the Union Addresses' deals with 'progress' and somewhat less than half discusses 'problems'. The proportion of what Biderman calls 'political, self-congratulatory, vindicating' elements has increased through the years.[51]

A considerable portion of the propaganda disseminated by the Soviet agitprop apparatus is, like the first part of the *Pravda* editorial, intended to give the citizen the impression that Soviet society is prosperous and strong, that progress and gains are continually being made. The purpose of such appeals seems to be to strengthen the citizen's identification with and loyalty to the political community. Pride in the development of his country functions as a diffuse moral stimulus. Similarly, the praise heaped upon various occupational groups – the Soviet worker, the Soviet writer, the Soviet railwayman, etc. – appears to be intended to arouse professional pride, which in turn serves to stimulate increased efforts. This interpretation, to which Ionescu subscribes, seems more convincing than the view that appeals to such groups should be regarded as reflecting efforts to liberate the professions and mould them into independent interest groups in Soviet politics.[52] Accounts of progress in the Soviet economy do indeed satisfy certain psychological needs of the occupational groups by providing them with a positive image of their professions, but it does not seem possible to regard such reports as subjective expressions of self-affirmation. They should rather be understood as Party communications addressed to the social sector in question, as integral parts of a political socialisation process that besides general civic training also embraces the exertion of selective influence on the different groups.

Using economic terminology, these general impulses might be described as *political investments*. By raising politically conscious, patriotic and proud Soviet citizens and encouraging a strong feeling of professional pride in all occupational groups, the leadership builds a base for its political actions; it lays a moral foundation for future activity. The concrete and specific impulses in the latter parts of *Pravda*'s editorials might be designated with the same terminology as a form of *political consumption.*[53] Here it is no longer a matter of building up an action reserve, but rather of utilising or mobilising that reserve; the capital of confidence accumulated through a painstakingly conducted process of socialisation is spent to encourage the citizen to act. This 'capital', of course, is amassed not only by means of positive accounts in newspaper editorials, but also through very complex social processes. It need only be noted in this context that the generally formulated phrases in the coverage of high-priority areas in the mass media belong to the category of impulses which attempt in the most general sense to develop the citizen's moral incentive. The purpose of criticising shortcomings and issuing directives aimed at the correction of such faults, on the other hand, is to tell them who is to do what, and where and how it should be done.

In the discussion below we shall refer to the negative part of *Pravda*'s editorials as *criticism* and to the constructive part as *directives*. Together they will be known as *Pravda*'s instructions. Before examining in more detail how these instructions are employed, it might be appropriate to compare their informational content with that of other sources.

### 3.1.5 *Pravda*'s Instructions as a Source

In making an inventory of the political problems of a community we can theoretically choose between various cuts into the problem-solving process. The course of a problem through the political institutions can be tapped at different stages, first of all at the points of input to and output from the higher power centres. If one is interested in the early phases of demand-voicing or the implementation of decisions it is of course possible to make other cuts, but that involves the difficulty of treating enormous bodies of data. In most instances the output from the central power apparatus should be the most economical point of approach, since the observer can then take advantage of the sifting that has already occurred in the political system. Information that in one way or another summarises the leaders' decisions does not register all the political problems considered by that leadership, but it does indicate which problems have passed through the aggregation and filtering processes present in all political systems. In other words, what we find at the output is a posthumous résumé of the most important questions on the political agenda.

The output can be studied through the use of several different sources. *Pravda*'s editorials were selected here as the most suitable indicator of the Soviet leaders' perception of political problems, their interpretation of the causes of those problems, their allocation of political energy and their choice of instruments of control. This decision was based on a detailed evaluation of the characteristics of several types of material.

According to certain criteria, other indicators are better or just as good as the *Pravda* instructions, but a total comparison shows that *Pravda* is more valuable than any of its 'competitors'. The criteria taken into consideration were as follows:

*(a) Availability.*

An elementary demand on any body of materials is that it be available. The primary sources that best reflect Soviet politics may in this respect be divided into three categories. The first group consists of materials that are normally secret and are rarely put at the researcher's disposal. These include minutes from internal Party discussions and internal Party correspondence. Fainsod's study of the Smolensk Party archives (which the Germans captured intact and which were later brought to the United States) provides us with a good deal of information on the instructions and reports that circulated among various levels of the Party apparatus, but we have no such materials for the period after 1937.[54] The types of communications sent are fairly well described in modern studies of the internal operation of the Party, but the specific contents of such documents are not available.[55]

The second category consists of sources available on the spot. Soviet archives are rather restrictive in admitting foreign observers interested in twentieth-century politics, but newspapers and periodicals are generally available, as are most of the books published during the Soviet period. The third type of source includes printed matter also available outside the Soviet Union. Only the central and republican press is represented here among the daily newspapers. The regional papers are under an export ban, probably because in spite of censorship they are considered to contain too much information of potential military interest. Economic data of value to the study of appropriations, plan indicators, and other instruments of economic control are available outside the Soviet Union only at a high level of aggregation.

Certain sources are troublesome in that they fall partly into the first and partly into the second or third categories. Thus, many Party resolutions are printed in the daily press, the Party journal *Partiinaya Zhizn* and the yearly *Spravochnik partiinogo rabotnika,* while others appear only in special publications or are communicated through sealed channels.[56] There exists no complete list of Party resolutions.[57] Judging by the imperfect agreement between decree number and diary number in the government's statute-book *Sobranie postanovlenii pravitel'stva SSSR*, only a quarter or a fifth of all governmental decrees are registered there. Only a very small part of all departmental and ministerial acts are published in *Byulleten' normativnykh aktov ministerstv i vedomstv SSSR.*

*(b)  Centrality*

A source close to the political leadership is naturally a better indicator of their views than one that is farther away. This puts *Pravda* ahead of the other mass media, with the possible exception of the periodicals *Kommunist* and *Partiinaya Zhizn'*. Even if all Soviet publications are presumed to express the Party line and follow its instructions, the chief organ of the Central Committee is obviously the most authoritative voice. The newspaper's proximity to the Party leaders, the frequency of the contacts between them, and the degree of control exercised over the publication make *Pravda* a more faithful reflection of the Politburo's positions than the papers and journals controlled through direct or indirect written decrees. This is further enhanced by the fact that *Pravda* itself serves as one of the channels by which signals are transmitted to other media. The contents of what is in one sense or another the peripheral press, therefore, are less indicative of the attitude of the political leadership, since such material is based upon instructions that have been filtered and perhaps distorted by a long chain of transmission. On the other hand, these papers contain more information than the central press on political goals and ambitions within individual geographical and economic areas, and this makes them very valuable for specialised studies.

Several sources may with respect to the criterion of centrality be ranked together with or above *Pravda*. These include resolutions adopted by Party congresses, the Central Committee and the Politburo, speeches by members of the supreme Party leadership and certain governmental decisions that may be assumed to have been thoroughly discussed within the Politburo, e.g. questions relating to the budget and economic planning.

*(c)  Authority*

The value or position of a given source in the established 'normative hierarchy' is another closely related criterion.[58] Authority is to some degree a function of the centrality of an indicator, but there are obvious differences among sources at the same distance from the supreme leadership. Experienced Soviet readers are adept at interpreting texts and can easily orient themselves in the regular flood of information.[59] Authority is closely connected to the depth and degree of will and intent that readers perceive in a given text. It is a subjective characteristic that can only be measured in the reader's attitude toward a source, and this also lends it a certain predictive significance. An authoritative communication not only reflects desires at the top of the Party, but also serves as a basis for prognosticating the activities of lower levels. If, as many observers assure us, the Central Committee's main press organ really is read carefully by inferior echelons of the Party hierarchy and by officials within other hierarchies, and if its directives really do result in activities at various levels, then the newspaper tells us something about what is happening or will happen in Soviet society. The actual impact of the message, of course, can only be assessed on the basis of empirical observations, but the knowledge that signals are transmitted throughout the intricate communications network binding together the Soviet administration at any rate warrants the conclusion that the editorials in *Pravda* have a certain 'predictive' value in relation to the receivers in addition to their 'indicative' value in relation to the senders. The *Pravda* editorial is less authoritative than some decisions by leading Party organs (Congress, Central Committee and Politburo resolutions) and speeches by the General Secretary of the Party.

## (d) Equivalence

Content analysis is considerably easier when the textual materials are homogeneous and all units of registration (coding) have approximately the same weight. Certain types of material are troublesome in this regard. An attempt to study Soviet politics through a content analysis of available decrees, for example, would produce peculiar results; important and unimportant decrees occur indiscriminately and in varying proportions at various times. From this point of view, the *Pravda* editorials are more worth while, since they are fairly consistent in size and intermittence and therefore constitute a 'symmetrical' data base. Since the space for communications through a single channel is limited, all transmitted directives have approximately equal value; the cost in terms of the space allotted and the ability of an editorial to attract attention are the same in all cases. With relatively few exceptions, the average editorial of recent years has measured 450 × 93 mm or about 120 lines. The length of the excerpts from *Pravda* editorials used in the present study, however, varies. They average nine sentences per editorial.

## (e) Informational value

A characteristic closely related to that described immediately above has important economic implications. If the work load is to be kept within reasonable bounds, the content analyst must utilise a body of materials in which informational value is high in proportion to volume. Consequently, it is necessary to find sources with a high degree of concentration. This goal cannot be maximised, however, since excessive concentration implies a loss in specific content. In other words, not only must the texts be concise, they must also contain an ample amount of information on the problems and strategies the study is attempting to illuminate. The *Pravda* editorial meets both requirements to a reasonable degree. Certain sources, such as the May Day slogans studied by Yakobson and Lasswell, are more concise; others, such as the long articles used by Stewart, contain more detailed information.[60] Earlier experiments conducted by the present author on 'leaner' texts (official speeches on May Day and the anniversary of the Revolution during a period of ten years), however, yielded unsatisfactory results, and a study of a more comprehensive body of newspaper materials was regarded as exceeding the economic and practical framework of our research project.

## *(f) Sensitivity*

The final significant factor is the sensitivity of the medium to changes in the political leadership's positions. This is affected by a number of variables, including frequency, proximity (centrality), and the ability of the editorial staff to interpret moods and reactions. *Pravda*'s suitability in this respect has a certain connection with the fact that it is used in particular for communications with a high priority. One of the most important functions of the Soviet Party apparatus is to act as a trouble-shooter — local organs are meant to channel energy toward sectors of the economy experiencing difficulties at a given moment. The Central Committee's mouthpiece contributes to these efforts by transmitting an order of the day to lower levels; by emphasising certain questions the paper points out the areas most urgently in need of attention. Figuratively speaking, *Pravda* helps Party officials to sort their mail. Since no *apparatchik* is capable of handling all the demands made upon him by superior organs, the Party paper is a serviceable aid in determining priorities. Its high degree of sensitivity allows it to reflect currents within the Party and indicate the tasks the Party Secretariat and Politburo feel to be essential at any particular time.[61]

None of these six 'desirable qualities' taken alone can point to any one type of source as an ideal indicator of the political content of the Soviet leadership's problem diagnoses and course of action. A comprehensive evaluation, however, shows the *Pravda* editorial to be considerably superior. It is not only, as Wolfgang Leonhard put it, 'the most important material in an analysis of Soviet politics', but also a source whose symmetry, precision and concreteness make it particularly suitable for computerised studies of large bodies of data.[62] Its instructions appear to be the best conceivable basis of analysis for our stated purposes. This base also has certain limitations, however, and it is therefore appropriate to dwell somewhat on the fundamental question of validity. What can we extract from the directives in *Pravda*'s editorials? How reliably do they reflect the political agenda?

Politicians do not voice their intentions in order to satisfy political scientists. When they express themselves clearly they usually have some 'instrumental' purpose in mind; they speak in order to influence. This is in no small measure true of how they formulate their goals. In organisations where several élites vie for the favour of the membership, such declarations sometimes function as instruments of political competition. To the extent that the pluralist model is applicable to the Soviet Union, therefore, we should be able to expect that the *Pravda* instructions seek to strengthen the popularity of the leaders among the various groups of society. But goal formulations also have action-related functions. If the leaders of an organisation can only attain their ends through an effective mobilisation of its membership, they must articulate themselves in order to indicate the course of action they desire.

The extensive and greatly differentiated goal catalogues in *Pravda* testify to the existence of a high level of articulation in the Soviet Union. But not all the problems treated by the leaders and not all their decisions require mobilisation of the active stratum to which *Pravda* is addressed. The leadership itself can implement certain measures more or less directly, while others demand action on the part of very limited sectors of the Party or administrative apparatus. A third group of decisions often affect a great many people but may be of such a nature that it is deemed unsuitable to give them extensive publicity. Thus, matters connected with foreign trade and internal and external security are very seldom treated in editorials. The political agenda that can be gathered from *Pravda* – like everything else published in the Soviet Union – is marked by a deep-rooted tradition of censorship.

Besides openly announced priorities, therefore, there must be others not available to us through *Pravda*'s editorials. We do not know the extent of this latter category, but the scope of *Pravda*'s treatment of social problems suggests that the part of the whole thus withheld from the public is not very significant, an impression that is confirmed by the results of our institutional analysis in Chapter 7 below. In spite of *Pravda*'s enormous circulation – over 10,000,000 copies – the Soviet leaders do not hesitate to discuss there questions relating to very limited groups of society such as individual ministries or civil service departments.

The instructions in *Pravda*, then, offer us a slightly doctored résumé of the most important problems on the political agenda. They do not summarise all the problems considered by the Soviet leadership, but they do indicate those which the leaders try to tackle by means of an open mobilisation of political and administrative organs. As an order of the day, therefore, the *Pravda* editorial is a fairly good reproduction of the total political agenda.

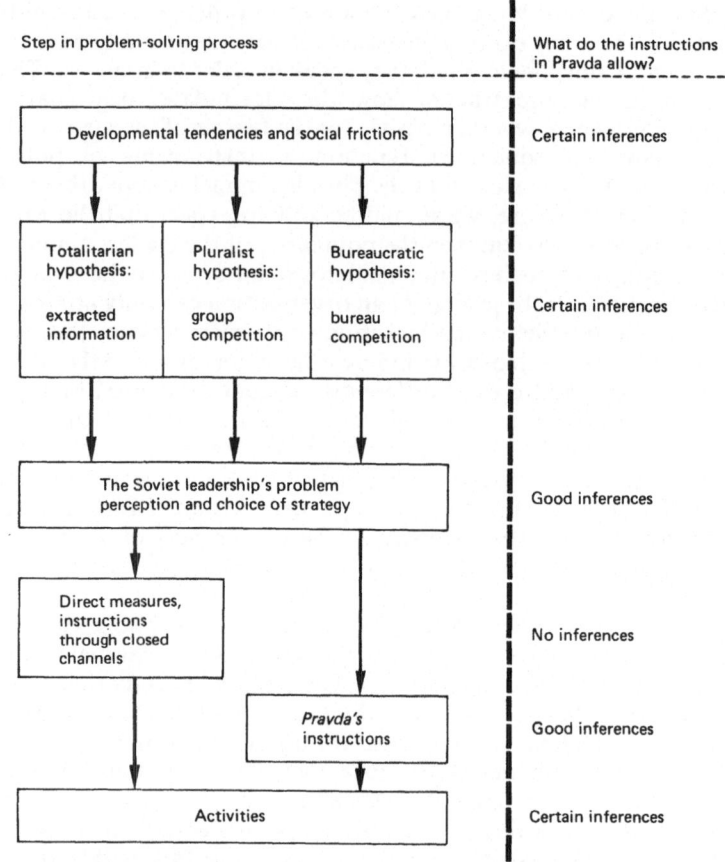

Fɪɢ. 3.1.5.1 Source Value of the Instructions in *Pravda*

## 3.1.6 Period of Time

The three years chosen for analysis are 1950, 1960 and 1970. The primary motives for that selection may be summarised as follows:
1. One of the points from which the study departed was an interest in changes in the political agenda over a long period of time. From a specifically Soviet point of view the question concerned the development of the country's problems during a period when the Stalin regime was replaced by a relatively more liberal order, when an economy plagued by shortages developed into relative prosperity and the legitimacy of the system was by all indications stabilised. From a more general viewpoint

the interesting question was how social problems change as a political order 'matures' and how this 'maturing' affects the diagnoses, analyses and strategies of the leaders. This developmental perspective made a longitudinal study natural, but limited resources prevented an examination of the entire population of editorials during a ten or twenty-year period. It was necessary to choose between a stratified selection (for example, every twentieth editorial) and several longer, continuous periods of time. The latter alternative was preferred, since it would presumably provide a better picture of the coherency of the campaigns sometimes undertaken in Soviet politics. The same reasoning favoured selecting periods of an entire year in length; shorter segments might have distorted the treatment given certain seasonal subjects such as sowing and harvesting.

2. The original intention was to cover the longest possible period from the Russian Revolution onwards. Two factors, however, made it difficult to go farther back in time than the Second World War. In the first place, the collections of older issues of *Pravda* in Swedish libraries are incomplete, and the microfilms obtained from Helsinki also proved to contain certain gaps. Secondly, differences in themes and journalistic rhetoric were discovered in the earlier material which seemed to complicate comparisons with later years. Moreover, in the very first period – from the founding of the newspaper to the early 1930s – *Pravda* did not function to the same degree as later as the official organ of the supreme Party leadership, but at times assumed a relatively autonomous position. For these reasons the temporal scope of the study was restricted to the post-war years.

3. The choice of a ten-year period and the years 1950, 1960 and 1970 was doubtless in some measure influenced by the appeal of even numbers. But there were other criteria which motivated the selection of these years. Firstly, there was their distribution over three regimes – Stalin's, Khrushchev's, and Brezhnev's. Secondly, they were free from Party congresses. During the post-war years when such congresses were held (1952, 1956, 1959, 1961, 1966, 1971, and 1976), the editorials in *Pravda* dealt with their preparation to such an extent that other specific, thematic editorials were proportionately few. Only after excerpting was it possible to establish that the intense foreign policy activity of 1960 had a similar effect, and that the editorials concerned with domestic matters were consequently fewer than in 1950 and 1970.

## 3.2 METHOD

### 3.2.1 Qualitative *v.* quantitative methods

Throughout the history of Soviet studies, *Pravda* has been used as a source of information on the political behaviour of the Party leadership. As early as in the 1920s, when the 'Kremlinological' tradition was founded by analysts who had personally participated in Soviet politics (Nikolaevsky, Borkenau, etc.), perceptive observers attempted to read between the lines of the main Party organ to gain insights into the power struggle then in progress. The source value of the paper in this regard increased when it was put under total Party control in the early thirties, and it has been an important instrument for the observation of reshufflings and alterations in course ever since. The 'Kremlinologists' have been particularly interested in questions of power and personalities, and they have used the official material in *Pravda* and other leading publications in an attempt to identify rival camps. The genre has often and not entirely unjustly been scoffed at, but it has none the less registered some successes within its limited field. 'Perhaps Beriya doesn't like opera,' the *New York Post* noted sarcastically when the failure of the Secret Police Chief to attend a Bolshoi Theatre performance generated speculations of a struggle among the Party leadership. Perhaps not, but a few days later Beriya was eliminated all the same.[63]

'Kremlinology', with its concentration on the personal aspects of Soviet politics, is still widely practised among journalists and professional observers of the Soviet Union, but it is definitely losing ground at the level of serious research. Yet even in expanding politological fields – such as the study of Soviet interest groups, individual sectors and local and regional politics – *Pravda* is often used as a source. Here as well many analysts try to apply the method of 'esoteric reading', but since such an approach requires a broad and detailed knowledge of Soviet politics and political parlance, it leads to considerable difficulties, especially in the case of younger analysts with no personal experience of Soviet society.[64] Awareness of the risk of incorrect subjective interpretations and interest in analyses at the systems level have contributed to focusing attention on quantitative techniques of gathering information. Lasswell and Yakobson's early content analysis of May Day slogans has been followed by many other attempts to study Soviet politics with the instruments of behaviouralism. Examples include Gati's study, 'Soviet Elite Perception of International Regions', Lodge's work on the emancipation of interest groups and Evans's analysis of history textbooks used in Soviet secondary schools.[65]

Social scientists and students in the humanities have been debating the relationship between qualitative and quantitative methods for some time now. Only 'esoteric reading' can bring the researcher close to his material, highlight nuances and pave the way for profound understanding and insights. On the other hand, this approach can never provide the broader sweep and greater precision offered by analyses of large bodies of data. It must always be kept in mind when evaluating quantitative studies that their precision and hence validity are often illusory because of arbitrary premises, but this is not a decisive argument against the method as such. Traditional and behaviouralist research complement each other; together they can provide valuable insights which cannot be attained by close reading or broad surveys in isolation.

The balance of quantitative and qualitative elements in the analytical method of the present study emerged through a laborious trial-and-error process. Considering the macro-political problems with which we are ultimately concerned, it originally seemed natural to employ a traditional quantitative content analysis. A number of such methods were consequently studied and tested over a long period of time, but results were meagre. The questions posed to the materials and the answers obtained from test analyses of limited bodies of data proved simply to be so numerous that the preliminary coding schemes collapsed. Moreover, the process became unreasonably cumbersome, as coding the data required so many and such complicated classifications in order to take into consideration all the types of information desirable in a numerical analysis of the text. As the experiments progressed and more nuances and potentially interesting informational categories were dscovered, it became increasingly clear that reliability would be unsatisfactory and that the bulkiness of the coding procedure would greatly exceed available resources. The large number of the variables also threatened to reduce figures to the point where statistical analyses would become meaningless. It therefore seemed necessary to lower our ambitions considerably in order to complete the project in accordance with original methodological intentions.

At this point we investigated whether it might not be possible to make a switch. Taken within the limits of available resources for coding, no known method of quantitative content analysis seemed capable of providing sufficiently comprehensive and reliable information on the substance of the *Pravda* materials. Since the preliminary tests showed that the information received as answers to questions constantly generated new questions, it was also a great drawback to have to restrict the study to certain predetermined problems. It therefore seemed desirable to find a method which would permit continuous alterations in hypotheses. For that purpose it appeared practical to establish an information bank which could be used in a number of ways, something like the data bases employed in bibliographical research. The inventory of suitable techniques was therefore resumed and focused on a comparison of information retrieval methods.[66]

At this stage considerations of availability weighed most heavily. The system that could most easily be utilised was the CORSAIR III developed by the Swedish Institute of Defence Analysis. CORSAIR III could be used both for determining frequencies in a text and for searches with a large number of questions by means of the so-called IRMA function. Special search programmes allowed the retrieval of short passages containing indicated words or word groups from a large textual mass. This made it possible to retrieve all sentences in *Pravda* dealing with a particular subject in KWOC ('key-word out of context') form, which facilitated a total comparative analysis of the paper's treatment of a given problem over a long period of time.

This changeover from a 'locked' quantitative content analysis to an 'open' analysis of retrieved material shifted emphasis back toward a qualitative method. The computer was used primarily for a series of sortings of the data, while the final review of the information structured in such a form was performed 'manually'. This meant that automatised techniques could be used to process a large body of material, but that the many reliability and validity risks connected with sharply reducing the informational content of the material were avoided.

### 3.2.2 Structuring through Information Retrieval

The form of information retrieval used here is based on the searching of a stored textual mass. The process may be described briefly as follows:

First, all *Pravda* editorials for the years 1950, 1960, and 1970 were examined and a record was drawn up for each editorial dealing with domestic problems.[67] Here were included *in extenso* all sentences in the editorial containing either (1) a mention of faults in Soviet society ('criticism') or (2) an indication of measures that ought to be taken ('directive'). The text was copied in the original Russian, transliterated into the Latin alphabet.

All excerpting was done by the same person. The excerpted material was then reviewed by two other persons, who checked that all sentences were understandable even out of context. When they were not, they were slightly re-edited, usually by joining together several sentences. The material was then punched and transferred to magnetic tapes. Incorrect punchings were corrected by checking a frequency list, where most errors appeared with a frequency of one, two or three.

There were several types of reliability problem in this process. First of all, there was the possibility of simple copying errors, which, however, double-checking kept to a minimum. Secondly, there was the risk of 'under-excerption', meaning that sentences that should have been copied were not. The third danger was the opposite of this, or 'over-excerption'. These risks were neutralised through random controls and by instructing the excerpter to take too much rather than too little in doubtful cases. The text could then be cleansed at all later stages by eliminating irrelevant sentences. 'Over-excerption' was judged to be considerably less serious in an information retrieval analysis than in a traditional quantitative content analysis, since the superfluous material in the former case does not disappear into numerical aggregates but instead appears again during the searches. These security measures proved to be effective in practice, and very few 'over-excerpted' items were found in the retrieved material.

TABLE 3.2.2.1 Physical structure of the material

|                                         | 1950   | 1960   | 1970   | Total   |
| --------------------------------------- | ------ | ------ | ------ | ------- |
| Number of editorials                    | 216    | 142    | 254    | 612     |
| Number of instructions                  | 1,808  | 1,325  | 2,390  | 5,523   |
| Number of sign-strings                  | 48,616 | 28,512 | 58,586 | 135,714 |
| Number of instructions per editorial    | 8.37   | 9.33   | 9.41   | 9.02    |
| Number of sign-strings per instruction  | 26.89  | 21.52  | 24.51  | 24.57   |
| Number of sign-strings per editorial    | 225    | 201    | 231    | 222     |

Constructing questions to be addressed to a data base organised like this involved some difficulties. Homonyms, i.e. identical words and word forms with different meanings, present a common problem in information retrieval. It is theoretically quite possible to develop disambiguation routines which eliminate certain meanings of a given sign-string, but such a process was deemed to be too demanding. Instead, a certain number of 'false' answers to the questions posed were accepted and then eliminated through checking before the analysis was begun. Another, related, difficulty had to do with the many different inflected forms in Russian. This problem can also be solved by careful programming, but here as well it was thought more appropriate to choose a simpler and technically less refined method, namely truncation. In many instances truncated sign-strings that would cover all inflected forms, while in other cases the desired sign-strings were supplemented with blank spaces or negated sign-strings. In other words, it was possible to design the programme in such a way that the machine would seek all words in *vod,* which covered all inflected forms of the Russian word for 'water' (*voda, vody, vodu, vode, vodoi, vod, vodami, vodakh*) and all compounds with 'water-' (*vodo-*). Such a command, however, would also produce a number of undesired words beginning in vod (e.g. *vodit'*, 'lead, conduct', or *vodka*). To avoid such irrelevant information, search terms with negative operators were also introduced, which eliminated from among the retrieved words in *vod* those which continued with $k, i$, or certain other letters or combinations of letters.

Searching by means of the IRMA function is based on Boolean algebra. One or more questions form a profile. Questions consist of operands and operators. The operands are three-place numbers which refer to a term-list. The following operators may be used:

Conjunction          Search for occurrence of both *P and Q*
$P*Q$

| | |
|---|---|
| Inclusive disjunction | Search for $P$ or $Q$ or both |
| $P + Q$ | |
| Exclusive disjunction | Search for $P$ or $Q$, but *not* both together |
| $P;Q$ | |
| P but not Q | Search for $P$ but not $Q$ |
| $P\%Q$ | |
| Conditional | Search for $Q$ alone or including $P$, but exclude $P$ |
| $PQ$ | when *alone* |
| Equivalence | Search for presence *or* absence of both $P$ and $Q$ |
| $P = Q$ | *together* |
| Negation | Exclude everything containing $P$ |
| $-P$ | |
| $P/Q$ | Search for everything containing neither $P$ nor $Q$ |

Thus there are a number of conceivable search profiles. By combining operands and operators it is possible to retrieve in KWOC form, say, all sentences referring to the steel industry, or all sentences dealing with both the Party and the steel industry, or all sentences that mention the steel industry but not the Party, or all sentences referring to the steel industry which in addition contain a term indicating failure to fulfil the plan, etc. The prerequisite in all cases is that the vocabulary has been studied and that all terms referring to a given concept or theme (the steel industry, the Party, failure to fulfil the plan, etc.) are included on a term-list. The simplest such compilation is based on a frequency list including all sign-strings in the data base.

For the present study, three basic search lists were first developed for sectoral, geographical and institutional analyses. All terms connected with a given sector, geographical area or institution were entered into these lists grouped according to subject, which made it possible to retrieve all items dealing with a number of search words or truncated strings in chronological order. For example, in the sub-section of the sectoral list dealing with education there was the word *uchitel'* (teacher), and the computer produced a list of all sentences containing this word. A total study of *Pravda*'s treatment of various words connected with education thus made it possible to compare what the paper had to say about school problems at different times.

The text thus retrieved from the data base proved to be very long; the sectoral list resulted in more than 1000 pages of print-out. To make the text more surveyable, it was in many cases judged appropriate to develop more precise search profiles using more operators. In certain cases search profiles were cross-checked against one another, while at other times distinctions were introduced in order to test the working hypotheses generated when the preliminarily sorted material was examined. Many of these experiments yielded little, but others facilitated the analysis considerably. The low cost of the searches made it worth while to experiment a great deal with new search profiles, even if many of the answers had to be discarded.

In addition to the transcriptions in KWOC form, frequencies were also extraced from the data base. The same operators were used here, and a question might be forumulated as follows: count the frequency of instructions containing both a word connected with science and one connected with agriculture. Since there is a risk in such contingency searches that irrelevant combinations will influence the total, frequencies were sought only for words that had been checked earlier in KWOC form.

Punching 135,714 words is a long process, and constructing programmes and search profiles also proved to be an arduous task. When the technique tested here matures somewhat, however, it may become possible to win time in two ways. First, the transmission of data on to magnetic tapes by optic reading is both considerably cheaper and much more rapid than punching; secondly, standardised programmes simplify utilisation of the data base. The possibilities of using optic reading for the present study were investigated, but entry costs were found to be too high. When optic reading of printed texts makes a definite breakthrough – and that must happen in the not too distant future – it will greatly facilitate information retrieval analyses in a number of disciplines in the humanities and social sciences.

# 4 Three Years in the Life of the Soviet Union

The history of the Soviet Union between the World Wars was revolutionary in more than one sense. The political upheaval in 1917 was followed by a series of radical changes which in a few decades totally reshaped the social and economic structure of the country. During the period of so-called War Communism the monetary economy ceased to function, and the cities were instead supplied through requisitioning and bartering. In the NEP era there arose a kind of mixed economy, which, however, broke down under the pressure of price controls and other interventions in the market. This paved the way for forced collectivisation. Great waves of migration were triggered by forced industrialisation and the arrests of the late 1920s and the 1930s. At the same time, human resources were mobilised by an intense concentration on education, agitation and propaganda. In the course of just a few decades Soviet society underwent not only a political but also an agrarian, industrial and cultural revolution.

The period after 1945 appears on the surface less dramatic. Administrative and economic reforms have been implemented without agonising social conflicts. Forms of political struggle have gradually become milder, and ideological changes in course such as de-Stalinisation have been made without causing convulsive repercussions in the Party and society. Reconstruction in a number of areas has continued according to the plans drawn up before the Second World War. Dialectical breaks have been avoided, and the transformation of society has been guided into evolutionary channels.

In many respects, however, the post-war epoch has also been one of radical changes. Not until these decades does industrialisation really set its mark on Soviet society by fundamentally altering the living conditions of the population. Manual labour has diminished in scope and been replaced by mechanical and automated processes. Depopulation of the countryside has continued, so that a majority of Soviet citizens now live in cities and other densely populated areas. A significant expansion has occurred in housing and the consumer industries. The educational system has been developed considerably; the new means of communication such as aviation and television have contributed to a more rapid flow of information and firmer social integration. Distances in the enormous country have shrunk at the same time as new, peripheral areas have begun to be exploited in earnest through systematic colonisation. From a lacerated and starving nation at the end of the War the Soviet Union has come a long way on the road towards prosperity and modernity.

The conditions in which this reconstruction was begun were gloomier than in most European states.[1] The European part of the Soviet Union was hit harder by the Second than by the First World War, and the destruction in 1945 was greater than that which in 1917 had helped to cause two political revolutions. Stalingrad, Kiev, Khatkov, Minsk, Sevastopol, Odessa, Voronezh, Smolensk and many other cities lay in ruins. Leningrad had suffered greatly during the long blockade, and the enemy had penetrated to the outskirts of the city of Moscow. A total of six million buildings were destroyed and 25 million people lost their homes, and this in a country where overcrowding had been an acute problem even before the war. The water and energy supply systems were in many areas out of order. Communications were broken in large parts of the country – 65,000 km of railroad lines and 2000 km of streetcar tracks had been destroyed, the road network was severely damaged and fuel was in short supply. Agriculture was badly mauled in the occupied areas, where over 100,000 kolkhozes had been burnt. Livestock herds had been greatly reduced and seed had in many cases been consumed. A severe drought in 1946 brought the country to the brink of starvation.

Material losses were alleviated by extensive indemnities and requisitions from Eastern and Central Europe. One American analyst has calculated that such transfers may have been great enough to replace all the material destruction caused by the War.[2] Yet in no way could they compensate for the enormous loss of human resources. According to official statistics, approximately 20,000,000 Soviet citizens died as a result of the war, and to this figure must be added the millions who perished in Stalin's persecution campaigns. In *The Great Terror* (1968) Conquest estimates that the famine and deportations connected with collectivisation claimed roughly 7,000,000 victims, and that as many as 12,000,000 may have died in concentration camps in 1936–50. Approximately an additional 1,000,000 were executed in the thirties. Apart from the losses in the war, then, the Stalin regime may have cost the country as many as 20,000,000 people. Conquest himself considers this a cautious estimate which might need to be raised by as much as 50 per cent.[3] All in all, the war, famine, executions and the camps would account for 40–50 million lives. Of those who were spared, many were crippled for life.

Such atrocities have left wounds which neither five, fifteen nor twenty-five years have been able to heal. But reconstruction was also vigorous and 1950, 1960, and 1970 all have a distinctive character as three different steps in the developmental staircase from destitution to relative prosperity. In Stalin's last year the proximity of the war was still apparent in all parts of everyday Soviet life. The camps had been emptied of their dead but not of their living. The cities had lost a large part of their population, and in agriculture women, children, and the aged filled the vacuum left by the men killed in the war. The Khruschev era was in many respects different. By then the greatest destitution had been eliminated and the foundations of a modern consumer society had been laid. But goods were still very limited, and the goal of catching up with and passing the United States was in most areas extremely remote. This was a time when one production campaign followed another — victory in the peaceful competition between nations with different social systems was sought in outer space, in corn-farming, in Siberian oil fields and the newly cultivated expanses of Kazakhstan. The period under Brezhnev witnesses the consolidation of a Soviet welfare society with certain features of 'post-industrialism'. Extensive expansion has been replaced by a more intensive type of growth, the economy is swept by rationalisation campaigns. The service sector increases and the environmental effects of growth begin to attract notice. The 'post-war era' approaches its conclusion — it becomes increasingly irrelevant to view development against the background of a distant world war.

## 4.1 THE SOVIET UNION IN 1950

The year 1950 is a frosty one in world politics. The late forties represent an expansive period for Stalin and his allies. The communists have seized power throughout Eastern Europe, and in China Chiang Kai-shek has just been driven out. Mao Tse-tung spends the winter of 1949–50 in Moscow negotiating for Soviet aid to the new people's republic. In the European people's republics accounts have recently been settled with Titoism, and a number of leading revisionists have been executed. The time of the popular front has passed, and the division between Communists and Social-Democrats has hardened. The United States has begun its policy of 'containment'. The summer of 1950 witnesses the outbreak of the Korean War. The chilly atmosphere on the international scene spreads to domestic politics. Stalin's autocracy is solidly established and his personality cult unbroken. There is hardly even any pretence of following the Party statutes any longer. No congress has been held for eleven years, and the Politburo is practically inoperative. Not even Stalin's closest subordinates feel secure; Voznesenskii, who was a leading economic organiser during the war, and a number of high officials in the Leningrad Party organisations are dismissed and executed. Innumerable collectives and organisations congratulate Stalin on his seventy-fifth birthday in December 1949, and these eulogies are published in *Pravda* as a daily serial during the whole of 1950.

It is also a cold year in a more literal sense. Throughout the country there are shortages of food, clothing and housing. The production of foodstuffs has not yet reached the 1940 level, which itself was low in comparison with other pre-war years. In spite of the fact that the vast majority of all land belongs to co-operative and state agricultural concerns, meat, milk and eggs are for the most part still produced privately. There is a fair potato harvest in 1950 (88.6 million tons as against 76.1 million tons ten years earlier), but in the subsequent years it sinks below that of 1940. Although 48 per cent of the labour force is engaged in agriculture, hunger has not yet been eliminated.

The yield per hectare is low. There is little hope that the many small kolkhozes will be able to increase their productivity, so an extensive series of mergers is begun in 1950. The small sector of state farms, or sovkhozes, is also allowed to expand. Investments are made in foresting the steppes and the European part of the country in order to bind and dry land areas. In 1950 alone 560,000 hectares of new forest are planted. The project is named 'the Stalinist plan for the transformation of nature'.

Housing conditions are severely overcrowded, both in the cities and the countryside. Some of the destroyed buildings have been patched up, but there are neither materials nor means of transportation for any large-scale housing construction. Several families still commonly live together in a single room. In 1950, 1,073,000 apartments are built, most of them very small. Resources are at the same time channelled into showcase construction projects in Moscow such as subway stations and skyscrapers built in 'Stalin Gothic'. The greatest investments, however, are made in canals and hydroelectric stations. The Council of Ministers decides in 1950 to improve the irrigation of agricultural areas in the Rostov and Stalingrad regions and to create a new and important transportation route by constructing a canal between the Volga and the Don. Proposed canals in Turkmenistan and the Ukraine are approved at the same time. Huge power plants are planned on the Volga and the Dnieper. Such projects are called 'mighty construction works of communism' and are given highest priority.

Electricity is needed for both industrial and household use. In 1950 the countryside is still enveloped in darkness. Three decades have passed since Lenin defined Communism as Soviet power plus the electrification of the entire country and the GOELRO plan was set in operation, but only 15 per cent of the kolkhozes have electricity and only 21.5 per cent have telephones. The vastness of the country and a poorly developed road network also contribute to the isolation of the rural areas. The radio was important during the war as an instrument for influencing public opinion, but it has as yet penetrated but little into individual households. Public loudspeakers are common in 1950, but only one out of 50 Soviet citizens has his own radio set.

Household appliances have not yet been included in Soviet production plants. Only 6100 vacuum cleaners, 1200 refrigerators and 300 washing machines are manufactured in the entire country in 1950. Few grocery stores, let alone households, have a refrigerator. On the other hand, the shops and marketplaces have little that needs preserving, so quickly do their goods disappear from the counters.

Post-war Soviet society is a land of women. Even before the war they had a certain numerical dominance as a result of the previous World War, the Civil War, collectivisation and deportations, but by the end of the forties this majority is of quite a different order. At the end of the war only 31,000,000 men of draftable age remain, as against 52,000,000 women in the comparable age brackets. The ratio for this generation is therefore six to ten and about five to six for the entire population (43.9 per cent men and 56.1 per cent women in 1950). Women are forced to shoulder a heavy work load, accounting at this time for nearly one-third of the labour force in the building industry and over half in agriculture. Younger and older age groups and even invalids have also been extensively mobilised, and the working day is heavy. The forty-eight-hour week, which was reintroduced immediately before the war, is still the minimum norm. Labour discipline is maintained with harsh measures. Even trivial violations sometimes lead to deportation to the camps.

Nor is it difficult to fall into disfavour in the intellectual sphere. Lysenko's star is at its zenith in the natural sciences. A tight rein is kept on art and literature, even if the strangulation hold of the Zhdanov era has relaxed somewhat. In the area of linguistics, the established Marxist authority Marr is in 1950 dealt a crippling blow by Stalin, whose detailed criticism in *Marxism and Linguistics* is first published in an expanded issue of *Pravda* and then distributed in mass editions.

The year 1950 is difficult, but it is still one of noticeable progress. On 1 March considerable price reductions are announced for foodstuffs and a number of industrial products. Prices generally decrease 21–35 per cent, for milk by 10–35 per cent and for cooking fats by 30 per cent. This is the third major reduction since the war.

## 4.2 THE SOVIET UNION IN 1960

Ten years later the international climate has become milder. The Soviet Union no longer sees itself as a beleaguered fortress. Khrushchev has declared that the socialist camp is now strong enough to withstand attack and that aggression on the part of the big capitalist powers is therefore not inevitable. On the contrary, societies with different political systems can live in peaceful coexistence.

Tension between the two blocks has relaxed, and a cautious rapprochement has begun. The first thaw is interrupted by the revolts in Poland and Hungary in 1956, but afterwards contacts are resumed. A summit conference between the Soviet Union, Great Britain, France and the United States is held in Paris in the spring of 1960, but it soon breaks down when Eisenhower refuses to apologise for the violation of Soviet air space that comes to light in the U2 affair. Later in the year the disarmament conference in Geneva also runs aground. At the same time, the Soviet Union's relations with China begin to deteriorate seriously.

It is an eventful year for international politics. Sixteen new states are admitted to the United Nations. The declaration of independence in the Congo is followed by a violent civil war. Tension increases in Berlin, but the Soviet Union avoids pushing antagonisms to their extreme. The West assumes that the Russians are lying low pending the American presidential election, which results in a narrow victory for John F. Kennedy.

Three Soviet sputniks are launched into space. The space race has been intensified, but the time of manned flight has not yet arrived. The cosmos, however, provides attractive stuff for fascinating visions, and space flights leave a strong impression on Soviet science, culture, and social life.

Down on the ground the scars of war have begun to heal. Increases in production have been extremely rapid. Coal production has been doubled in the fifties, electricity has been tripled, petroleum quadrupled. Construction is in full swing. 45,000,000 tons of cement are produced, as compared with only 10,000,000 tons in 1950, and 2,500,000 apartments are now built each year. But urbanisation has also proceeded rapidly, and the housing shortage is far from solved. Industry has absorbed a large part of the new labour force. White and blue-collar workers have increased by 50 per cent in a single decade, from 40,000,000 to 62,000,000. The urban population has grown from 69,000,000 to 104,000,000, but a slight majority of Soviet citizens still live in the countryside.

A large part of the production increase has gone to investments. Consumers no longer experience any acute shortages of fundamental goods, but supply is uneven and quality products few. Some households have begun to purchase capital goods such as refrigerators and vacuum cleaners, but such things are still inconceivable luxuries for the vast majority. In 1960 500,000 refrigerators are manufactured, as many vacuum cleaners, 800,000 washing machines and 88,000 pianos. Soviet homes have a total of 27,800,000 radio sets – seven times more than ten years previously – but television has so far come to only a fraction of the population.

The transport system has been expanded. In 1960 the average Soviet citizen travels 1170 km yearly, as compared with only 550 km in 1950. There are bicycles to be had, and even 500,000 motorcycles are sold.

Collective traffic in the cities has been improved, but passengers have also increased in number. Buses are more overcrowded than ever. Railway traffic has expanded, but flying is still too exclusive for the average Soviet citizen.

Great changes have occurred in the countryside. The old machine and tractor stations (MTS) have been dissolved and handed over to the large new kolkhozes, which are far better equipped than the earlier small collective farms. Electrification has come a long way – more than half of all kolkhozes have received electricity during the past decade, and all but the most remote farms now have telephones. The collective farms, however, are still less effective than the state farms, and the transformation of kolkhozes into sovkhozes slowly continues.

Agricultural produce has not increased as expected. There is a setback in the cultivation of new areas in Kazakhstan as the natural nutritious substances of the thin topsoil are exhausted. Kazakhstan, Tadzhikistan and the Ukraine fail to meet their plan quotas in 1960. Abundant rainfall makes harvesting difficult, but the yield is on the average a normal one.

The mass media strongly emphasise competition with the United States in this year, and in all imaginable areas Soviet citizens are urged to dig in to help the Soviet Union equal and surpass American production figures. 'During the present seven-year plan a decisive step must be taken in the creation of the material and technical base of communism to ensure a Soviet victory in peaceful economic competition with the capitalist countries,' notes the theoretical Party journal *Kommunist*.[4] 1960 is the second year of the seven-year plan.

The ultimate goal of communism plays an important role in Party doctrine. The extraordinary 21st Party Congress in 1959 saw the proclamation of a new epoch in Soviet history – 'the intensified construction of communism'. An ideological renaissance emerged in connection with de-Stalinisation, and a great deal of attention is now devoted to the transformation the Soviet Union will undergo as it develops from socialism to a fully communist society characterised by equality between city and countryside, a moneyless economy, the complete satisfaction of material needs, and social autonomy.

Political reforms have already begun to be described as stages in this transition to communism. The ambition of breathing new life into public organisations and letting them assume certain functions from governmental organs, for example, is presented as a step on the road to the stateless society. Economic decentralisation is another significant structural change. By 1957 most of the ministries in Moscow have been dissolved and responsibility for the day-by-day management of the economy transferred to regional economic councils, the so-called *sovnarkhozes*. Functional co-ordination at the union level, however, is taken care of by so-called state committees, which in many cases correspond to the old ministries.

Soviet politics in the Khrushchev era is characterised by a certain degree of liberalism. The closed society has opened windows to the outside world. Efforts are made in the judicial sphere to strengthen 'socialist legality', which is a formula for justice without administrative arbitrariness or excessively broad notions of guilt. The climate of debate is relatively mild, and scholars have a certain freedom to experiment. Modernism in art and literature is granted a limited amount of elbow-room.

## 4.3 THE SOVIET UNION IN 1970

Ten years later Europe is no longer the hot spot of world politics. A balance has been established there that has been steadied rather than disturbed by the Soviet display of power in Czechoslovakia in 1968. The new regime in West Germany, which alters its foreign policy at this time, contributes to this stabilisation. In 1970 Brandt visits both East Germany and the Soviet Union. A non-aggression pact between the Soviet Union and West Germany is signed in Moscow. In other parts of the world, however, violence is all the more apparent. Nigeria is still being torn by devastating civil strife, and the war in Indochina has continued to escalate. In the spring, American and South Vietnamese troops invade Cambodia.

During the 1960s the Soviet Union acquired many of the characteristic features of a prosperous modern society. The birth rate has declined in a single decade from 24.9 to 17.4 per mille. It is highest in the Caucasus and Central Asia and lowest in the Baltic and other European republics. Divorces have doubled. The standard of living has risen considerably. Food is more plentiful and clothes are more elegant. Other stores also begin to be well stocked. Capital consumer goods are now purchased by households on a relatively large scale. In August 1970, the Volga factory in the large automobile manufacturing centre Togliatti begins production of the 'Zhiguli' passenger car, the fruit of Soviet and Italian co-operation. During the year are produced six million refrigerators, five million washing machines and six million television sets.

Light industry, however, is not the only expanding area; the heavy sector has also continued to grow steadily. Energy production has increased considerably – oil and electricity have more than doubled and natural gas has quadrupled since 1960. Huge new fields in Siberia are being tapped, and the pipeline system has been extended. Substantial investments have also been made in the chemical industry, where both artificial fertilisers and synthetic materials for the building and textile industries have become important product areas. The manufacture of chemical fibres has nearly tripled in a single decade.

Growth can still to a great extent draw on new labour. The industrial work force grows in the sixties from 22 to 31 million, while that of agriculture decreases from 29 to 27 million. But efforts are also made to increase productivity through rationalisation. The sixties represent a renaissance in Soviet labour science and by 1970 there are already 40 research centres occupied with increasing effectivity. The 'scientific organisation of work' is now a publicly established goal. It is reckoned that 85 per cent of the national economic growth in 1970 will be ensured by increased productivity. Concentrations and fusions are part of this effort. Kolkhozes have continued to decrease in number, and the tendency is the same in industry, where a great many small units are liquidated in 1970 in favour of larger integrated organisations. Certain forms of decentralisation, however, are also tested. More and more enterprises are allowed to keep their own books (*khozraschet*), and the planned economy has acquired certain elements of market socialism.

Technical achievements in a broad assortment of fields begin to approach the spectacular progress already achieved in narrow high-priority areas such as defence and space travel. By the time Luna-16 and Luna-17 land on the moon in 1970, there are also more adding machines in Soviet offices down here on earth, and industry has begun to make serious use of computerised techniques. The mass media, research and education devote considerable attention to the 'scientific and technological revolution'.

The 1960s were also a time of expansion within the educational system. By 1970 there are almost 80,000,000 Soviet students at all levels, of which 4,500, 000 are enrolled in the 800 institutes of advanced study. A raised level of education has also resulted in a more active cultural life and a more varied assortment of reading materials. Total newspaper circulation has doubled since 1960.

The great political event of the year is the centenary of Lenin's birth, celebrated on 22 April. But 1970 as a whole is Lenin's year. Demonstrations, campaigns and exhibitions follow one another in rapid succession, his works are published in commemorative editions, there is a steady stream of artistic works depicting him, Soviet publishers print a broad assortment of books on such themes as 'Lenin and art', 'Lenin and Uzbekistan', 'Lenin and the cotton industry', etc. Khrushchev's Party programme adopted by the 22nd Congress in 1962 has fallen into the background under Brezhnev, but Leninism lives on. Like 1967, 1970 is an anniversary year, and memories of the revolutionary past are a prominent theme in the mass media.

# 5 Political Problems: The Sectoral Dimension

The 5523 instructions on which the present study is based all deal with problems in Soviet politics. Degree of thoroughness varies, but almost all the instructions explicitly or implicitly register some fault, attempt a rudimentary diagnosis of the nature or most likely causes of the shortcoming, and indicate what must be done and who ought to do it. These components can be kept separate analytically, but to do so in the present discussion would result in pointless repetitions; faults, causes and solutions are often mentioned in the same breath. We shall instead examine Soviet political problems in three distinct divisions. In this chapter, the problems of the various economic sectors will be considered. The next chapter will treat the geographical distribution of the problems, and finally we shall turn to the role of political institutions in *Pravda*'s diagnoses and strategies.

## 5.1 IRON, STEEL AND THE ENGINEERING INDUSTRY

The metal industry is the base of industrial expansion in the Soviet Union. It is known in Party jargon as *osnova osnov* – 'the foundation of foundations'. The Donets-Dnieper region in the southern Ukraine, which still accounts for approximately half of the total iron production, was the chief area of development before the Second World War. During the war, however, supplies to the weapons industry came from a 'second metallurgical base' in the Urals which has continued to increase in significance. A 'third metallurgical base' has also been developed in Kazakhstan and in the Kuznetsk Basin in Siberia, and efforts have been made at the same time to spread the production of iron and steel to a number of smaller centres. The engineering industry has traditionally been localised near its consumers, and is concentrated in the central Russian industrial area around Moscow. Machines for Siberia are manufactured primarily in the European areas of the country. The iron and steel industry is a favourite target of criticism in *Pravda*. Azovstal and Zaporozhstal, two southern steel plants that had failed to store up fuel and raw materials for the winter, are severely reprimanded in the winter of 1950. These attacks continue throughout the year, and toward autumn new forceful warnings are issued to steelworks throughout the country advising them to amass sufficient winter supplies to avoid breaking production rhythm. The Krivorog Basin, the largest Soviet iron-ore field, is among the lagging areas. *Pravda* notes:

At one time the Krivorog Basin was famous for its Stakhanovite working methods: Now it is almost forgotten.

In addition to general complaints of poor results, there are also more specific demands for various products. An editorial entitled 'More Construction Materials for the National Economy' (50.206) emphasises the need for reinforcement steel and special roll-forged sections. The building and engineering industries express similar demands in the following years.

There is a certain shift in consumer demands for different types of products. In 1960, *Pravda* greatly emphasises the need for roll-forged steel and directs its summons to an unusually large number of groups – sovnarkhozes, local Party organizations, trade unions, the Komsomol, inventors, rationalisation experts, the press, and finally the entire Soviet public – exhorting them to engage themselves in this urgent economic problem. Ten years later new demands are discussed – steel pipe, new steel alloys, and a standardisation of curved sections. Specific requests increase during this period.

The iron and steel industry, however, also makes demands of its own. Coke is not good enough for the blast-furnaces. Coal deliveries are late. Ore transports are also unsatisfactory. In January 1970 *Pravda* states that steelworks were a million tons short of iron ore during the preceding month due to a lack of railroad cars. The supply of limestone and scrap metal is also uneven. The many directives in *Pravda* concerning the effective operation of the metal industry indicate that 1970 was a difficult year in this regard.

*Pravda* discusses the Soviet engineering industry every few weeks. The word 'machine' alone occurs 204 times in our material, and most cases have to do with faults in machine construction or unsatisfied demands for machines on the part of various branches of industry. It seems that a shortage of agricultural machines received highest priority in 1950, but the mechanisation of other industries also required increased production, as is emphasised by the editorials of later years. In 1960 *Pravda* stresses the need for machines for the chemical and consumer industries, and ten years later attention is directed to a number of work processes requiring mechanisation. During the entire period, however, agriculture remains one of the most important customers of the engineering industry, and *Pravda's* editorials constantly issue directives on the farmers' need of tractors, combines and other vehicles. The transition from mechanisation to automation is accompanied by demands for increased efforts in the areas of research and development in order to solve the problems of individual branches. There is a demand for completely equipped factories. One recurrent complaint in the latter two years is that new plants cannot be used due to defective equipment.

## 5.2 THE ENERGY SECTOR

The energy resources of the Soviet Union are vast but difficult to tap. Exploitation before the Second World War was concentrated in the regions near the large industrial areas in the European part of the country – coal came from the Donets Basin and oil from the Baku fields. The electrification campaign (GOELRO) launched by Lenin in the twenties significantly explained the production of electricity. A number of hydroelectric power plants were constructed on the rivers of the Ukraine and Russia. But electricity was never as important as coal, whose relative share of the energy balance continued to grow until the middle fifties.

After the war, however, the European reserves were no longer sufficient. The Donets Basin never regained its former significance. Instead new coalfields were exploited in the far north of Russia, in the Urals, in Kazakhstan and Siberia. The Baku oil fields began to dry up and petroleum extraction moved out into the Caspian Sea, but even more important was the opening of the 'second Baku' in the Volga-Urals area east of Moscow. Technical advances also made it possible to use the water power of Siberian rivers, and gigantic power plants were constructed on the Yenisei and Angara. Less spectacular fuelled power stations in European Russia, however, continued to account for the greater part of the Soviet Union's electricity production.

In spite of the fact that large industrial centres were established in the new peripheral power areas, this expansion put great strains on the Soviet transport system. The old industries were situated in parts of the country which were poor in natural energy resources. Coal was transported primarily by rail, accounting under Stalin for more than a third of all railroad freight. One of the major post-war projects is the huge pipeline system from the 'second Baku', which supplies both European and Siberian industries with petroleum. Considerable investments have also been made in natural gas, a resource that was previously unexploited. The large cities of Russia and the Ukraine receive gas through pipelines from the northern Caucasus and the Dashava region in the western Ukraine, and gas is also exported to other countries in Eastern Europe by means of the so called Druzhba network.

*Pravda*'s interest in coal is particularly lively in 1950. Mining is beset with serious difficulties. Some fifteen editorials during this year criticise the organisation and low productivity of the branch. It is noted that many mines are obsolete and lack modern technical equipment. *Pravda*'s principal remedy is 'complex mechanisation', and numerous directives demand rationalisation and an increased use of new techniques. The under-exploitation of machinery and poor management are common complaints.

| | 1950 | 1960 | 1970 | |
|---|---|---|---|---|
| COAL | 19 | 4 | 12 | absolute figures |
| | 0.39 | 0.14 | 0.21 | frequency per mille* |

\* where not indicated otherwise, per mille denotes per thousand words/year

Coal production has a lower priority in the remaining two years. In 1960 *Pravda* again notes technical deficiencies and still recommends 'complex mechanisation', but in addition to complaints about productivity, now we also find comments on the miners' work environment and living conditions. One editorial points out that certain of the largest mines in Kuzbass (the Kuznets Basin) still lack lunchrooms, while another notes housing shortages. By 1970 the production of coal has practically disappeared from the editorial page, but distribution, storage and use are topical subjects. Complaints of waste are common; faulty railcars, for example, drop much of their cargo en route. Deficiencies in the transport system have resulted in difficulties for receivers. The leading coalfields of the country have not fulfilled their raised haulage, and the Kazakhstan miners have not managed to ship out the quantities specified in their plan.

Items mentioning coke are few but evenly distributed. Criticism deals mainly with shortages (1950), waste and poor quality (1960), and lags in the development of the coke industry (1970). The message under Stalin is a simple one — work more to produce more. Socialist competition, the emulation of successful brigades and a more efficient use of available production resources are among the standard remedies. One editorial recommends more intensive drilling for new deposits, another notes that the new method of turbine drilling has not yet been employed. Twenty years later emphasis has shifted forward from production to distribution and utilisation. *Pravda* not only appeals for an increased use of modern techniques and greater productivity in petroleum extraction, it also discusses problems connected with the transportation and refinement of the raw material. The shortage of pipe is a central theme, inland navigation is another bottleneck. The petrochemical industry cannot meet its quotas due to a lack of equipment.

Gas is first discussed under Khrushchev and becomes particularly topical under Brezhnev. It is noted twice in January 1960 that the production of gas turbines is insufficient, and several complaints are made against the transport branches responsible for supplying distant parts of the country. Thus far the demands voiced in *Pravda* reflect problems connected with gas winning, but the waste in user branches such as the metal industry is also criticised. In 1970, reactions from individual households are registered — gas lines have often not been laid when new housing developments are ready for occupation. On one occasion, *Pravda* sharply denounces pipeline builders who neglect to restore the land around the pipes so that it can be used for agriculture. This is among the first and as yet uncommon discussion of the environment to appear in the paper.

Electricity is the subject of about ten editorials in each of the three years studied here. Lenin's old demand for the 'electrification of the whole country' recurs every year but is not given high priority. During the early post-war period the needs of the farmers and consumers come after those of industry. Kolkhoz workers are offered more or less symbolic satisfaction:

> The patriotic duty of the Soviet peasant class is through work in the fields and the prompt fulfilment of its obligations to the state to strengthen our beloved Fatherland, which will further the speedy completion of the gigantic power stations on the Volga. (50.250)

Construction workers are important in *Pravda*'s appeals in 1950, but so are a number of operational problems. It is emphasised on several occasions that damaged turbines must be repaired and that the collectives of the fuelled power stations must lay up sufficient stores of fuel. Rationalisation is needed both in the operation of power plants and in the utilisation of electricity in industry. Several editorials call for extreme economy in resource consumption. The national ministry responsible for power stations is also rebuked for paying insufficient attention to the housing needs of plant workers. A strong interest in forced investments, high operational reliability, and good productivity in the field of electric production is in line with the signals sent in the same year to the coalmines. 1950 is a year when the Soviet leaders are keenly aware of problems of energy supply.

Interest a decade later in new plants and economical operation is almost null. Instead, *Pravda* discusses problems connected with the industrial utilisation of electric power. A shortage of electrotechnology seems to cause the greatest worries. The shoe and textile industries lack the electric machines needed to mechanise a number of stages of production, and the chemical industry expresses similar complaints. Schools also need more electric equipment. There is a shortage of electric locomotives, and *Pravda* discusses the need for electric motors. In 1970 the main emphasis is still on the utilization of electric energy, but there is also a renewed stress on economy. Industry is exhorted on several occasions to devote more attention to efficiency and to use locally available fuels to generate electricity.

Nuclear power is not considered at all.

Households occupy a subordinate position in *Pravda*'s treatment of energy problems. The needs of the transport sector are also given little attention, and agriculture is discussed relatively seldom. The predominant question is how to stretch energy resources to guarantee the smooth operation of industry. Political interest shifts during the period towards new sources of energy (from coal to gas and in some measure to oil) and from early to later stages of the production, distribution and utilisation chain. Energy problems seem to be important in 1950 and 1970, but they are less conspicuous in 1960.

## 5.3 THE CHEMICAL INDUSTRY

The chemical sector is one of the most rapidly expanding areas in the post-war Soviet economy, especially in the past two decades. The country is self-sufficient with respect to all essential chemicals. The use of artificial fertilisers has increased greatly, particularly after the failures in the newly cultivated virgin lands of Central Asia. Fertilisers have been enriched nutritionally in an attempt to reduce transport costs. Apatite rich in sulphuric acid is brought from the Kola Peninsula to superphosphate plants throughout the European part of the country, while Siberia and especially the cotton fields of Central Asia are supplied by newly discovered deposits in Kazakhstan. Nitrogenous fertilisers are produced around the large coal basins, but their share of the total production is smaller and growing less rapidly than in other countries.

The light chemical sector has also expanded considerably in recent decades, but the Soviet Union lags in this area. As late as 1970 production of plastics and synthetic resins was under the world average per capita (underdeveloped countries included), and calculated in absolute figures it was only somewhat over a third of West Germany's and a fourth of Japan's. Exploitation of large new oilfields, however, has also facilitated an expansion in the petrochemical industry, and the development of a pipeline system for gas distribution has provided a base for the production of synthetic fibres in the central industrial area. Nevertheless, in this sector as well Soviet production is low in relation to that of other industrialised countries.

*Pravda* devotes little attention to the chemical industry in 1950. The only specific complaints concern a shortage of nitrate of ammonia and printer's ink for the printing industry. By 1960 the industry receives considerably more comment. Two editorials contain detailed directives on the successful expansion of the branch. It is noted that Party organisations, soviets, and economic organs in a number of unidentified republics pay entirely too little attention to investments in the chemical industry. Machine construction is behind schedule; construction divisions that should have concerned themselves with the chemical industry have instead accepted other projects. The quality of machines and instruments is inferior; examples are mentioned of installations that have collapsed after a short time. Plants already in use often lack the necessary blueprints and specifications. There are also faults farther back in the production chain – the machinery industry is short of metal.

|  | *1950* | *1960* | *1970* |  |
| --- | --- | --- | --- | --- |
| CHEMICAL INDUSTRY | 5 | 24 | 41 | absolute figures |
|  | 0.10 | 0.84 | 0.70 | per mille |

Ten years later the chemical sector is still very much in the limelight. Investment problems are still given the most space. A steady stream of directives deal with construction that must be accelerated, machines that must be designed and equipment that must be delivered and broken in. In addition to these objectives, *Pravda* exhorts factories to make use of all available reserves to satisfy demand. Fertilisers, which in 1960 still aroused little attention, are now the most frequently discussed product. Under Khrushchev, *Pravda* urged most of all a better utilisation of locally available resources, but by 1970 the emphasis is on synthetic substances. A 'sharp rise' in the quality of such products is needed if agriculture is to benefit from these highly concentrated preparation. Insecticides and pesticides are another new area. The need of chemical products in the building industry is also discussed, but now for the first time the printing industry is ignored. Poorly run dry-cleaners are a new source of irritation to which *Pravda* returns a number of times.

*Pravda*'s editorials relatively seldom concern themselves with specific products, but clearly addressed appeals do sometimes occur. In 1960 it is noted twice that the synthetic rubber industry is developing too slowly, and on another occasion the chemical industry is called upon to produce more phenolic resin to be used in the development of a lighter rock wool for the building industry. Here, as in many other appeals to the chemical industry, other branches have obviously experienced difficulties. *Pravda*'s treatment of the sector reveals repeatedly the vital role chemicals play in the expansion of the Soviet economy.

5.4 THE CONSTRUCTION SECTOR

With an investment quota that has risen from about 21 per cent in 1950 to a little over 30 per cent in 1970, the Soviet building industry is steadily increasing its share of the national economy.[1] Although considerable expenditures have been made on industrial construction, the greater part of investments have gone into the housing sector. Little was done in the inter-war period to alleviate the traditionally overcrowded situation in Russia, and the war only served to aggravate the shortage. From 1950 to 1970 housing area per capita increased from seven to eleven square metres. That may seem to be a modest expansion, but the process appears in a new light when it is considered that during this period Soviet cities increased their population by 66,000,000, which represents almost a doubling. Soviet cement production – another indicator of the size of the building industry – increased by 900 per cent in the same period.

A considerable part of Soviet housing construction is done privately. Official statistics include housing built by the state and co-operative enterprises, housing built privately by workers and salaried employees, and housing built by kolkhozes, kolkhoz farmers and the 'rural intelligentsia'. As late as 1960, the latter two categories accounted for over half of all construction, while after that date the governmental sector has been allowed to expand considerably more rapidly, embracing more than three fourths of new housing projects by 1970. Over half of all housing, however, seems to be still in private hands.[2]

This rapid growth has necessitated a substantial expansion in the building materials industry, and in a number of areas – e.g. bricks, timber, window glass and construction steel – the Soviet Union has passed American production figures to become the world's largest manufacturer. At the same time, Western observers often note that the Soviet building sector is plagued by inherent weaknesses. Wilczynski has recently pointed out five weak points in the system. First of all, especially before the reforms of the sixties, there existed a *jolie de grandeur* that made itself felt in both public monumental architecture and the construction of industrial plants as 'work palaces'. Secondly, the building sector as a whole has been characterised by high material intensity. The low quality of building materials is a third troublesome factor, insufficiently mechanised construction techniques are a fourth. Finally, construction projects are often greatly delayed by a lack of co-ordination among the production components.[3]

Of the five problems postulated above, *Pravda*'s editorials concentrate above all on the last one. Prolonged construction projects are frequently mentioned, especially toward the end of the period. In 1970, for example, the paper attacks the *oblispolkom* (regional government administration) of the Novosibirsk region, which began building six hotels some five or six years previously, and criticises a number of specified ministries that are just as far behind in their projects. Disruptions in the distribution of financial resources, lags in planning and poor work management are sometimes mentioned as causes of such delays.

Wilczynski's other points are treated less directly. Appeals for economy and efficiency occur regularly in editorials dealing with construction, which also increase in number during the period. The strategy for successful construction in the earlier material seems to be a kind of 'Operation Persuasion'. The relevant Party organisations are exhorted to devote more energy to the construction workers' ideological and organisational training, and especially in 1960 there is an emphasis on the significance of intense socialist competition and a stress on moral incentives. In 1950 such appeals are addressed to a wider audience. If the building sector is to become effective it is not enough that only the construction workers dig in – they must also be given all possible support from the population as a whole. Manufacturers of cement, concrete, and bricks are often criticised for the poor quality of their products. The building materials industry and all other contractors are called upon to do their utmost for 'mighty construction works of communism'. The large investments of 1950 in energy and industry acquire a deep symbolic meaning.

One tendency throughout the period – discernible already in 1960 and clearer in 1970 – is that the diagnosis of problems in the construction sector deepens to include a greater interest in motivational and organisational aspects. In 1960 discussions begin to touch upon rationalisation and innovation in production processes and rhythm and continuity in the supply of materials. Ten years later *Pravda* has become strikingly frank not only about carelessness, but also about tendencies to insubordination and corruption. Waste and theft at construction sites are mentioned on several occasions, and in one editorial, entitled 'Take Care of the Property of the People', it is hinted that private building nearby is responsible for a surprisingly high consumption of materials on certain projects. The paper is also criticial of local organisations which have managed to obtain sums for construction that has never been planned or which use appropriated funds for other than specified purposes. It is noted that in a number of republics and regions showy administrative buildings, gymnasiums, and swimming pools have been constructed instead of schools, hospitals, and nurseries. Such transgressions show that better discipline is needed. Other problems in the building sector such as delays, or uneconomical methods and planning, however, can only be solved by greater creativity and flexibility on the part of local organisations. Faults in the administrative and organisational structure, deficient economic responsibility on the part of construction enterprises and the incompetent utilisation of material incentives are among the inherent shortcomings of the system most commonly mentioned in 1970.

Housing construction receives but scant interest in *Pravda*'s editorials in 1950. The needs of rural areas are most prominent. After harvesting in the fall the paper returns on three occasions to the lamentable state of housing on the kolkhozes, calling upon Soviet architects to design house types suited to the specific character of different geographical regions. The authorities responsible for housing construction are also instructed not to accept any half measures:

> Instead of sturdy, well-built houses certain leaders are building all manner of temporary shacks. Such nonsense must be stopped. (50.221)

*Pravda* orders Party organisations to get a good grip on housing construction. They must pay particular attention to economic considerations and make maximum use of locally available materials. In 1950 the paper is especially concerned about the thrifty employment of resources:

> It is the solemn duty of our builders and architects to furnish the Soviet people with attractive, economical, simple and comfortable housing, but they must at the same time avoid excesses that might make construction more expensive. (50.271)

The same chords are struck in 1960, when *Pravda* criticises the construction of unnecessarily expensive brick and stone apartment houses in certain republics. But now the quality of housing is of greater concern. Too many apartments are incomplete or defective at the time of occupation. Hygienic standards have been ignored, heating systems function poorly, local authorities neglect repairs and maintenance. A certain shift of interest toward older housing can be noted in 1960, and this trend continues and intensifies ten years later.

There is considerable emphasis in 1960 on industrialising housing construction. Time and again the newspaper notes that the building materials industry is underdeveloped. The most urgent need is for an increased production of prefabricated components. Multi-storey blocks have first priority in 1960. One editorial complains that entirely too many one-family houses are being built even in the large cities. In 1970 the reverse is true — *Pravda* is of the opinion that enthusiasm for constructing multi-storey houses has got out of hand, noting that buildings of up to nine storeys have been erected even in small communities and villages, in disregard of the general townscape and technical and economic considerations.

*Pravda*'s directives concerning housing construction pay noticeably more attention to aesthetic and functional aspects in the last year of our two-decade period. Several editorials express irritation over the careless use of land; houses have been built without a thought to possible effects on the environment or to whether the land could have been used better for other purposes. Others note that many cities and communities have no general plans and that those that do exist are not always followed. 'Discipline in city planning' is a new editorial slogan in 1970.

Discipline is also needed in the construction process itself. Delayed building projects and interrupted repairs are discussed several times in this year. Better planning and a more flexible use of economic incentives are the recommended cure for such ailments. Building enterprises should be given greater responsibility for their cost estimates, one of *Pravda*'s suggestions being a type of total contract system (*raschet za polnostyu gotovye ob''ekty*) (70.192).

The three leaders dealing with architecture, one for each of the years studied, offer us an interesting view of Soviet housing policy. In 'The Soviet Architect' (50.271) the members of the profession are called upon to improve their theoretical knowledge and study the traditions of Russian architecture. The classical heritage must be absorbed, but this must not be allowed to degenerate into a mechanical and uninspired copying of 'the artistic forms of the past'. The Academy of Architecture is exhorted to 'strengthen its contacts with life'. According to 'The Solemn Duty of Soviet City Planners' (60.013), it is important that architects and builders develop new and efficient materials for multi-storey houses. The style must be simple, without any embellishments or showy ornaments. Experts must be given a bigger say in construction matters – *Pravda* stresses that the chief architects of the cities must be granted greater responsibility and authority. In 'The Soviet Master-Builder' (70.303), it is emphasised that architects must learn to understand and utilise the latest scientific and technical advances. Architecture must be modernised and made more efficient – buildings should be beautiful and expressive but also economical and functional. It is the architect's solemn duty, therefore, to pay careful attention to the needs and interests of the people. But construction must also satisfy ideological demands:

> Soviet architects, their associations and Party organisations must protect the architect from alien ideological influence, develop the theory of their fields on the firm basis of Marxist aesthetics and help strengthen international ties with builders in the fraternal socialist countries and with progressive architects elsewhere in the world. (70.303)

Thus, while architects are encouraged in 1950 to study the national heritage, their colleagues in 1970 are to be sensitive to international impulses, as long as this stimulation does not contain alien ideological elements. The differences in shades of meaning are subtle but noticeable.


5.5 LIGHT INDUSTRY

A retardation of the development of consumer products was one price Soviet society was forced to pay for rapid industrialisation. After a relatively expansive development during the NEP period, light industry received extremely limited investments in the thirties. The war caused a further serious depression in the standard of living.

According to Janet Chapman's calculations, the production of consumer products per capita in 1945 had sunk to 43 per cent of the 1937 level. [4] The decline was even sharper in the textile and clothing industries; during the remainder of Stalin's life less than one item per person and year was manufactured of such articles as underwear. [5]

Great resources have been allotted to the consumer industries during the following decades, and at several points the official course has been described as giving light industry priority over the heavy sector. But the consumer industries have had a higher growth rate than heavy industry in only two of the twenty years between 1950 and 1970 (1953 and 1970), while in one year (1968) expansion was equal in both sectors. The average increase in production for the period is 9.3 per cent for light industry and 10.9 per cent for heavy industry. [6] Growth in both sectors is greatest during the first post-war decade. This is of course natural, considering the battered state of the Soviet economy in 1945, but since Stalin's successors have often been associated with a special emphasis on light industry, it may be worth noting that its growth rate in the past two decades has never surpassed that of his last year.

The *Pravda* material used here agrees better with the conventional image of developments than with the economic statistics. Interest in consumer products in 1950 is almost nil. On one occasion the clothing industry is urged to be more careful with its raw materials, on another the White Russian knitwear industry is reproached for not fulfilling its second quarter plan, but there is otherwise total silence. Attention to textiles and clothing is considerably more keen in 1960, but the discussion is centred on the problems of the industry rather than those of the consumers. *Pravda* mentions a number of factors which hamper production – shortages of mechanical equipment, thread, dyes, etc. – and addresses repeated appeals to research institutes and development departments in the engineering and chemical industries to satisfy these needs. In some editorials, however, consumers' viewpoints are also voiced. Demands are made for more children's clothes, more modern fashions, brighter colours, and better ready-made garments.

Demands for quality and variety predominate in 1970. Complaints are made about the meagre assortment of children's summer clothes, and in November *Pravda* reports that there is a shortage of good skiing outfits. An editorial entitled 'Better Quality in Production' (70.070) tells of a factory, 'The Red Urals', which was forced to take back a large part of its production for restitching. Contractors to the textile and clothing industries are still often made the scapegoat for shortcomings in the branch. 'High-Quality Raw Materials for the Consumer Industries' (70.219) contains several examples of passing the buck backward in the production process. The demands of the textile factories for high-quality linen fibres are just, *Pravda* notes. More good cotton is also needed. The need for fine-fibred cotton is three-fifths higher than supply. It is therefore the duty of agriculture in the cotton-growing regions to further expand cultivation of the best types of cotton and to raise their yield. If demands for linen are to be satisfied, the Ministry of Agriculture and the textile research institutes will have to develop better processing techniques. In addition, the textile industry needs more orlon and dacron.[7] *Pravda* returns several times in 1970 to the shortage of synthetic fibres.

Another branch that *Pravda* helps by pressuring suppliers is the shoe industry, which is the subject of no fewer than five editorials in 1960. Appeals are directed to various parties: the machine builders are urged to provide the shoe workers with better equipment, research institutes are urged to develop mechanical and automated techniques, and the chemical industry is exhorted to guarantee the shoe industry an adequate supply of dyes and artificial leather. Gosplan RSFSR (the planning authority in the Russian Soviet Federal Socialist Republic) is also encouraged to acquire electric equipment to rationalise production. But there is also criticism of the shoe industry in *Pravda* that evidently springs from reactions on the part of retailers or consumers: models are old-fashioned and unattractive, quality is low, the range poor. The shortage of children's shoes is mentioned on two occasions. By 1970 consumer opinion is even more important. Complaints are made of poor shoes and poor repair shops, and as usual there are gaps in the range — ski boots and children's shoes.

The stronger voice of consumer demands in 1970 is also confirmed by a number of directives dealing with various consumer articles. *Tovary* ('consumer goods') are treated in four editorials in both 1950 and 1960, but they are the subject of no fewer than fourteen editorials in 1970. The writers of the articles in the last year also seem to have been more deeply impressed by letters from angry consumers — references to such complaints now begin to be common. Nor do they any longer hesitate to condescend to speak of such everyday matters as shortages of china, eating utensils, and drinking glasses. Direct references to consumer desires are rare in all three years, however, and they do not become more frequent towards the end of the period. In spite of a growing interest in consumer goods, directives calling upon light industry and retailers to pay closer attention to consumer demands are if anything fewer in 1970 than in the other two years.


## 5.6 THE TRANSPORT SECTOR

The Soviet transport system differs in significant respects from those of developed Western countries. Railways and inland navigation account for a very large share of freight traffic, while road transport is less important. Considerable sections of the rail network were built during tsarist times. It has reassumed its central significance in the Soviet economy since the war. The major transport routes run east to west, primarily through the southern Ukraine and western Siberia. The transportation of coal and ore is important in these areas. Only a modest part of the rail network is electrified.

The share of all transportation accounted for by inland navigation was greater before the Revolution than now, but its decrease in the Soviet Union has been less marked than in many other parts of the world. On the contrary, huge dam and canal projects have been undertaken to expand inland navigation; the capacity of the Volga system, for example, has been greatly increased by new connections with the Moskva and the Don. Other new canals have opened navigation between the Baltic, the White Sea and the Black Sea. Siberian waterways are also being used to a greater extent. Cargoes there consist chiefly of timber, minerals, and oil.

Road haulage (reckoned in tons per mile) has increased by ten times during the period between 1950 and 1970, but it still represents only a small part of the entire sector. Trucks are most often used for short runs to connect other types of transportation. 'Roadless Russia', as it was once called, is still very much with us – the highway network is of poor quality, and road maintenance in rural areas has long been the responsibility of individual agricultural collectives. A decree issued in 1958 extended these duties to industrial enterprises and also allowed for maintenance responsibilities to be discharged in the form of taxes. Large areas of the country lack paved roads.

Hunter, an American expert on Soviet transport policy, stresses the impressive gains in productivity that have been made during recent decades. The railways in particular show an extraordinarily high capacity-utilisation.[8] *Pravda*'s editorials, however, illuminate an aspect of this utilisation that is not evident in the statistics, namely overload. Criticism of the railways is severe in both 1950 and 1970, and many complaints have to do with shipments that could not be delivered on schedule. Slack labour discipline on the railways is troublesome in 1950, and the need for better political work among the employees is noted often. In 1960 there is nothing whatsoever about the railways in the *Pravda* editorials, but ten years later the sector has again become an important problem. The list of goods that have arrived late or been carelessly handled is a long one, including iron ore, liquid fuels, fertilisers, coal, salt, chemical products, school equipment, metals, etc. On several occasions the newspaper discusses breakdowns in the transportation of foodstuffs – grain has been left lying in the warehouses, fruit and vegetables have been spoilt by delays, food has not reached the large cities in the north. Diagnoses now point more to technical and organisational faults than to breaches of discipline. Rolling stock is insufficient and unsuitable for certain cargoes, loading and unloading facilities are in many places deficient, and there is a lack of co-ordination between the railroads and the inland waterways. Better planning is needed in all areas.

|  | 1950 | 1960 | 1970 |  |
| --- | --- | --- | --- | --- |
| RAILWAYS | 22 | 0 | 18 | absolute figures |
|  | 0.45 | 0 | 0.31 | per mille |

Loading and unloading are in 1970 also a problem for inland navigation. Ports do not function satisfactorily. The principal worries in the area of transportation by road seem to be inadequate loading techniques, poor vehicles and faulty organisation. Farm trucks lose too much grain en route, and when they do arrive at their destination a lack of storage space often causes delays in reloading. One proposed remedy recommends transportation in 'vehicle-trains' trucks (*avtopoezd*) – or tractors with several trailers or wagons – as a means of overcoming the most serious problems. There is a slight increase during the period in the number of items dealing with road haulage, but the sector as a whole is not a common topic. *Pravda* has nothing at all to say about highway construction.

There is an interesting note in 1970 on the need of raising the social status of the transport sector that shows that by then such questions have acquired a higher rank in Soviet politics. In their reports of successes in agriculture, *Pravda* writes, it is not enough that newspapers deal with the best harvest workers and tractor drivers. The mass media should also portray leading skilled workers in the transport sector. The names of our best drivers, railwaymen, engineers, ship's captains and dock workers must be known throughout the country, notes an editorial addressed to the moulders of public opinion. (70.190)

Passenger traffic never receives nearly the same attention as freight haulage, but several items in 1950 and 1970 reflect a concern for holidaymakers and tourists. *Pravda* is more interested in local public transportation in the latter year, pointing out some of the reasons communications are still unsatisfactory in certain areas: poor management, careless drivers who fail to observe their schedules and a lack of garages and depots that necessitates leaving buses and coaches out in the open are among the factors mentioned. City traffic has now also been assigned a weak position on the political agenda, and *Pravda* observes that urban planning must allow for efficient communications.

### 5.7 AGRICULTURE

The dramatic revolution in Soviet agriculture occurred in the late 1920s and early 1930s, when millions of peasant households were combined into collective units. No structural revolution of comparable proportions has taken place since then, but it may still be maintained that the real collectivisation has in many respects been accomplished after the Second World War. The collective sector of Soviet agriculture has steadily expanded, and its dominance over private production is in many areas fairly recent. The production of such foodstuffs as potatoes and eggs, however, is still for the most part in private hands.

Post-war collectivisation has been realised chiefly by expanding state and co-operative production and allowing the private sector to stagnate or grow only slightly. A series of structural rationalisations has been implemented. Around 1950 the number of kolkhozes was reduced from approximately 250,000 to about 125,000. Mergers have continued since then, so that by 1970 only about 33,000 remained. Moreover, many collective farms have been transformed into state farms. The expansion of the sovkhoz sector has also been furthered by the cultivation of vast new areas, projects which have generally been accomplished under state management. All in all, the total cultivated area of the Soviet Union increased from 146,300,000 hectares in 1950 to 202,900,000 hectares in 1960 and 206,600,000 hectares in 1970. Sovkhozes and kolkhozes account at the latter date for approximately half of that area. Private land represents only about 3–4 per cent of all cultivated acreage, but its yields are of considerable significance in the national economy. In his study of Soviet agriculture, Wädekin notes that the private and state and co-operative sectors are closely interlocked, performing complementary functions in the total production process.[9] Table 5.7.1. shows the extent of 'quiet' collectivisation during the past two decades.

Private production has decreased considerably but is still significant. It should be added that a large part of it is for the individual use of the producing households. The private share of marketed produce is in all cases substantially lower than the figures in the table.[10]

Concomitantly with this development – 'quiet' collectivisation, larger

TABLE 5.7.1 The 'Quiet' Collectivisation of Agriculture 1950–70

| Foodstuffs and livestock | Private production in % 1950 | Private production in % 1970 | Year when private production falls under 50% |
|---|---|---|---|
| Sugar | 0 | 0 | Before 1940 |
| Grain | 7 | 1 | Before 1940 |
| Sheep | 21 | 21 | 1938 |
| Wool | 21 | 20 | Before 1940 |
| Horses | 8 | 5 | 1932 |
| Hogs | 43 | 25 | 1948 |
| Vegetables | 44 | 38 | 1945–50 |
| Meat | 67 | 35 | 1959 |
| Cattle | 70 | 39 | 1961 |
| Milk | 75 | 36 | 1959 |
| Potatoes | 73 | 65 | – |
| Eggs | 89 | 53 | – |

According to Clarke, op. cit., pp. 99–144 *passim*.

units, the growth of the sovkhoz sector and the cultivation of vast new areas, primarily in Central Asia – Soviet agriculture since the war has also been considerably mechanised. In 1950 over half of the working population was still employed on kolkhozes and sovkhozes. Twenty years later, the figure was less than a third. Agriculture has received extensive technical resources, first through the machine and tractor stations (MTS), each of which supplied several collective farms and was at the same time an instrument of political control, and later through the technical repair stations (RTS), successors to the MTSs, which aid the farms in utilising technical equipment they have acquired for themselves. Agricultural experts have also multiplied. In 1950 agronomists were connected with the MTSs, while in 1970 all kolkhozes had their own groups of trained specialists.

The kolkhozes are not formally part of the governmental apparatus, but this has never inhibited the ambitions of the Soviet leadership to control agricultural development. To guarantee supplies to the state the Party has constantly sought to influence local organisational forms and work methods, the choice of crops and means of production, the rotation of fallow fields and the use of fertilisers, sowing and harvesting times and techniques, etc. These efforts have often taken the form of nationwide campaigns for newly established solutions. Conflicting opinions in agricultural questions have greatly affected both research policies (for example, the Lysenko controversies) and clashes among political leaders and constellations of leaders. The role of agriculture in political struggles is the subject of several special studies, such as those by Ploss (1953–63) and Hahn (1960–70).[11] Official attitudes toward the private plots of the kolkhoz farmers – relatively liberal under Stalin and Brezhnev, more restrictive under Khrushchev – have been investigated by Wädekin.

The need for political intervention in agriculture has been partly determined by low bulk-purchase prices, which fail to stimulate the kolkhozes to produce. A 'low-price line' has characterised Soviet agricultural policy ever since the NEP era. There have been periodic attempts to increase material incentives, but the kolkhoz farmers' economic lag does not seem to have disappeared. It is impossible to be any more precise on that point, however, since Soviet income statistics only account for incomes in the different state sub-sectors. The lot of the sovkhoz farmers improved considerably in the sixties. Whereas their average income in 1950 and 1960 was lower than that of all other economic sub-sectors, by 1970 they had reached an average monthly wage of 100 roubles which was above the average in retail, communications, housing maintenance, and the health and communal services.

The importance the Party attaches to agricultural problems is apparent both in its organisation and in the thorough consideration such questions receive at congresses, conferences, and plenary sessions. Each regional Party organisation (*obkom*) has an agricultural section responsible for both the sovkhozes and kolkhozes of the region and purchase and service agencies. During Khrushchev's last year in power these sections were granted a certain autonomy through the division of regional Party organisations into an industrial and an agricultural part, but this dichotomy was abandoned after his fall. Party publications, however, continue to devote a great deal of attention to agriculture at all levels, and coverage of the sector by the Soviet press far exceeds that of non-specialized Western newspapers.

This is also reflected in *Pravda*, which regularly discusses agricultural problems in its editorials. An average of some four such articles appear each month, and the problems of the sector are in addition often treated in comments on general economic and rural problems. Subjects and themes generally follow the rhythm of the agricultural year – machine repairs and preparations for sowing are discussed in the late winter and early spring, organisation of the harvest is a typical summer topic, while themes in the fall include transport problems, sowing, construction, and other measures taken in preparation for the winter. Appeals are particularly frequent during busy seasons, but a great deal is also written about tasks that can be performed during calmer intermediate periods. Much is said about the importance of establishing an even rhythm in agricultural work, but the newspaper never fails to fan enthusiasm during those weeks that most critically affect the yield of the yearly harvest.

*Pravda*'s agricultural editorials are usually addressed to broad groups, often to all kolkhoz and sovkhoz farmers or all rural workers, but categories with especially important functions in production, such as agricultural technicians and tractor drivers, are sometimes singled out for particular attention. Another ordering is according to crop. Many directives indicate which agricultural sectors the political leadership regard as most urgent, and frequencies here are so great that fairly clear tendencies can be discerned. A count of the number of times various crops are mentioned shows that in 1950 and 1960 the *Pravda* editorials were most intensely concerned with fodder production, whereas grain was considerably more important in 1970. There is another clear shift with respect to fruit, vegetables, and potatoes, which are hardly mentioned at all in the earlier materials but which have advanced as an area of interest in 1970. The rank of the different crops is presented in Table 5.7.2 below.

TABLE 5.7.2. Crops ranked according to frequency

| 1950 | 1960 | 1970 |
|---|---|---|
| 1. Fodder | 1. Fodder | 1. Grain |
| 2. Grain | 2. Grain | 2. Fruit and vegetables |
| 3. Cotton | 3. Cotton | 3. Fodder |
| 4. Technical cultures* | 4. Technical cultures* | 4. Cotton |
| 5. Fruit and vegetables | 5. Fruit and vegetables | 5. Technical cultures* |

\* Sugar beets, flex, hemp, sunflowers, etc.

This order of precedence may be said to correspond in some degree to the share a given product represents in the total agricultural production, but it is not a wholly reliable reflection. The proportion of all Soviet agricultural acreage devoted to fodder increases sharply at the same time as *Pravda*'s interest in fodder decreases. The converse is true of grains — their acreage decreases, but their cultivation simultaneously becomes more urgent politically. The acreage statistics show no significant change with respect to fruit, vegetables, and potatoes, but in this area there is a considerable shift from private production on a small scale to large-scale state management. Parallel to this nationalization, the product group advances to a much higher position on the political agenda.

To get a picture of the relative weight of the various crops, an 'attention coefficient' has been calculated according to the formula:

$$Qc_1 = \frac{\dfrac{Fc_1}{F\Sigma c}}{\dfrac{Ac_1}{A\Sigma c}}$$

where $Q$ stands for attention coefficient, $F$ for observed frequency of instructions in *Pravda*, $c$ for crops and $A$ for acreage.

Other methods of reckoning, of course, would have been possible and would have produced somewhat different results. Instead of acreage, for

| | 1950 | 1960 | 1970 | |
|---|---|---|---|---|
| CORN | 0 | 1 | 2 | absolute figures |
| | 0 | 0.49 | 0.03 | per mille |

example, one would have been justified in measuring value, which would have resulted in a lower coefficient for the more expensive crops, but the statistics needed for such a calculation, unfortunately, were not available. Tables 5.7.3 and 5.7.4 present the attention coefficients of the most important crops. It is noticeable that cotton tops the list all years, that fodder declines throughout the period, and that the significance of vegetables is on the increase. Cotton appears to be the 'political' crop par excellence.

TABLE 5.7.3 Crops ranked according to attention coefficients

| 1950 | 1960 | 1970 |
|---|---|---|
| 1. Cotton | 1. Cotton | 1. Cotton |
| 2. Fodder | 2. Technical cultures* | 2. Fruit and vegetables |
| 3. Technical cultures* | 3. Fruit and vegetables | 3. Technical cultures* |
| 4. Grain | 4. Fodder | 4. Grain |
| 5. Fruit and vegetables | 5. Grain | 5. Fodder |

* See Table 5.7.2, note

TABLE 5.7.4 Attention coefficients for vegetable produce

| | Observed frequencies | | | Observed frequencies, % | | | Expected frequencies, % | | | Attention coefficients | | |
| --- | --- | --- | --- | --- | --- | --- | --- | --- | --- | --- | --- | --- |
| | 50 | 60 | 70 | 50 | 60 | 70 | 50 | 60 | 70 | 50 | 60 | 70 |
| Cereals | 36 | 42 | 55 | 32.1 | 33.3 | 42.3 | 70.3 | 56.9 | 57.7 | 0.41 | 0.59 | 0.73 |
| Cotton | 11 | 19 | 15 | 9.8 | 15.4 | 11.5 | 1.6 | 1.2 | 1.3 | 6.13 | 12.83 | 8.85 |
| Technical cultures* | 8 | 11 | 6 | 7.1 | 8.9 | 4.6 | 6.8 | 5.2 | 5.7 | 1.04 | 1.71 | 0.81 |
| Fruit, vegetables, potatoes | 1 | 8 | 32 | 0.9 | 6.5 | 24.6 | 7.1 | 5.5 | 4.9 | 0.13 | 1.45 | 5.02 |
| Fodder | 56 | 44 | 22 | 50.0 | 35.8 | 16.9 | 14.2 | 31.2 | 30.4 | 3.52 | 1.15 | 0.56 |
| Total | 112 | 124 | 130 | 99.9 | 99.9 | 99.9 | 100.0 | 100.0 | 100.0 | | | |

* See Table 5.7.2, note.

Certain shifts within the five groups may be worth noting. In the fodder category, corn reaches a predictable peak in 1960 – although Khrushchev's campaign for that cereal grain had not yet culminated, it was in full swing, and many *Pravda* editorials urged farmers to learn the profitable art of corn-growing. In the fruit and vegetable group, potatoes increase slightly but editorials in 1970 are particularly keen on the need for more expensive produce. They discuss problems connected with the transportation, storage and distribution of fruit and vegetables, and both eating establishments of all kinds and retailers are urged to pay more attention to the legitimate demands of consumers. Other 'green' directives emphasise the importance of mechanisation.

*Pravda*'s interest in animal products is strong and rises throughout the period. In 1950 and 1970 concern is expressed over a reduction in livestock herds in certain areas of the country. The supply of milk is a problem to which *Pravda* returns on 21 occasions in 1960. Meat is hardly discussed at all in 1950, but is an important theme in the other two years.

|        | *1950* | *1960* | *1970* |                 |
|--------|--------|--------|--------|-----------------|
| MILK   | 2      | 21     | 12     | absolute figures |
|        | 0.04   | 0.74   | 0.21   | per mille       |

Eggs and poultry are seldom considered before 1970, when, however, they receive a good deal of attention. Fishing, apart from one sharp reprimand to the Ministry of Fisheries in 1950, is rarely discussed.

|                  | *1950* | *1960* | *1970* |                 |
|------------------|--------|--------|--------|-----------------|
| EGGS AND POULTRY | 4      | 2      | 22     | absolute figures |
|                  | 0.08   | 0.07   | 0.38   | per mille       |

Diagnoses of the problems of the animal sector vary considerably during the period. In 1950 *Pravda* discusses the fodder shortage, exhorting the appropriate officials to make use of all available feeds. The need for better stalls and shelters is another frequent topic. Ten years later fodder is still the overshadowing problem. In editorial after editorial *Pravda* returns to the stocking of reserves in various republics and regions, stressing that an increase in meat production is directly dependent on an adequate 'fodder base'. 'In certain republics livestock have been allowed to increase more rapidly than the fodder base', notes one editorial in January 1960 (60.023), and this theme is varied in a long series of articles in the latter half of the year. Emphasis is entirely on the amount of fodder produced, not on its quality.

The discussion of animal production in 1970 has a more 'modern' character. The quality of fodder, chemical additives and technical equipment are new areas of interest. A shortage of milking machines and feed-spreaders is mentioned on several occasions. Nutritious feeds are regarded as essential to successful stock-raising, while the frequency of words such as 'pasture' has naturally decreased. The feed supply is still a problem, however, especially in poultry-raising. *Pravda* complains that supply and bulk-purchase agencies pay insufficient attention to private producers, whose poultry are needed to satisfy consumer demand.

*Pravda*'s appeals to Soviet agronomists further illustrate changes in agricultural strategies. In 1950 these specialists are regarded as a kind of teacher whose main job is to instruct the farmers. Party organisations are obliged to see to it that agronomists are ideologically stable, that they receive adequate training and that they work as much as possible on the kolkhozes so as to be able to spread their knowledge. The need for agronomic propaganda in the mass media is emphasised; on one occasion *Pravda* complains that recommendations issued to farmers by the press are often too general.

Ten years later agronomists are assigned a more active role in production. Their educational functions are greatly reduced and replaced by more important duties at the level of management. According to *Pravda*, agricultural experts should participate in the day-to-day supervision of the kolkhozes and sovkhozes. They are responsible for ensuring the correct use of modern technology and the adaptation of new methods to local conditions. Efficient crop rotation demands expert organisation. In 1970, by which date there has emerged what *Pravda* calls 'a great army of agronomists', the demand for independent analyses is even more pronounced. Although many recommendations are still issued centrally, the newspaper is keenly aware that such prescriptions must be varied according to climate and soil conditions. Agronomists, therefore, must spend more time on fieldwork and a thorough investigation of which crops are best suited to each individual area. They must profit from experience and correctly apply achievements in the field of chemistry. What is needed, *Pravda* writes, is 'creative initiatives'; 'stereotyped thinking' must be avoided. Certain agricultural specialists seem to have fallen out with their sovkhoz and kolkhoz managers, for leading officials are urged to listen more to their agronomists and to put more confidence in the younger cadres just graduated from the universities and technical schools. Otherwise, unsatisfactory working conditions often result in 'drifting' (*tekuchest kadrov*); one specified sovkhoz in the Karaganda region is reported to have lost twenty specialists in the course of four years.

There is also a clear tendency to further intensive growth through the application of differentiated approaches. The agricultural editorials of 1970 stress that scientific methods are the chief prerequisite of new successes. Plant breeding and the improvement of soil conditions are regarded as very important, as is agricultural technology in the broad sense. Two aspects in particular come to the fore in 1970 – water and fertilisers. Clay pipes for the drainage of flooded fields are an article in short supply in 1970, and *Pravda* criticises the Ministry for Construction Materials for its inability to guarantee adequate production of the item. Another complaint is levelled against the farmers – many drainage facilities are sub-standard. Drought is the major problem in other areas, and considerable investments are being made in irrigation. Such projects depend on a great many factors, and *Pravda* directs its appeals to a number of sectors and groups – the engineering industry, the construction industry, experts in soil improvement. Water has in general become an interesting political topic by 1970, its frequency series being 1–2–16. If it was ignored earlier, now there is an awareness that it is a scarce and valuable resource that must not be polluted or wasted.

|       | 1950 | 1960 | 1970 |                  |
|-------|------|------|------|------------------|
| SOIL  | 0    | 2    | 9    | absolute figures |
|       | 0    | 0.07 | 0.15 | per mille        |
| WATER | 1    | 2    | 16   | absolute figures |
|       | 0.04 | 0.07 | 0.27 | per mille        |

Interest in fertilisers also rises dramatically in 1970. The thorough discussion of artifical manuring in that year contrasts with the isolated articles earlier in the period recommending the utilisation of natural substances. Problems are distributed fairly evenly through the chain from manufacturer over transporter to consumer. The fertiliser industry is criticised for insufficient production and a shortage of machines, the railroads for poor cars and deficient loading facilities, and the farmers for their inefficient use of available resources. Knowledge and techniques are still thought to be inadequate as is evidenced by *Pravda*'s recurring appeals to the press and agitprop apparatus to devote more attention to artificial manuring.

Mechanical agricultural equipment is discussed in all three years, least thoroughly, however, in 1960. The most acute problem is that tractors

|  | *1950* | *1960* | *1970* |  |
|---|---|---|---|---|
| ARTIFICIAL | 2 | 3 | 60 | absolute figures |
| FERTILISERS | 0.04 | 0.11 | 1.02 | per mille |

and combines stand idle for want of repair. A shortage of spare parts is one reason for this, but maintenance are repairs are often neglected even when parts are available. It is also reported in 1970 that the tractor industry is experiencing a shortage of rolled steel, alloys, and weather-proof enamels. Another recurrent problem in 1960 and 1970 concerns grain elevators which have either not been built fast enough to satisfy demand or have been constructed poorly and broken down. The ministries responsible for agricultural machines and construction are often the target of *Pravda*'s attacks.

## 5.8 THE SERVICE SECTOR

An underdeveloped retailer network and a considerable shortage of goods are part of the price Soviet citizens have been forced to pay for rapid industrialisation. Services have been particularly weak in rural areas, where households have traditionally been fairly self-sufficient. The shop network, however, has expanded during the past few decades. The turnover of the retail trade per capita tripled between 1950 and 1970, and employees increased from 2,2000,000 to 5,700,000 in the same period.[12] This growth has occurred entirely within the state and co-operative sector – private kolkhoz trade has stagnated and decreased in relative importance.

The collective share of other services has also increased. There were about 8,100,000 day nursery and kindergarten places in 1970, compared with somewhat over a million twenty years earlier.[13] The number of employees per capita in the health services has nearly doubled in the same period. There are no figures for the so-called domestic services (*bytovye uslugi*) during the 1950s, but a considerable expansion has occurred here in especially the early sixties.

Corresponding to this development, *Pravda*'s editorials show a faintly rising interest in the everyday life of the average citizen. The frequency series for 'services' is illustrative.

|  | *1950* | *1960* | *1970* |  |
|---|---|---|---|---|
| SERVICES[14] | 6 | 13 | 36 | absolute figures |
|  | 0.12 | 0.46 | 0.62 | per mille |

Toward the end of the period, the Party mouthpiece also reflects the change that has occurred from a shortage of consumer goods to a relative abundance. Specific faults in supply, hygiene in shops and public eating establishments, service-mindedness and politeness towards customers – such matters appear in the paper now, albeit not very frequently. In 1970 as in 1950 distribution is much less interesting than production in *Pravda*'s scale of values.

Many of the instructions in *Pravda* dealing with services are connected with the needs of production. In one editorial on mines, for example, it is pointed out that many mines lack lunchrooms; in another on agriculture in Kazakhstan deficient service is mentioned as having a detrimental effect on results. The driving motive in such contexts seems to be concern for productivity. Directives associated with production occur in all three years, but in the latter two there is increasing competition on the part of more 'welfare-oriented' demands for better service, which justifies speaking of a consumer breakthrough. *Pravda*'s decrees in 1970 dealing with repair shops discuss not only the need for serviceable combines and tractors, but also give some attention to consumer demands for the repair of household machines, etc. It is clearer now than before that the Soviet Union has a large urban population which depends on a developed system of collective services for its everyday necessities.

The consumer is conspicuous throughout the period, although in varying forms. In 1950 and 1960 retailers and light industry are regularly advised to study consumer desire in order to avoid producing the wrong goods. In 1970 there are some references to consumer demands, and now one often suspects that *Pravda* is basing its comments on irritated letters to the editor. 'Demand' is a more important notion in analyses, but it often denotes demand on the part of wholesale purchasers for producer goods. The newspaper stresses several times the need for better co-ordination between industry, wholesalers and retailers. Well-established communications and greater flexibility are needed if recurrent interruptions in supply are to be avoided.

|  | 1950 | 1960 | 1970 |  |
|---|---|---|---|---|
| DEMAND | 4 | 6 | 27 | absolute figures |
|  | 0.08 | 0.21 | 0.46 | per mille |

Certain retail and service branches come under especially intense fire. In 1960, for example, two long editorials attack shortcomings in public eating places. Dry-cleaning establishments are another target; the most severe criticism is aimed at a newly built installation in Armenia used to produce soft drinks rather than for laundry. As for the retail trade, no branch is discussed more often than the bookstores and press distribution network, which are on numerous occasions criticised for poor organisation. Several editorials even note that some types of literature are lacking in certain regions or republics.

Due to the limited extent of our materials, it is difficult to discern tendencies throughout the period in the various branches of the sector. It can be observed, however, that the range of goods treated by the instructions is broadened, and there is a gradually increasing emphasis on quality. The distribution of foodstuffs, both in the shops and in eating places, is given greater space. In 1970 *Pravda* calls for more self-service stores and pre-packed foods. Interest in leisure activities also grows somewhat. In 1950 the newspaper strongly advocates gymnastics, but in 1960 the accent is more on other sports. Skiing is a popular topic in 1970. *Pravda* is somewhat cool toward the construction of large athletic facilities in this year, however; biting criticism is made of cases where funds intended for housing construction have been diverted to extravagant cultural palaces and gymnasiums.

|  | 1950 | 1960 | 1970 |  |
|---|---|---|---|---|
| GYMNASTICS | 17 | 5 | 4 | absolute figures |
|  | 0.35 | 0.18 | 0.07 | per mille |

There is a long editorial dealing with children's summer camps in 1950, but daily child care appears on the political agenda only in 1960, when, however, it has a high priority. *Pravda* returns constantly to the shortage of day nurseries, appealing to all planning agencies to take such needs into consideration. Ten years later these calls have ceased. Nor does the paper have anything to say about senior citizens – pensioners are an unnoticed group in *Pravda*'s editorials.

There are so few items about medical service – the subject of one editorial each year – that no trend can be discerned. Institution heads are named and criticised in 1950, while recommendations in the following year deal in more general terms with better prophylactic measures, better care of patients and the development of new medicines and treatments. A decree in 1960 stating that notes of admission to sanatoriums must be issued in strict accordance with medical criteria suggests that such was not generally the practice.

5.9 EDUCATION AND RESEARCH

At the time of the Revolution, about half of the population of Russia was literate. By Stalin's death illiteracy had been practically eliminated, and four years later the first sputnik aroused apprehensions in the West of a growing education and research gap between East and West. The standard of Soviet education, however, was not yet that high. The vast majority of the inter-war generation had only had four years of schooling. By 1950 the six-year primary school had become more or less universal, and about one out of five pupils continued their education. Obligatory education was further lengthened during the next two decades to eight years. Forty per cent of the pupils completed ten years, either in the ordinary school or in various types of vocational schools, and about 20 per cent went on to receive higher education. There were approximately 4,500,000 students in Soviet universities and institutes of advanced study in 1970. The majority of these students, however, studied in their leisure time. Evening and correspondence courses combined with full-time employment are a common phenomenon in the Soviet Union.

Views on the relationship between work and study have varied somewhat during the period. There was a good deal of discussion under Khrushchev on 'polytechnicising' education, that is, making it more practical and more a form of vocational training. Various forms of work, therefore, became an important component, and a period of practical experience was made obligatory. After Khrushchev's fall there was a certain return to an all-round, general system, but there was continued emphasis on close contacts between the schools and practical employment. Beside the formal educational system, there are several other forms of adult education and political training. These include an extensive range of public lectures, an organisation for private studies, a variety of popular scientific literature and last but not least, instruction under the direct management of the Party, from simple agitprop activities and the so-called political schools (*politshkoly*) to more advanced Party schools and the Academy of Social Sciences of the Central Committee.

The *Pravda* editorials devote considerable attention to problems of education. One or more leaders are regularly published at the beginning of the academic year, sometimes also at its conclusion. During the year such questions are often treated in connection with other topics. The focus of this coverage, however, shifts rather sharply during the period. The most prominent form of education in 1950 is that provided by the Party – agitprop organisations, lectures, private political studies and the *politshkoly*. Detailed directives specify the level of pedagogical proficiency to which adult education instructors should aspire and the methods Party organisations should use to establish contact with the masses. Primary and secondary education is less important; demands voiced in this area seem to have flaked off from higher doctrinal disputes. Language teachers, for example, are warned against spreading Marr's false theories, and biology teachers are urged to adhere to the tenets of progressive physiology. There are also complaints that philosophy is not given due attention, but teachers in this area are rarely advised more specifically. The most frequently named educationalist in *Pravda* during this year is the great teacher Stalin.

|  | 1950 | 1960 | 1970 |  |
| --- | --- | --- | --- | --- |
| SCHOOLS | 46 | 74 | 60 | absolute figures |
|  | 0.95 | 2.60 | 1.02 | per mille |

By 1960 the educational system proper has quite a different position in *Pravda*'s directives. Both primary and secondary schools and higher institutions are now discussed frequently, and many instructions suggest the presence of severe growing pains. The planning, construction, and even furnishing of schools are the dominant themes. Shortages of textbooks and furniture are a recurrent topic. *Pravda* also expresses opinions on the work of the teachers. The profession must recruit the right kind of people, and instructors with some experience need supplementary training. One editorial holds up as a negative example the Bransk Institute for the Construction of Transport Vehicles, where lectures in the social sciences are said to be characterised by 'academic formalism and dullness'.

Co-operation is another prominent theme. Teachers must try to help the Komsomol, the Party, factories, kolkhozes, and parents. They in turn deserve all the support they can get. 'Soviet teachers receive daily help and support from Party and public organisations in preparing for the new school year', urgingly observes one editorial (60.238). Adult education and institutes of advanced study are also discussed. Interest in the school system as a whole is greater in 1960 than in either of the other two years.

Comments on education in the 1970 editorials do not have the same emphasis on expansion. The problems of the sector are instead discussed on a broader and more varied plane. Textbooks, pedagogical methods, the pupils' leisure time, contacts between schools and parents, etc., are among the many aspects considered. *Pravda* is still actively engaged in questions relating to teachers' education and additional training, pointing out that improvements in methodology are needed if the new curricula are to succeed. Normal schools must increase their efforts, and the schools themselves must give more help to newly graduated teachers. On one occasion *Pravda* recommends that teaching staffs collectively study the new educational regulations. Change, it is emphasised, requires involvement at the lowest levels.

|  | 1950 | 1960 | 1970 |  |
|---|---|---|---|---|
| STUDENTS | 0 | 25 | 10 | absolute figures |
|  | 0 | 0.88 | 0.17 | per mille |

Higher education receives the most attention in 1960, when there is a flood of exhortations and admonitions to university students dealing with both their moral and intellectual training and material and technical deficiencies in higher education such as the difficulty of finding housing, the shortage of lunchrooms, etc. Ten years later there is considerably less discussion; students are most often mentioned as a labour reserve for various kinds of voluntary projects.

A more important theme is research, which in the Soviet Union is not extensively connected with higher educational institutions. *Pravda* expresses frequent demands for more research, better research and closer contact between research and production in all three years, with an increase toward the end of the period. Numerous volleys are discharged in 1950 against named bigwigs in various disciplines. Here *Pravda* is echoing the turbulent doctrinal struggles of the period. These personal polemics later give way to a more general and constructive journalism. The problem with research is no longer that it rests on false ideological foundations or produces undesirable results, but rather that it is inadequate and that new findings cannot be assimilated rapidly enough into the economy. The tone of a number of editorials addressed to scientific education is strikingly mild, almost as if it were felt that gentle persuasion is the means of inciting scientists to make discoveries.

|  | 1950 | 1960 | 1970 |  |
|---|---|---|---|---|
| SCIENCE | 105 | 67 | 202 | absolute figures |
|  | 2.16 | 2.35 | 3.45 | per mille |

Research seems to be sluggish in many areas. Ministries are occasionally called upon to reflect upon their responsibility for scientific work in their sectors, and Party committees at the republican level are in 1970 urgently requested to give more support to the republican academies of sciences. Difficulties in co-ordination at various research centres are a major topic. Inefficient scientific research is sometimes attributed to an excessive division of resources. The type of co-ordination discussed particularly often, however, is that between researchers and users. A typical article in 1970, for example, demands better contact between the Ministry of Agriculture and the agricultural research departments at the academies of sciences.

The attention *Pravda* devotes to the problems of the researcher sometimes deals with inadequate assistance on the part of other agencies, poor equipment, and unsatisfactory buildings and laboratories. Most comments, however, derive from research consumers. Complaints concern failures to develop machines and methods or to solve acute production problems. Researchers are criticised for not paying enough attention to practical applications. Strengthening the ties between science and 'life' is a constant refrain in *Pravda*'s editorials.

There are certain thematic shifts in the instructions on research during the period. In 1950 agriculture is most central, and 'agronomical science' is regarded almost as a panacea for the economic ailments of Soviet society. Propagating scientific findings among the farmers and training them to adopt a scientific outlook are presented as among the Party's most important tasks. Especially in the summer and fall *Pravda* tries to stimulate a broad popular scientific educational campaign. Energy production, in particular coalmining, is another area in want of research. Other industries attract little attention in 1950, but by 1960 appeals for research have attained quite a different breadth. Now the paper is concerned about sectoral research and development in such areas as the steel industry, the building industry, the textile industry, and the engineering industry. Different types of special machines are in great demand. The same spectrum occurs in 1970, with a slight tendency toward even more specialised requests. Raw materials are no longer so interesting as in 1950, the stress having shifted instead to later links in the production chain. Demands in the agricultural area are to a greater extent than before concerned with individual stages of the labour process ('combine-harvesting must be raised more rapidly to a truly scientific level', 70.358) and special practices adapted to different soils, climates, and crops.

## 5.10 THE MASS MEDIA

The Party's monopoly of the printed and spoken word sets its mark on Soviet society. The basis for this dominance was laid during the interwar period, when the small underground Bolshevik press developed into an intricate network of newspapers and periodicals. Changes after the Second World War have been primarily quantitative in nature – instead of 201 papers per thousand inhabitants in 1950, 578 per thousand were sold in 1970. [15] The development of television, of course, has signified a considerable qualitative development in the broadcast media, but this new medium had not yet attained full capacity by 1970. As early as 1966, however, there were more television sets per capita than there had been radio receivers per capita in 1950. [16]

*Pravda*'s significance in the control of the mass media derives to a great extent from its position as the national standard. Instructions to journalists are often communicated implicitly through its evaluation of news materials and views on various questions. Other signals are transmitted by surveys of newspapers and journals which, even if they deal primarily with certain specified organs, are like other such attacks intended as mementos to broader groups. The explicit directives in Pravda's editorials constitute a third category of impulses. They contain exhortations directed at both functionally specialized organs ('the agricultural newspapers must devote more attention to the use of chemical insecticides') and the press in general at the republican, regional and local levels. These messages are especially interesting, since they not only reflect the Party's ambitions with respect to the mass media as a branch, but also indicate a broader range of priorities. Newspapers and the broadcast media function as instruments of control; when they are used intensively and on a mass scale to attain certain ends, this is obviously an expression of a very strong determination on the part of the Party leadership.

Most appeals to the mass media are related to the economy. Specific directives to press organs connected with particular branches demanding that they pay more attention to the problems of their sectors are very common in 1950. Coalmining is an important question in that year, and the newspaper *Kuzbass* in the Kemerovo region, for example, is criticised in *Pravda* for not allotting enough space to a discussion of mechanisation. The Uzbek republican newspaper *Pravda Vostoka* is urged to write more about the mechanisation of cotton-growing, and *Kazakhstanskaya Pravda* is attacked for its inadequate coverage of stock-raising. Agricultural problems are particularly frequent in such instructions, but the development and application of industrial technology is another major theme. In 1960 *Pravda* criticises the branch newspapers of the timber and paper industries for not paying enough attention to Stakhanovite work methods.

*Pravda*'s instructions in 1970 are seldom so specific. Criticism of individual organs has practically ceased. The functions of the mass media are often discussed in general terms, however, and their significance in the training of good Soviet citizens is frequently emphasised. Economy, efficiency, responsibility, enterprise, loyalty, and concern for public property are among the virtues the press should seek to encourage. *Pravda* also stresses the duty of the mass media to stimulate socialist competition between enterprises. The solemn obligations to which collectives commit themselves should be publicised and followed by reports on their efforts to fulfil these promises.

On other occasions it is special incidents or events which demand attention. The *Pravda* editorials are used to switch on the agitprop megaphone – through its directives to the mass media of the country the central leadership seeks to ensure the involvement of all citizens in symbolically important happenings. Numerous appeals, for example, deal with the role of the mass media in election campaigns, including their coverage of contacts between the candidates and the people. Even an undertaking such as the 1970 census is regarded as an important national event, and *Pravda* emphasises that it must be given a prominent place in the news. The role of the press in the agitprop apparatus is stressed in demands that newspapers support activities at the grass-roots level such as agitational meetings and the widespread wall-newspapers published by the local organisations of the Party and Komsomol.

*Pravda*'s appeals to the mass media, then, are concerned first of all with production problems and secondly with reinforcing the citizen's feeling of national and political solidarity. Questions of social and private morals occupy a more modest position, but they are occasionally considered. In 1960, for example, it is emphasised that the radio should seek to foster Soviet citizens in the true communist spirit and to combat parasitism and sloth wherever they appear in society. Ten years later the press, radio, and television are urged to propagate works of culture which echo happy familial and conjugal relationships. *Pravda* has more to say about the new man and the pedagogical functions of the mass media toward the end of the period than at its beginning.

|  | *1950* | *1960* | *1970* |  |
|---|---|---|---|---|
| TELEVISION | 0 | 36 | 53 | absolute figures |
|  | 0 | 1.26 | 0.91 | per mille |
| RADIO | 23 | 47 | 53 | absolute figures |
|  | 0.47 | 1.65 | 0.91 | per mille |

Another change occurs in the relative share of attention devoted to the various media. *Pravda*'s most important target group in 1950 is journalists and editors-in-chief on the daily newspapers, while the broadcast media are less significant. This balance is upset in 1960, by which time both radio and television have achieved priority as propaganda channels. If *Pravda*'s communications to the press tend to become more abstract and general, the opposite is true of its signals to the broadcast media, which contain numerous specific viewpoints on the planning of programmes and the selection of materials and topics. The significance of firm and competent control by lower Party agencies is also emphasised – media as effective as radio and television must not be left to take care of themselves. In 1970 alone television is discussed in 40 editorials.

A number of articles in *Pravda* put the spotlight on mass media technology. In 1950 and 1960 especially there are complaints of raw material shortages, poor machines, and inadequate distribution. The paper industry is criticised for insufficient deliveries, the colours and inks produced by the chemical industry do not meet the requirements of the printers, radio tubes constantly burn out, etc. The factories responsible for supplying the TV stations with equipment must shoulder their share of the blame. The national press distributor Soyuzpechat is reproached for its management of the sale of newspapers and magazines, as is the network of bureaux which handle subscriptions. The many severe comments in the newspaper on the production and distribution of the mass media suggest that the Party leadership – or at least that part of it responsible for *Pravda* – regards the moulding of public opinion as an extremely vital matter.

### 5.11 CULTURAL LIFE

Art, literature, the theatre and film have always had an important role in the building of Soviet society. Culture is regarded first and foremost as an arena for the moulding of political opinion and social mobilisation. Both its extent and its content, therefore, are of great concern to the leaders, and cultural policy has consequently ever since the Revolution been shaped on the basis of careful consideration of the effects of artistic creation on society in general. Considerable energy has been expended on the development of a rich variety of art forms and a well-organised cultural life in all parts of the union, while at the same time artistic production has been held under close surveillance. The 'creative intelligentsia' is required not only to take an active stand, but also to contribute to the Party's efforts to develop the new Soviet man. The doctrine of politically neutral art has been emphatically rejected. Demands for docility in form and content have varied in strength but have never been weak.

There is a fairly modest quantitative cultural expansion during the twenty years between 1950 and 1970. The number of theatres is more or less the same, while attendance rises from 0.38 to 0.46 visits per inhabitant and year. There is some increase in the number of museums and clubs. Book publication increases from 4.6 to 5.6 copies per capita. Clubs, which are the centre of local cultural activities, increase numerically, but while in 1970 there is one club per 1800 inhabitants, twenty years earlier there was one club per 1400. Public libraries do not increase in number, but their total holdings rise by 500 per cent. The most radical quantitative change occurs in the cinema. Only fifteen full-length films were produced in the entire Soviet Union in 1950, whereas the corresponding figure for 1970 (including feature films for television) is 181. Attendance rises from six visits per capita in 1950 to nineteen in 1970.

Fluctuations in Soviet cultural policy are often described in terms of changes in climate or temperature. Stalin's final year is usually characterised as the end of the chilly period introduced in 1946 by the so-called Zhdanov decrees, which called upon artists to stiffen their guard against bourgeois and Western impulses. Commissar of Culture Zhdanov died in 1948, but the so-called *zhdanovshchina* continued until the dictator's death in 1953. The middle fifties were characterised by a relatively mild cultural climate often known as 'the Thaw', a name taken from a novel by Ilya Ehrenburg. The Khrushchev era had its cold spells, of course, but it was predominantly marked by a criticial settlement of accounts with Stalin which was in some measure allowed to penetrate literature, the theatre, and film. Tolerance of such works narrowed under Brezhnev, and the Prague Spring and the ensuing intervention in Czechoslovakia in 1968 has been accompanied by a more vigilant attitude toward liberal and revisionist tendencies.

*Pravda*'s editorials clearly reflect the importance the Party attaches to culture. The 'creative intelligentsia' receives a steady stream of admonishments and exhortations. The standard appeals call in abstract terms for high artistic quality and keen ideological consciousness (*vysokaya ideinost* ), but often *Pravda* also specifies what the leadership would like to see. The chief target groups are professional artists and persons responsible for cultural propagation and distribution, but amateur activities also receive a certain amount of attention, especially in the earlier years. Creativity is a quality the newspaper wants to spread beyond the area of artistic creation proper.

The theatre is the main theme of five editorials and a sub-theme in many others. In 1950 the paper attacks a number of institutions which have not measured up to the Party's demands. Earlier calls for improvement, *Pravda* declares, have not been answered; the theatres have contented themselves with making a few formal changes in their one-sided and banal repertoires. Two Moscow theatres, for example, have invested all their resources in a single play, and things are just as bad in the theatres in Rostov, Orel and Grodno. Heavier demands should be made on Soviet stage folk, the newspaper continues.

Moreover, the press must print more reviews and give more support to local theatres. Artistically inferior plays must be taken off the stage. A few months later *Pravda* returns with some new criticism, declaring that even some of the best Soviet artists produce weak plays. Thus, the theatre of the Moscow Soviet is featuring a play by a talented young writer, but the people responsible for its staging have not studied the text closely enough. Nor do young producers and actors receive adequate training. One of the main themes in both these editorials is a call to support young talents and new innovations in the theatre. Aesthetic quality is the primary criterion; demands for ideological purity are fairly unobtrusive.

Comments on the theatre ten years later produce a similar impression. *Pravda*'s criticism of the theatre in 1960 is relatively sparing, but there are a few interesting observations. On the one hand, the door is opened wide to progressive foreign authors:

All that is progressive in modern foreign drama is worthy of being shown in the Soviet theatre (60.255).

On the other hand, national themes must not be neglected. The same editorial complains that many theatres overlook works 'permeated with the pathos of our heroic era'. Other recommendations concern broadening the theatre-going public. On one occasion it is noted that certain theatres unreasonably resist having their plays televised. In another editorial *Pravda* urges institutes of advanced study to organise their instruction so as to allow the students time to visit the theatre.

In 1970 *Pravda* stresses the duty of Party members and leaders to improve theatrical repertoires and raise their ideological level. The theatre is a collective artistic form; actors, producers, playwrights, composers and artists must therefore work together in 'creative communities'. Plays should provide 'a true and talented portrayal of life, work, and struggle in Soviet society' (70.263). One editorial, entitled 'No Compromises With Bourgeois Ideology' (70.327), contains a summary of criticism voiced at a recent Party meeting in Moscow of 'ideologically immature works, attempts to conceal the artistic and ideological content of the classics behind new interpretations'.

Film is the topic of two editorials (1950 and 1960) and is also discussed in many other leader articles on agitprop or cultural activities in general. Here as well opinions on the technical and ideological content of the cinema are interspersed with calls for the treatment of more or less specific subjects. Demands for aesthetic improvement are especially pronounced in the two earlier years, when *Pravda* complains that Soviet films are often stereotyped and dull. More talent and better training are needed; in addition, the film division of the Union of Writers should give Soviet film-makers more active guidance. Another topic in 1960 is inferior studio equipment. Film-makers are repeatedly urged to give technical assistance to television, which indicates that the leadership is particularly concerned about the quality of the new medium.

The groups of film people in which *Pravda* is most interested are those which determine content – authors, directors, producers, etc. Some prescriptions to these gatekeepers deal with general questions – such as demands that films better comply with Soviet morals or contribute to sound attitudes toward the family – but there are also specific desires which seem to derive from the needs of individual branches of the economy. It is stressed in 1950 that the cinema is an important means of popularising new agricultural methods. Ten years later it is observed that films should be used more in agitprop activities, and there is particular emphasis on the need for films about Lenin. In 1970 there is a demand for films dealing with the approaching census, and more popular-science films are wanted to supplement lectures and other cultural work in rural areas. Relatively specific requests are made for artistic films as well. For example, there is a need for films which encourage better labour morale and for cinemas to stimulate professional pride among grain farmers.

Books and book publication receive more attention than any other cultural subject. In this area as well *Pravda* often addresses the responsible gatekeepers. Appeals to publishers are therefore frequent, especially in the first two years of the period. The year 1950 is particularly severe in this respect. Publishers are accused of producing 'waste paper', of being 'isolated from life' and of turning out goods of a wretchedly low technical quality. Time and time again the paper discusses the failures of the printing industry, but other links in the chain of production also receive their share of the blame. One viewpoint expressed in both 1950 and 1960 concerns the need for better-trained editors of non-fictional books, who – it is added in the latter year – must also be experienced and high-principled. The publishing houses are criticised in 1960 for printing outdated books, ignoring content and quality, overemphasising foreign books and displaying an excessively commercial attitude. Duplication is another source of irritation – different local publishers print the same books. The remedy recommended is better co-ordination, better communications among the publishing houses and more information for the consumers.

Many appeals to publishers deal with areas they have ignored. In 1950 *Pravda* calls for more books on music, economy, technology, ideology, agitation and propaganda, pedagogy, metallurgy, and rural architecture. The most acutely felt shortages are in the fields of textbooks and scientific literature. Demands ten years later are for works on Lenin, the theatre, music, and for children's literature and night-school textbooks. Another noteworthy request in 1960 is for Khrushchev's speeches, which it is felt ought to be published in larger editions. Deficiencies in the regional publishing houses are also noted; for example, a shortage of political literature is observed in bookstores in the North Caucausus. Among the less frequent directives to publishers in 1970 may be mentioned demands for school-books, teachers' handbooks, handbooks for wall-newspaper editors and lecturers, special literature on work training and books on drama.

Advice on screening is the most prominent element in *Pravda*'s directives to publishers. For the influence known in Soviet terminology as 'working with writers', the paper relies more on other organisations, primarily the Union of Writers and its local subdivisions. These agencies are held responsible for literary deficiencies and inadequate social engagement on the part of writers. In 1950, for example, the Union of Writers is urged to train more reviewers in the various republics, and dissatisfaction is expressed with the individual writers' unions for not having developed into forums for constructive literary criticism. The Union is not sufficiently concerned about organising 'the critical spirit', the editorial complains; it devotes too little effort to promoting the development of a thematically many-sided and ideologically sound literature and fails to provide writers with effective leadership. Demands a decade later stress 'practical social involvement'. The Union of Writers must see to it that its members actively participate in adult education and cultural affairs and that writers appear on the radio to answer workers' questions. Desirable literary tendencies are also indicated in 1970, when the writers' organisations are urged to instil in their younger members a spirit of fidelity to the Socialist Realist traditions of Soviet literature.

Last but not least, *Pravda* often appeals directly to the writers. Signposts are especially numerous in the first and last years of the period; here as in many other areas 1960 represents an intermediate stage of relatively weakly articulated demands for orthodoxy. In 1950, on the other hand, there is no lack of official views on the duties of the Soviet writer. He must put heavier demands on his work; he must learn to generalise from isolated examples; he must struggle for a high level of ideological awareness in literature; he must strive to perfect his artistic skill; he must seek to develop Bolshevik criticism and self-criticism in those around him; in his gratitude to the Party, the government and Stalin for their paternal concern he must create works which edify the reader politically; he must continue the traditions of the great Mayakovskii; he must study life more profoundly to be able to create historically correct portrayals of reality in its revolutionary development; etc. Appeals are numerous, repetitive, and abstract – writers are given few specific instructions as to what they should write or how they should approach their material. Yet through the presence of certain signal words with connotations known to all Soviet authors, the message is usually clear.

The instructions issued to writers in 1970 are somewhat more specific. They mention not only ideological purity and high aesthetic standards but also specify important components of literary creation. Writers are expected to further the reader's patriotism and internationalism; they must contribute to developing the Soviet people's spirit of heroic devotion to the Socialist Fatherland; they must combat alien cultural influences; they must give particular attention to subjects such as work, the life and struggle of the working class, everyday life in rural areas, changes in the situation of the kolkhoz farmers and the intelligentsia, etc. *Pravda* also takes up the cudgels for more penetrating literary description and more modern stylistic devices – 'schematism' and 'outdated approaches' are declared to be undesirable. Individual writers, however, appear to be a less important group in 1970 than in the earlier years. *Pravda* increasingly concentrates its attention on institutions – the publishing houses and the Union of Writers.

Literature, film, and the theatre seem in Pravda's estimation to be the most important art forms for moulding public opinion, and this accounts for a strong interest in production and distribution. Libraries, for example, are discussed regularly, and bookstores, as mentioned above, are treated more extensively in editorials than any other retail branch. The visual arts, sculpture, handicrafts, and music, in contrast, are almost entirely ignored. Composers and painters get no advice from *Pravda*.

5.12 PROPORTION AND EMPHASIS IN SECTORAL PROBLEMS

Economic problems strongly dominate the Soviet political agenda. Raw materials shipped behind schedule, inoperative plants, undelivered consignments of goods, abortive planning, inefficient management – such deficiencies are constantly criticised in *Pravda*'s editorials. A large part of its instructions deal with how opinion must be moulded to ensure the performance of vital social functions. The Soviet leadership's principal remedy for disturbances in the economy is to influence attitudes at the source of the trouble.

The changes registered *within* the eleven sectors reflect several facts of the country's economic and social development. They show that attention has progressed from a limited group of 'survival problems' – questions related to the supply of food and energy – to a broader scale of concern, that interest in 'superior goods' has grown, that problems in the production process itself have to some extent been eclipsed by problems in distribution and that modern methods of production and means of communication have introduced new complications into the Soviet economy. But underneath these shifts there is also a stable continuity in the way problems are selected, diagnosed and tackled.

Many themes that are subdued under Khrushchev reappear in 1970, which in several respects more resembles 1950 than 1960. There are signs of modernisation in all of the sectors, but each branch appears to have an 'eternal' set of problems, questions which are constantly discussed but which never seem to be solved satisfactorily.

The shifts *among* the different sectors are not dramatic, but certain features deserve to be noted. A count of the number of instructions mentioning any of the seven most common concepts in each sector (in certain cases more than one term was allowed to denote a single concept) suggests that interest in industrial problems rises sharply between 1950 and 1960, after which it declines somewhat towards 1970. Agriculture has clearly higher frequencies in 1950 than in any of the following two years, while the total value for questions of public opinion in the broad sense – the mass media, culture, education and research – is high during the first two years and lower during the third. The relative position of these three main sectors is presented in Table 5.12.1.

TABLE 5.12.1 The three main sectors ranked according to number of instructions containing seven key concepts*

| 1950 | 1960 | 1970 |
|---|---|---|
| 1. Opinion (27.21) | 1. Opinion (27.29) | 1. Opinion (20.62) |
| 2. Agriculture (19.96) | 2. Industry (21.60) | 2. Industry (17.46) |
| 3. Industry (12.60) | 3. Agriculture (13.06) | 3. Agriculture (14.17) |

* The figures in parentheses refer to percentages of all instructions of the year. The main sector industry has five sub-sectors, opinion has three and agriculture one. This makes the basis for comparison uneven, since terms associated with seven key concepts were sought for each sub-sector.

The table must be interpreted with caution, because the frequency of the agricultural sector is based on fewer search terms than those of the opinion and industrial sectors. In Table 5.12.2, which shows the corresponding frequencies for the eleven sub-sectors, the standard of comparison is more equitable.

The trends that can be discerned in these frequencies are summarised in Figure 5.12.3. Between 1950 and 1960 are registered a falling trend for the mass media, agriculture, services, energy, and transport; a stable trend for culture; and a rising trend for the building industry, consumer industries, iron, steel and engineering, the chemical industry and education and research. Interest in the mass media continues to decline between 1960 and 1970, and the same tendency is registered for culture, the building industry and the consumer industries. Agriculture, services, iron, steel and engineering, the chemical industry, education and research remain at about the same level, whereas energy and transport receive more attention. It must be kept in mind that these observations are based on measurements which, due to the fact that they are restricted to seven key concepts, do not provide a precise reflection of *Pravda*'s coverage of the various sectors; a sector where any of the seven key notions figures in practically every instruction shows a higher frequency than a sector where concepts are distributed more evenly.

TABLE 5.12.2 The eleven sub-sectors ranked according to number of instructions containing seven key concepts*

| 1950 | 1960 | 1970 |
|---|---|---|
| 1. Agriculture (19.96) | 1. Agriculture (13.06) | 1. Agriculture (14.17) |
| 2. Mass media (9.73) | 2. Education and research (11.74) | 2. Education and research (11.04) |
| 3. Culture (8.96) | 3. Building | 3. Iron, steel and industry (8.83) |
| 4. Education and research (8.52) | 4. Culture (8.83) | 4. Building industry (5.68) |
| 5. Building industry (4.37) | 5. Mass media (6.72) | 5. Mass media (5.02) |
| 6. Iron, steel and engineering (4.20) | 6. Iron, steel and engineering (6.27) | 6. Culture (4.56) |
| 7. Transport (2.77) | 7. Consumer industries (2.87) | 7. Transport (3.76) |
| 8. Energy (2.65) | 8. Chemical industry (2.57) | 8. Chemical industry (2.68) |
| 9. Services (2.60) | 9. Services (1.74) | 9. Services (1.96) |
| 10. Consumer industries (0.94) | 10. Transport (1.66) | 10. Energy (1.50) |
| 11. Chemical industry (0.44) | 11. Energy (1.06) | 11. Consumer industries (1.25) |

* The figures in parentheses refer to percentage of all instructions of the year. At least one of the 11 × 7 search concepts occurred in 65.14 per cent of the instructions in 1950, in 65.35 per cent of the instructions in 1960, and in 57.97 per cent of the instructions in 1970.

How much significance may be attached to the number of times the central concepts of a given sector is mentioned is a moot question. Measurements of frequency say something about degree of attention but nothing about degree of engagement. In order to penetrate the latter dimension – the intensity of the messages in the *Pravda* editorials – a contingency search was made for key sectoral concepts and indicators of deep involvement. As indicators were selected some thirty strong command-words such as 'responsibility', 'duty', 'sacred', 'absolute', 'necessary', etc.

Fɪɢ. 5.12.3 Development trends in the eleven sub-sectors

*Trend 1950–60*                    *Trend 1960–70*

| | Falling | Stable | Rising |
|---|---|---|---|
| Falling | Mass media | Agriculture Services | Energy Transport |
| Stable | Culture | | |
| Rising | Building industry Consumer industries | Iron, steel and engineering Chemical industry Education and research | |

After the contingency search it was established how many mentions of key sectoral concepts occurred in the same instructions as mentions of deep-involvement indicators. An 'intensity coefficient' was calculated according to the formula

$$I = \frac{100(N_s + I_{se})}{N_s}$$

where $I$ denotes the intensity coefficient, $N_s$ the number of instructions with a mention of any of the seven key concepts in a given sector, and $(N_s + I_{se})$ represents the number of instructions containing both any of the seven key concepts and one of the thirty deep-involvement indicators. The result of these calculations is presented in Table 5.12.4.

A high intensity coefficient suggests that many of *Pravda*'s messages on a given subject express considerable determination. Of the three years, 1950 has the highest coefficient and 1960 the lowest. A comparison of the eleven sectors shows that the tone of instructions to agriculture and the opinion sector tends to be heated, while industry seems to be discussed in more sober terms. *Pravda* invokes obligations and duties especially often in its appeals to persons and organisations concerned with culture, while the lowest intensity is noted for texts dealing with iron, steel and engineering.

Differences in frequency and intensity may be interpreted in several different ways. If we approach the figures from the viewpoint of 'power politics', the newspaper's interest in the various sectors might be connected with the relative political strength of the different sectors of

TABLE 5.12.4 The eleven sectors ranked according to intensity coefficients

|  | 1950 | 1960 | 1970 | Average | Rank |
|---|---|---|---|---|---|
| Culture | 56.17 | 57.26 | 54.22 | 55.88 | 1 |
| Agriculture | 56.79 | 47.40 | 60.47 | 54.89 | 2 |
| Mass media | 55.68 | 41.57 | 58.33 | 51.86 | 3 |
| Services | 51.06 | 52.17 | 51.06 | 51.43 | 4 |
| Transport | 46.00 | 50.00 | 54.44 | 50.15 | 5 |
| Education and research | 51.95 | 38.61 | 55.30 | 48.62 | 6 |
| Building industry | 55.70 | 35.90 | 49.26 | 46.95 | 7 |
| Chemical industry | (62.50)* | 29.41 | 40.63 | 44.18 | 8 |
| Energy | 45.83 | (35.71)* | 36.11 | 39.22 | 9 |
| Consumer industries | (52.94)* | 31.58 | (30.00) | 38.17 | 10 |
| Iron, steel and engineering | 38.16 | 34.94 | 37.50 | 36.86 | 11 |
| Average | 52.13 | 41.32 | 47.94 | 47.12 | |

* $n = 10$

production. The 'agriculture lobby', for example, might be able to ward off criticism of its own agencies while at the same time it uses *Pravda* as a megaphone to amplify its demands on other branches such as transport and the chemical industry. As no separate measurements of critical instructions and 'cross-demands' among different branches have been made, such a hypothesis cannot be tested, but it does not seem very plausible. High branch agencies may be capable of blocking undesirable comments on their own sector, but in view of the breadth of *Pravda*'s criticism, only a few branches appear to be privileged in this respect. The considerable reserve exercised with regard to instructions connected with the armed forces can, of course, be interpreted to support the 'power politics' hypothesis, but it is more reasonable to assume that such topics are suppressed for security reasons.

On the basis of an 'objective' interpretation, the tendencies we have observed would instead appear to be expressions of shifts in the structure of production itself. It is clear, at least, that a stronger interest in industry in the two later years corresponds to the increasing role of industry in the national economy. It can also be maintained that the demotion of agriculture from second in rank among the three main sectors in 1950 (cf. Table 5.12.1, p. 120) to third in 1960 and 1970 reflects its actual significance – harvests were not to the same extent a question of life and death in the later years as in 1950. According to the same interpretation, the declining frequencies for opinion would correspond to a relative decrease in its use by the regime as a general instrument of control.

On the whole, there is little doubt that shifts in the political agenda correspond to general developmental tendencies in the Soviet economy. When the economy is broken down into branches and forms and types of product, however, it becomes clear that neither GNP shares nor other quantitative production indicators provide a suitable basis for predicting which problems will be included on the political agenda. Just as it was shown in Section 5.7 that certain crops – e.g. cotton, fruit, vegetables, and the so-called technical cultures – are more 'political' than others, the entire chapter has indicated that certain goods and services have a high specific gravity in Soviet politics. Some of them are presented (unranked) in Table 5.12.5.

TABLE 5.12.5 Important product areas in 1950, 1960, and 1970 (unranked)

| 1950 | 1960 | 1970 |
|------|------|------|
| Coal | Steel | Steel |
| Coke | Chemical industry | Iron ore, scrap metal |
| Oil | Textile and clothing | Oil |
| Fodder grain | Shoes | Natural gas |
| Agricultural machines | Machines for the | Chemical industry |
| Rail transport | consumer and chemi- | Textiles and clothing |
| Research | cal industries | Shoes |
| Newspapers | Housing | Railroad transport |
|  | Milk | Inland navigation |
|  | Meat | Local communications |
|  | Education | Fodder grain |
|  | Radio and TV | Fruit and vegetables |
|  |  | Cereals |
|  |  | Eggs and poultry |
|  |  | Research |
|  |  | Radio and TV |

# 6 Political Problems: The Geographical Dimension

The place-names in *Pravda*'s editorials suggest something about where the problems regarded as urgent by the leadership are located and where remedial measures are thought to be necessary. Although geographical names are sometimes chosen merely as examples and criticism of a particular region is often intended as a mere general memento, it is of interest to determine which 'problem areas' the newspaper identifies. To get an idea of the geographical problem map, therefore, we have sorted the material according to mentions of various administrative areas. A first search produced all items containing a reference to republics, a second extracted those mentioning regions, territories and districts. In the latter search identifiable cities, districts and enterprises were traced to their respective regions. Thus by combining the republican and regional materials it became possible to look at large aggregates and republics or economic areas in which all items either mentioned the aggregate by name or identified any of its parts.

## 6.1 THE REPUBLICS

The Soviet Union is divided into fifteen republics, of which the Russian Soviet Federal Socialist Republic (RSFSR), with its capital in Moscow, is by far the largest. The RSFSR extends from the enclave Kaliningrad in the west to the Chukotsk National Area on the Bering Sea in the east, embracing both European Russia and most of the Asian part of the country. The second largest republic is the Ukraine. There are also five European republics (Estonia, Latvia, Lithuania, Belorussia [White Russia] and Moldavia), three in the Caucasus (Georgia, Armenia and Azerbaijan) and five in Central Asia (Turkmenistan, Uzbekistan, Kazakhstan, Tadzhikistan and Kirgizia). Karelia, which for a time after the Second World War was the sixteenth Soviet republic, was demoted in 1956 to the rank of autonomous republic within the RSFSR.

125

Fourteen of the fifteen republics, then, are non-Russian. None of them, however, has a homogeneous ethnic composition. A considerable part of the population of the non-Russian republics is Russian – in Kazakhstan Russians and Ukrainians are even in the majority – and there are similarly many non-Russian ethnic groups in the RSFSR. In 1970 some 22 million non-Russians (17.2 per cent of the population) were living in the RSFSR and there were about as many Russians in the non-Russian republics.

The RSFSR, of course, is the republic mentioned most often in *Pravda*'s editorials, while the small republics, the least of which are more or less equivalent to regions within the RSFSR, occur fairly seldom. Table 6.1.1 shows the frequencies for the different republics in absolute figures and by percentage. The size of the population must be taken into account to be able to interpret these figures correctly. 'Attention coefficients' have been calculated for the republics according to the formula

$$A_r, \text{year} = \frac{\dfrac{F_r}{F_{sssr}}}{\dfrac{P_r}{P_{sssr}}}$$

where $A$ denotes the attention coefficients, $F$ observed frequency in *Pravda*, $P$ population, $r$ republic and $sssr$ the entire Soviet Union. The results are presented in columns $B$ and $C$ for each year in Table 6.1.1.

In Table 6.1.2 the fifteen republics are ranked according to their attention coefficients. Certain considerations must be kept in mind when reading the table. First of all, the population of some republics is so small that their coefficients are greatly affected by slight variations. Only 31 mentions of Turkmenistan during all three years are enough to give it a secure first place in the table. When Estonia occurs six times in *Pravda*'s editorials in 1960 instead of only once in 1950, the coefficient rises from 0.26 to 2.05 and its rank from 15 to 5. Secondly, there is little room for variation in the coefficients of the large republics. Even if all editorials in 1950 had dealt with the RSFSR, it could not have attained a coefficient higher than 1.76, while the corresponding 'theoretical maximum' is as high as 12.18 for the Ukraine and 97.09 for a small republic such as Kirgizia. The actual value of 1.25 attained by the RSFSR in 1950 is in view of this remarkably high, and it indicates, in spite of its modest rank of 5, considerable interest in the Russian republic in that year. Its coefficient decreases later, but never to the mean value of 1, which implies that the attention the leaders devote to the Russian areas of the country remains greater that what might have been

Table 6.1.1 Geographical names in the *Pravda* instructions by republics

| | 1950 | | | | 1960 | | | | 1970 | | | |
|---|---|---|---|---|---|---|---|---|---|---|---|---|
| | A | B | C | D | A | B | C | D | A | B | C | D |
| | Number of instructions | Instructions in % | Population, % of USSR | Attention coefficient B/C | Number of instructions | Instructions in % | Population, % of USSR | Attention coefficient B/C | Number of instructions | Instructions in % | Population, % of USSR | Attention coefficient B/C |
| RSFSR | 276 | 71.00 | 56.8 | 1.25 | 279 | 57.30 | 56.0 | 1.02 | 212 | 57.00 | 53.8 | 1.06 |
| Ukraine | 32 | 8.21 | 20.5 | 0.40 | 37 | 7.60 | 20.0 | 0.38 | 23 | 6.20 | 19.5 | 0.32 |
| Belorussia | 13 | 3.33 | 4.3 | 0.77 | 8 | 1.64 | 3.8 | 0.43 | 3 | 0.81 | 3.7 | 0.22 |
| Uzbekistan | 10 | 2.56 | 3.5 | 0.73 | 12 | 2.46 | 4.0 | 0.62 | 16 | 4.30 | 4.9 | 0.88 |
| Kazakhstan | 27 | 6.92 | 3.7 | 1.87 | 59 | 12.10 | 4.6 | 2.63 | 38 | 10.20 | 5.3 | 1.92 |
| Georgia | 1 | 0.26 | 2.0 | 0.13 | 13 | 2.67 | 1.9 | 1.41 | 13 | 3.49 | 1.9 | 1.84 |
| Azerbaijan | 5 | 1.28 | 1.6 | 0.80 | 12 | 2.46 | 1.8 | 1.37 | 18 | 4.84 | 2.1 | 2.30 |
| Lithuania | 1 | 0.26 | 1.4 | 0.19 | 3 | 0.62 | 1.3 | 0.48 | – | – | 1.3 | – |
| Moldavia | 2 | 0.51 | 1.3 | 0.39 | 8 | 1.64 | 1.0 | 1.64 | 7 | 1.88 | 1.3 | 1.25 |
| Latvia | 3 | 0.77 | 1.1 | 0.70 | 5 | 1.02 | 1.0 | 1.02 | 2 | 0.53 | 1.0 | 0.53 |
| Kirgizia | 4 | 1.30 | 1.0 | 1.03 | 16 | 3.28 | 1.0 | 3.28 | 7 | 1.88 | 1.2 | 1.57 |
| Tadzhikistan | 4 | 1.03 | 0.8 | 1.29 | 7 | 1.44 | 1.0 | 1.44 | 9 | 2.42 | 1.2 | 2.02 |
| Armenia | 4 | 1.03 | 0.8 | 1.29 | 10 | 2.05 | 0.9 | 2.28 | 10 | 2.68 | 1.0 | 2.68 |
| Turkmenistan | 7 | 1.79 | 0.7 | 2.56 | 12 | 2.46 | 0.7 | 3.51 | 12 | 3.23 | 0.9 | 3.58 |
| Estonia | 1 | 0.26 | 0.6 | 0.43 | 6 | 1.23 | 0.6 | 2.05 | 2 | 0.53 | 0.6 | 0.88 |
| Total | 390 | 100.51 | 100.1 | | 487 | 99.97 | 99.6 | | 372 | 99.99 | 99.7 | |

TABLE 6.1.2 Republics ranked according to attention coefficients

| 1950 | | 1960 | | 1970 | |
|---|---|---|---|---|---|
| 1. Turkmenistan | 2.56 | 1. Turkmenistan | 3.51 | 1. Turkmenistan | 3.58 |
| 2. Kazakhstan | 1.87 | 2. Kirgizia | 3.28 | 2. Armenia | 2.68 |
| 3. Tadzhikistan | 1.29 | 3. Kazakhstan | 2.63 | 3. Azerbaijan | 2.30 |
| 4. Armenia | 1.29 | 4. Armenia | 2.28 | 4. Tadzhikistan | 2.02 |
| 5. RSFSR | 1.25 | 5. Estonia | 2.05 | 5. Kazakhstan | 1.92 |
| 6. Kirgizia | 1.03 | 6. Moldavia | 1.64 | 6. Georgia | 1.84 |
| 7. Azerbaijan | 0.80 | 7. Tadzhikistan | 1.44 | 7. Kirgizia | 1.57 |
| 8. Belorussia | 0.77 | 8. Georgia | 1.41 | 8. Moldavia | 1.25 |
| 9. Uzbekistan | 0.73 | 9. Azerbaijan | 1.37 | 9. RSFSR | 1.06 |
| 10. Latvia | 0.70 | 10. RSFSR | 1.02 | 10. Uzbekistan | 0.88 |
| 11. Estonia | 0.43 | 11. Latvia | 1.02 | 11. Estonia | 0.88 |
| 12. The Ukraine | 0.40 | 12. Uzbekistan | 0.62 | 12. Latvia | 0.53 |
| 13. Moldavia | 0.39 | 13. Lithuania | 0.48 | 13. The Ukraine | 0.32 |
| 14. Lithuania | 0.19 | 14. Belorussia | 0.43 | 14. Belorussia | 0.22 |
| 15. Georgia | 0.13 | 15. The Ukraine | 0.39 | 15. Lithuania | 0.22 |

expected given a proportional distribution. The decrease in concentration on the RSFSR is shown in Table 6.1.3.

TABLE 6.1.3 Attention coefficients for the RSFSR and other republics

|                 | 1950 | 1960 | 1970 |
|-----------------|------|------|------|
| RSFSR           | 1.30 | 1.02 | 1.06 |
| Other republics | 0.70 | 0.98 | 0.94 |

Most prominent in the non-Russian group are the Central Asian and Caucasian republics. Turkmenistan tops the list in all three years, and Kazakhstan also has a high rank. The Caucasian republics show a gradual rise. Georgia's last place in 1950 – the Stalin year in the study – is worth noting.

The Ukraine has low coefficients both under Khrushchev and under Brezhnev, but these figures correspond well to the pattern for the western part of the Soviet Union, which generally receives little attention in the *Pravda* editorials. The Ukraine and Belorussia together account for almost a quarter of the Soviet population, but in 1950 only a tenth of the geographically-specified critical items in the paper deal with these republics, and their frequency continues to decline in the subsequent years.

In view of the distribution among the republics that can be determined on the basis of Tables 6.1.1 and 6.2.2, it seems natural to ask whether interest in a given geographical area is related to the priority given to various economic sectors. For example, it can hardly be a coincidence that both cotton and the cotton-growing Central Asian republics have high attention coefficients. A study of the sectors considered in criticism of the various republics, however, gives the impression that such remarks extend over a broad range of areas – industry, agriculture, construction, investments, education, services, housing conditions, Party work, etc. If we compare two republics at the top and bottom of the list – Turkmenistan and Belorussia, respectively – we find that there is no striking difference at all with respect to subjects, apart from distinctions arising from the specific economic and geographical structure of the republics. True, *Pravda* returns on several occasions to certain problems in Turkmenistan such as the construction of schools and stock-raising, but during the three years studied here the paper discusses so many different problems in the republic that practically none of the sections in its Party committee escape criticism. Thus, *Pravda*'s coverage of the different republics is very broad, and judging by the attention they are given in its editorials, no part of the country seems to be regarded as merely a bread-basket, producer of raw materials or industrial centre.

## 6.2 THE ECONOMIC AREAS

Even in tsarist times, Russia was divided for statistical purposes into different economic areas. Attempts have been made on various occasions during the Soviet epoch to use this division for administrative ends as well, but it has for the most part remained purely geographical in nature. In addition, the boundaries between certain regions have been adjusted and the number of areas has varied, generally between 15 and 17.[1]

Regrouping the *Pravda* material from republics to economic areas serves two purposes. Combining the smallest republics into larger units reduces random variations, and we also obtain a better picture of the RSFSR, which is divided into ten areas. This makes it easier to see which non-Russian areas attract increased notice and which parts of the huge Russian republic are given decreasing attention.

The frequencies for the different areas are presented in Table 6.2.1. In 1950 the list is topped in absolute figures by the central region around Moscow and the Volga region, which includes Stalingrad and parts of the new industrial area east of the Volga. Ten years later attention is focused instead on the Central Asian areas — Kazakhstan and the rest of Central Asia. These two areas still show high figures in 1970, but now they are accompanied by the Caucasus and the central region around Moscow.

Here again these observations must be set in relation to the population of the various areas in order to get a balanced view of the significance of the absolute frequencies. Attention coefficients have therefore been calculated according to the same formula as before. The results of the operation are presented in Table 6.2.1, which shows the coefficients, and Table 6.2.2, which lists the economic areas in ranked order.

Kazakhstan also has a prominent position in the coefficient tables. The list is headed in 1950 by a coherent block of areas south and west of Moscow, which includes both the newly-tilled virgin lands in Central Asia and the expanding industrial area in southern Russia and western Siberia. The coefficients for this zone are high in the two later years as well, but emphasis on the Volga-Ural area weakens. The Caucasus is an area that rises in rank, while the western parts of the Soviet Union attract but little attention. Here, as in the list of coefficients for the republics, low values are noted for the Ukraine, Belorussia and the Baltic States. Other 'peripheral' areas which register weakly in *Pravda*'s

TABLE 6.2.1 Geographical names in the *Pravda* instructions: economic areas

| Economic areas | Observed frequencies | | | | | | | | Expected frequencies | | | Attention coefficients | | |
|---|---|---|---|---|---|---|---|---|---|---|---|---|---|---|
| | 1950 | % | 1960 | % | 1970 | % | All years | % | 1950 | 1960 | 1970 | 1950 | 1960 | 1970 |
| Kazakhstan | 27 | 7.03 | 59 | 12.55 | 38 | 11.11 | 124 | 10.37 | 3.70 | 4.60 | 5.30 | 1.90 | 2.73 | 2.10 |
| Central black-earth belt | 29 | 7.55 | 24 | 5.11 | 23 | 6.73 | 76 | 6.35 | 4.28 | 3.65 | 3.30 | 1.76 | 1.40 | 2.04 |
| Georgia, Azerbaijan, Armenia | 10 | 2.60 | 35 | 7.45 | 41 | 11.99 | 86 | 7.19 | 4.31 | 4.60 | 5.09 | 0.60 | 1.62 | 2.36 |
| E. Siberia | 13 | 3.39 | 24 | 5.11 | 10 | 2.92 | 47 | 3.93 | 2.73 | 2.70 | 2.67 | 1.24 | 1.89 | 1.09 |
| Uzbekistan, Tadzhikistan, Turkmenistan | 25 | 6.51 | 47 | 10.0 | 44 | 12.87 | 116 | 9.70 | 5.98 | 6.71 | 8.25 | 1.09 | 1.49 | 1.56 |
| Povolzhskii-area | 51 | 13.28 | 37 | 7.87 | 31 | 9.06 | 119 | 9.95 | 7.53 | 7.54 | 7.55 | 1.76 | 1.04 | 1.20 |
| Urals | 36 | 9.38 | 29 | 6.17 | 25 | 7.31 | 90 | 7.53 | 6.55 | 6.12 | 5.69 | 1.43 | 1.01 | 1.28 |
| W. Siberia | 22 | 5.70 | 44 | 9.36 | 13 | 3.80 | 79 | 6.60 | 5.74 | 5.38 | 5.02 | 0.99 | 1.74 | 0.76 |
| N. Caucasus | 21 | 5.47 | 30 | 6.38 | 13 | 3.80 | 64 | 5.35 | 4.68 | 4.91 | 5.14 | 1.17 | 1.30 | 0.74 |
| N. W. area | 19 | 4.95 | 20 | 4.26 | 17 | 4.97 | 56 | 4.68 | 4.78 | 4.72 | 4.66 | 1.04 | 0.90 | 1.07 |
| Central area | 57 | 14.84 | 37 | 7.87 | 36 | 10.53 | 130 | 10.87 | 12.85 | 12.02 | 11.48 | 1.15 | 0.65 | 0.92 |
| Volga-Viatskii area | 14 | 3.64 | 13 | 2.77 | 7 | 2.05 | 34 | 2.84 | 3.74 | 3.38 | 3.02 | 0.97 | 0.82 | 0.68 |
| Far East | 8 | 2.08 | 4 | 0.85 | 7 | 2.05 | 19 | 1.59 | 2.12 | 2.28 | 2.44 | 0.98 | 0.37 | 0.84 |
| Belorussia, Baltic republics | 18 | 4.69 | 22 | 4.68 | 7 | 2.05 | 47 | 3.93 | 7.46 | 7.00 | 7.71 | 0.63 | 0.67 | 0.27 |
| Ukraine, Moldavia | 34 | 8.86 | 45 | 9.57 | 30 | 8.77 | 109 | 9.11 | 21.77 | 21.12 | 20.97 | 0.41 | 0.45 | 0.42 |
| Total | 384 | 100.01 | 470 | 100.00 | 342 | 100.01 | 1196 | 99.99 | 98.22 | 96.73 | 98.29 | | | |

TABLE 6.2.2 Economic areas ranked according to attention coefficients

| 1950 | | 1960 | | 1970 | |
|---|---|---|---|---|---|
| 1. Kazakhstan | 1.90 | 1. Kazakhstan | 2.73 | 1. Georgia, Azerbaijan, Armenia | 2.36 |
| 2. Central Black-earth belt | 1.76 | 2. E. Siberia | 1.89 | 2. Kazakhstan | 2.10 |
| 3. Povolzhskii area | 1.76 | 3. W. Siberia | 1.74 | 3. Central Black-earth belt | 2.04 |
| 4. Urals | 1.43 | 4. Georgia, Azerbaijan, Armenia | 1.62 | 4. Uzbekistan, Kirgizia, Tadzhikistan, Turkmenistan | 1.56 |
| 5. E. Siberia | 1.24 | 5. Uzbekistan, Kirgizia, Tadzhikistan, Turkmenistan | 1.49 | 5. Urals | 1.28 |
| 6. N. Caucasus | 1.17 | 6. Central Black-earth belt | 1.40 | 6. Povolzhskii area | 1.20 |
| 7. Central area | 1.15 | 7. N. Caucasus | 1.30 | 7. E. Siberia | 1.09 |
| 8. Uzbekistan, Kirgizia, Tadzhikistan, Turkmenistan | 1.09 | 8. Povolzhskii area | 1.04 | 8. N. W. area | 1.07 |
| 9. N. W. area | 1.04 | 9. Urals | 1.01 | 9. Central area | 0.92 |
| 10. W. Siberia | 0.99 | 10. N. W. area | 0.90 | 10. Far East | 0.84 |
| 11. Far East | 0.98 | 11. Volga-Viatskii area | 0.82 | 11. W. Siberia | 0.76 |
| 12. Volga-Viatskii area | 0.97 | 12. White Belorussia, Baltic republics | 0.67 | 12. N. Caucasus | 0.74 |
| 13. Belorussia, Baltic republics | 0.63 | 13. Central area | 0.65 | 13. Volga-Viatskii area | 0.68 |
| 14. Georgia, Azerbaijan, Armenia | 0.60 | 14. Ukraine, Moldavia | 0.45 | 14. Ukraine, Moldavia | – |
| 15. Ukraine, Moldavia | 0.41 | 15. Far East | 0.37 | 15. Belorussia, Baltic republics | 0.27 |

editorials include the extreme eastern part of Siberia and the northwestern corner of European Russia. In 1960 and 1970 the coefficients of the central area around Moscow fall below the average.

### 6.3 THE REGIONS

By breaking the material down further it is possible to establish the distribution of *Pravda*'s interest among the various regions in the Soviet Union. These units are usually known as *oblasts*, but several other names also occur – autonomous republic, autonomous *oblast'*, *okrug* (national area), *krai* (territory), *gorod* (city). The regional structure changes occasionally, which in a number of cases makes comparisons between different years difficult. Most regions, however, are stable during the period.

Owing to the large number of regions in the Soviet Union, the frequency for each region is fairly small. Few of them, however, are totally absent in the material. Of the 70 regions of the RSFSR, for example, only three are never mentioned (Tuva, Komi and Magadan), and they are among the most sparsely populated. Of the 70 regions in the RSFSR only 44 are addressed in *Pravda* in all three years.

Absolute frequencies, percentages and attention coefficients for the different regions are presented in Table 6.3.1. Table 6.3.2 is an unranked list of the regions with an attention coefficient greater than 1 in all three years. That is, they are mentioned more often in *Pravda*'s editorials than one would be led to expect on the basis of their population. Sixteen of the seventeen regions in this category belong to the RSFSR, while one – Karaganda – is in Kazakhstan. The Ukraine and Belorussia are absent, as are the Central Asian republics divided into regions. If the seven smallest republics not divided into regions are added to the list, it can be stated that the coefficient of Armenia and Azerbaijan is also higher than 1 in all three years. The respective figures for all republics are presented in Table 6.1.1.

The sixteen intensely observed regions in the RSFSR are among the most densely populated of the republic. All but one (Orel) are above the mean with respect to population. A majority are primarily industrial. Seven of the regions (Orel, Kursk, Voronezh, Tambov, Penza, Saratov and Kuibyshev) form a connected belt south of Moscow, while another five (Sverdlovsk, Cheliabinsk, Karaganda, Omsk and Novosibirsk) are located in the western Siberian industrial area. The zone in the RSFSR to which *Pravda* devotes particular attention approximately coincides with the parts of the Soviet Union designated already in the early 1920s as centres of industrial expansion in plans such as GOELRO.[2]

Seven of the ten largest regions in the RSFSR are missing from the list in Table 6.3.2: Moscow, Leningrad, Krasnodar, Rostov, Perm', the

Table 6.3.1 Regional attention coefficients

| | 1950 | | | | 1960 | | | | 1970 | | | |
|---|---|---|---|---|---|---|---|---|---|---|---|---|
| | Population, % of USSR* | Number of instructions | Instructions in % | Attention coefficient C/A | Population, % of USSR | Number of instructions | Instructions in % | Attention coefficient C/A | Population, % of USSR | Number of instructions | Instructions in % | Attention coefficient C/A |
| | A | B | C | D | A | B | C | D | A | B | C | D |
| Altaiskii krai | 1.46 | 4 | 1.11 | 0.76 | 1.28 | 12 | 2.82 | 2.20 | 1.10 | 1 | 0.29 | 0.26 |
| Arkhangelskaya obl. | 0.62 | 2 | 0.56 | 0.90 | 0.60 | 1 | 0.23 | 0.38 | 0.58 | 6 | 1.74 | 3.00 |
| Astrakhanskaya obl. | 0.32 | — | — | — | 0.34 | 4 | 0.94 | 2.76 | 0.36 | — | — | — |
| Amurskaya obl. | 0.35 | 3 | 0.83 | 2.37 | 0.34 | — | — | — | 0.33 | 1 | 0.29 | 0.88 |
| Belgorodskaya obl. | 0.64 | — | — | — | 0.58 | 4 | 0.94 | 1.62 | 0.52 | 3 | 0.87 | 1.67 |
| Brianskaya obl. | 0.85 | 6 | 1.67 | 1.96 | 0.72 | 3 | 0.71 | 0.99 | 0.65 | 2 | 0.58 | 0.89 |
| Vladimirskaya obl. | 0.69 | 4 | 1.11 | 1.61 | 0.66 | — | — | — | 0.63 | 1 | 0.29 | 0.46 |
| Volgogradskaya obl. | 0.81 | 7 | 1.94 | 2.40 | 0.89 | 1 | 0.23 | 0.26 | 0.97 | 5 | 1.45 | 1.49 |
| Vologodskaya obl. | 0.69 | 3 | 0.83 | 1.20 | 0.61 | 4 | 0.94 | 1.54 | 0.53 | — | — | — |
| Voronezhskaya obl. | 1.32 | 9 | 2.50 | 1.89 | 1.11 | 6 | 1.41 | 1.27 | 1.04 | 5 | 1.45 | 1.39 |
| Gorkovskaya obl. | 1.86 | 10 | 2.78 | 1.49 | 1.69 | 8 | 1.88 | 1.11 | 1.52 | 4 | 1.16 | 1.14 |
| Ivanovskaya obl. | 0.69 | 2 | 0.56 | 0.81 | 0.62 | 2 | 0.47 | 0.76 | 0.55 | 3 | 0.87 | 1.58 |
| Irkutskaya obl. | 0.98 | 5 | 1.39 | 1.42 | 0.97 | 7 | 1.65 | 1.70 | 0.96 | 1 | 0.29 | 0.30 |
| Kaliningradskaya obl. | 0.29 | — | — | — | 0.30 | — | — | — | 0.31 | — | — | — |
| Kalininskaya obl. | 0.91 | 8 | 2.22 | 2.44 | 0.83 | 2 | 0.47 | 0.57 | 0.71 | 1 | 0.29 | 0.41 |
| Kaluzhskaya obl. | 0.47 | 4 | 1.11 | 2.36 | 0.44 | 2 | 0.47 | 1.07 | 0.41 | 3 | 0.87 | 2.12 |
| Kamchatskaya obl. | 0.10 | 1 | 0.28 | 2.80 | 0.11 | — | — | — | 0.12 | — | — | — |

TABLE 6.3.1 (contd)

| | 1950 | | | | 1960 | | | | 1970 | | | |
|---|---|---|---|---|---|---|---|---|---|---|---|---|
| | Population, % of USSR* (A) | Number of instructions (B) | Instructions in % (C) | Attention coefficient C/A (D) | Population, % of USSR (A) | Number of instructions (B) | Instructions in % (C) | Attention coefficient C/A (D) | Population, % of USSR (A) | Number of instructions (B) | Instructions in % (C) | Attention coefficient C/A (D) |
| Kemerovskaya obl. | 1.50 | 5 | 1.39 | 0.93 | 1.35 | 8 | 1.88 | 1.39 | 1.20 | 3 | 0.87 | 0.72 |
| Kirovskaya obl. | 0.99 | 1 | 0.28 | 0.28 | 0.85 | 5 | 1.18 | 1.39 | 0.71 | 1 | 0.29 | 0.41 |
| Kostromskaya obl. | 0.49 | 7 | 1.94 | 3.96 | 0.42 | 1 | 0.23 | 0.55 | 0.35 | — | — | — |
| Kuibyshevskaya obl. | 1.04 | 7 | 1.94 | 1.87 | 1.10 | 9 | 2.12 | 1.93 | 1.16 | 7 | 2.03 | 1.75 |
| Kurganskaya obl. | 0.49 | 1 | 0.28 | 0.57 | 0.47 | 2 | 0.47 | 1.00 | 0.45 | 1 | 0.29 | 0.64 |
| Kurskaya obl. | 0.93 | 12 | 3.33 | 3.58 | 0.70 | 7 | 1.65 | 2.36 | 0.61 | 5 | 1.45 | 2.38 |
| Leningradskaya obl. | 2.10 | 4 | 1.11 | 0.53 | 2.18 | 11 | 2.59 | 1.19 | 2.26 | 4 | 1.16 | 0.51 |
| Lipetskaya obl. | 0.57 | — | — | — | 0.54 | — | — | — | 0.51 | 5 | 1.45 | 2.84 |
| Magadanskaya obl. | — | — | — | — | 0.11 | — | — | — | 0.15 | — | — | — |
| Moskovskaya obl. | 4.98 | 3 | 0.83 | 0.17 | 5.18 | 13 | 3.06 | 0.59 | 5.38 | 12 | 3.48 | 0.65 |
| Murmanskaya obl. | 0.22 | 1 | 0.28 | 1.27 | 0.28 | — | — | — | 0.34 | 1 | 0.29 | 0.85 |
| Novgorodskaya obl. | 0.36 | 2 | 0.56 | 1.56 | 0.33 | 1 | 0.23 | 0.70 | 0.30 | 3 | 0.87 | 2.90 |
| Novosibirskaya obl. | 1.16 | 8 | 2.22 | 1.91 | 1.10 | 9 | 2.12 | 1.93 | 1.04 | 4 | 1.16 | 1.12 |
| Omskaya obl. | 0.82 | 4 | 1.11 | 1.35 | 0.79 | 11 | 2.59 | 3.28 | 0.76 | 4 | 1.16 | 1.53 |
| Orenburgskaya obl. | 0.91 | 8 | 2.24 | 2.46 | 0.88 | 1 | 0.23 | 0.26 | 0.85 | 2 | 0.58 | 0.68 |
| Orlovskaya obl. | 0.62 | 7 | 1.94 | 3.12 | 0.43 | 3 | 0.71 | 1.65 | 0.38 | 2 | 0.58 | 1.53 |
| Penzenskaya obl. | 0.77 | 7 | 1.94 | 2.52 | 0.70 | 6 | 1.41 | 2.01 | 0.63 | 4 | 1.16 | 1.84 |

Table 6.3.1 (contd)

| | 1950 | | | | 1960 | | | | 1970 | | | |
|---|---|---|---|---|---|---|---|---|---|---|---|---|
| | Population, % of USSR* (A) | Number of instructions (B) | Instructions in % (C) | Attention coefficient C/A (D) | Population, % of USSR (A) | Number of instructions (B) | Instructions in % (C) | Attention coefficient C/A (D) | Population, % of USSR (A) | Number of instructions (B) | Instructions in % (C) | Attention coefficient C/A (D) |
| Permskaya obl. | 1.58 | – | – | – | 1.41 | 8 | 1.88 | 1.33 | 1.24 | 6 | 1.74 | 1.40 |
| Pskovskaya obl. | 0.48 | 4 | 1.11 | 2.31 | 0.42 | 3 | 0.71 | 1.69 | 0.36 | 2 | 0.58 | 1.61 |
| Rostovskaya obl. | 1.60 | 4 | 1.11 | 0.69 | 1.60 | 10 | 2.35 | 1.47 | 1.60 | 4 | 1.16 | 0.72 |
| Ryazanskaya obl. | 0.92 | 7 | 1.94 | 2.11 | 0.68 | 1 | 0.23 | 0.34 | 0.58 | 2 | 0.58 | 1.00 |
| Saratovskaya obl. | 1.04 | 7 | 1.94 | 1.87 | 1.03 | 6 | 1.41 | 1.37 | 1.02 | 10 | 2.90 | 2.84 |
| Sakhalinskaya obl. | 0.32 | – | – | – | 0.29 | – | – | – | 0.26 | 3 | 0.87 | 3.35 |
| Sverdlovskaya obl. | 2.07 | 8 | 2.22 | 1.07 | 1.93 | 9 | 2.12 | 1.10 | 1.79 | 7 | 2.03 | 1.13 |
| Smolenskaya obl. | 0.57 | 3 | 0.83 | 1.46 | 0.51 | 1 | 0.23 | 0.45 | 0.45 | 4 | 1.16 | 2.58 |
| Tambovskaya obl. | 0.82 | 8 | 2.22 | 2.71 | 0.72 | 7 | 1.65 | 2.29 | 0.62 | 5 | 1.45 | 2.34 |
| Tomskaya obl. | 0.35 | – | – | – | 0.34 | 2 | 0.47 | 1.38 | 0.33 | – | – | – |
| Tulskaya obl. | 0.96 | 3 | 0.83 | 0.86 | 0.89 | 3 | 0.71 | 0.80 | 0.81 | 1 | 0.29 | 0.36 |
| Tyumenskaya obl. | 0.45 | 1 | 0.28 | 0.62 | 0.52 | 2 | 0.47 | 0.90 | 0.59 | 1 | 0.29 | 0.49 |
| Yaroslavskaya obl. | 0.70 | 3 | 0.83 | 1.19 | 0.64 | 6 | 1.41 | 2.20 | 0.58 | 7 | 2.03 | 3.50 |
| Bashkirskaya assr | 1.61 | 9 | 2.50 | 1.55 | 1.60 | 5 | 1.18 | 0.74 | 1.59 | 2 | 0.58 | 0.36 |
| Buriatskaya assr | 0.32 | – | – | – | 0.33 | – | – | – | 0.34 | 1 | 0.29 | 0.85 |
| Dagestanskaya assr | 0.48 | – | – | – | 0.54 | 2 | 0.47 | 0.87 | 0.60 | 2 | 0.58 | 0.97 |
| Kabardino-Balkarskaya assr | 0.17 | 2 | 0.56 | 3.29 | 0.21 | 2 | 0.47 | 2.24 | 0.25 | – | – | – |

TABLE 6.3.1 (contd)

| | 1950 | | | | 1960 | | | | 1970 | | | |
|---|---|---|---|---|---|---|---|---|---|---|---|---|
| | Population, % of USSR* (A) | Number of instructions (B) | Instructions in % (C) | Attention coefficient C/A (D) | Population, % of USSR (A) | Number of instructions (B) | Instructions in % (C) | Attention coefficient C/A (D) | Population, % of USSR (A) | Number of instructions (B) | Instructions in % (C) | Attention coefficient C/A (D) |
| Kalmytskaya assr | 0.07 | — | — | — | 0.09 | 1 | 0.23 | 2.55 | 0.11 | — | — | — |
| Karelskaya assr | 0.31 | 3 | 0.83 | 2.68 | 0.30 | — | — | — | 0.29 | 1 | 0.29 | 1.00 |
| Mariiskaya assr | 0.34 | 1 | 0.28 | 0.82 | 0.31 | — | — | — | 0.28 | — | — | — |
| Mordovskaya assr | 0.49 | — | — | — | 0.46 | — | — | — | 0.43 | 2 | 0.58 | 1.35 |
| Severo-Ostenskaya assr | 0.21 | — | — | — | 0.22 | 1 | 0.23 | 1.04 | 0.23 | — | — | — |
| Tatarskaya assr | 1.41 | 9 | 2.50 | 1.77 | 1.36 | 3 | 0.71 | 0.52 | 1.31 | 2 | 0.58 | 0.44 |
| Udmurtskaya assr | 0.67 | — | — | — | 0.63 | 1 | 0.23 | 0.36 | 0.59 | — | — | — |
| Checheno-Inguskskaya assr | 0.33 | 1 | 0.28 | 0.85 | 0.39 | 1 | 0.23 | 0.59 | 0.45 | 2 | 0.58 | 1.29 |
| Chuvashskaya assr | 0.55 | 2 | 0.56 | 1.02 | 0.53 | — | — | — | 0.51 | 2 | 0.58 | 1.14 |
| Yakutskaya assr | 0.20 | — | — | — | 0.24 | 1 | 0.23 | 0.96 | 0.28 | — | — | — |
| Krasnodarskii krai | 1.72 | 3 | 0.83 | 0.48 | 1.80 | 3 | 0.71 | 0.39 | 1.88 | 2 | 0.58 | 0.31 |
| Krasnoyarskii krai | 1.27 | 7 | 1.94 | 1.53 | 1.25 | 7 | 1.65 | 1.32 | 1.23 | 6 | 1.74 | 1.41 |
| Primorskii krai | 0.57 | — | — | — | 0.65 | — | — | — | 0.73 | — | — | — |
| Stavropolskii krai | 0.86 | 11 | 3.06 | 3.56 | 0.91 | 11 | 2.59 | 2.85 | 0.96 | 7 | 2.03 | 2.11 |
| Khabarovskii krai | 0.51 | 4 | 1.11 | 2.18 | 0.54 | 4 | 0.94 | 1.74 | 0.57 | 3 | 0.87 | 1.53 |
| Ulyanovskaya obl. | 0.53 | 5 | 1.39 | 2.62 | 0.52 | 5 | 1.18 | 2.27 | 0.51 | 1 | 0.29 | 0.57 |
| Chelyabinskaya obl. | 1.50 | 12 | 3.33 | 2.22 | 1.43 | 12 | 2.82 | 1.97 | 1.36 | 7 | 2.03 | 1.49 |

Table 6.3.1 (contd)

| | 1950 | | | | 1960 | | | | 1970 | | | |
|---|---|---|---|---|---|---|---|---|---|---|---|---|
| | Population, % of USSR* (A) | Number of instructions (B) | Instructions in % (C) | Attention coefficient C/A (D) | Population, % of USSR (A) | Number of instructions (B) | Instructions in % (C) | Attention coefficient C/A (D) | Population, % of USSR (A) | Number of instructions (B) | Instructions in % (C) | Attention coefficient C/A (D) |
| Chitinskaya obl. | 0.48 | 1 | 0.28 | 0.58 | 0.48 | 1 | 0.23 | 0.48 | 0.48 | 3 | 0.87 | 1.81 |
| Khersonskaya obl. | 0.35 | — | — | — | 0.39 | — | — | — | 0.43 | 1 | 0.29 | 0.67 |
| Vinnitskaya obl. | 1.12 | — | — | — | 1.00 | 1 | 0.23 | 0.23 | 0.88 | 2 | 0.58 | 0.66 |
| Volynskaya obl. | 0.45 | 1 | 0.28 | 0.62 | 0.43 | — | — | — | 0.41 | — | — | — |
| Dnepropetrovskaya obl. | 1.24 | 4 | 1.11 | 0.90 | 1.32 | 3 | 0.71 | 0.54 | 1.40 | 1 | 0.29 | 0.21 |
| Zhitomirskaya obl. | 0.81 | 1 | 0.28 | 0.35 | 0.74 | — | — | — | 0.67 | — | — | — |
| Zakarpatskaya obl. | 0.46 | — | — | — | 0.45 | — | — | — | 0.44 | — | — | — |
| Zaporozhskaya obl. | 0.67 | 6 | 1.67 | 2.49 | 0.71 | 2 | 0.47 | 0.66 | 0.75 | 1 | 0.29 | 0.39 |
| Kievskaya obl. | 1.26 | — | — | — | 1.36 | 2 | 0.47 | 0.35 | 1.46 | 2 | 0.58 | 0.40 |
| Kirovogradskaya obl. | 0.62 | — | — | — | 0.57 | — | — | — | 0.52 | 2 | 0.58 | 1.12 |
| Krymskaya obl. | 0.43 | 3 | 0.83 | 1.93 | 0.60 | — | — | — | 0.77 | — | — | — |
| Voroshilovgradskaya obl. | 1.24 | 4 | 1.11 | 0.90 | 1.19 | 3 | 0.71 | 0.60 | 1.14 | 1 | 0.29 | 0.25 |
| Lvovskaya obl. | 1.00 | 1 | 0.28 | 0.28 | 1.01 | — | — | — | 1.02 | — | — | — |
| Nikolaevskaya obl. | 0.48 | 1 | 0.28 | 0.58 | 0.48 | 1 | 0.23 | 0.48 | 0.48 | — | — | — |
| Odesskaya obl. | 0.92 | 2 | 0.56 | 0.61 | 0.96 | 1 | 0.23 | 0.24 | 1.00 | — | — | — |
| Poltavskaya obl. | 0.81 | 1 | 0.28 | 0.35 | 0.76 | 1 | 0.23 | 0.30 | 0.71 | — | — | — |
| Donetskaya obl. | 2.06 | 3 | 0.83 | 0.40 | 2.05 | — | — | — | 2.04 | 2 | 0.58 | 0.28 |

Table 6.3.1 (contd)

| | 1950 | | | | 1960 | | | | 1970 | | | |
|---|---|---|---|---|---|---|---|---|---|---|---|---|
| | Population, % of USSR* (A) | Number of instructions (B) | Instructions in % (C) | Attention coefficient C/A (D) | Population, % of USSR (A) | Number of instructions (B) | Instructions in % (C) | Attention coefficient C/A (D) | Population, % of USSR (A) | Number of instructions (B) | Instructions in % (C) | Attention coefficient C/A (D) |
| Ivano-Frankovskaya obl. | 0.54 | — | — | — | 0.53 | 2 | 0.47 | 0.89 | 0.52 | — | — | — |
| Sumskaya obl. | 0.80 | — | — | — | 0.71 | — | — | — | 0.62 | 1 | 0.29 | 0.47 |
| Ternopolskaya obl. | 0.56 | — | — | — | 0.52 | — | — | — | 0.48 | — | — | — |
| Kharkovskaya obl. | 1.20 | 2 | 0.56 | 0.47 | 1.19 | 7 | 1.65 | 1.39 | 1.18 | 8 | 2.32 | 1.97 |
| Khmelnitskaya obl. | 0.83 | — | — | — | 0.75 | 1 | 0.23 | 0.33 | 0.67 | 1 | 0.29 | 0.43 |
| Cherkasskaya obl. | — | — | — | — | 0.69 | — | — | — | 0.64 | 1 | 0.29 | 0.45 |
| Chernigorskaya obl. | 0.80 | 1 | 0.28 | 0.35 | 0.72 | — | — | — | 0.64 | — | — | — |
| Chernovitskaya obl. | 0.39 | — | — | — | 0.37 | — | — | — | 0.35 | — | — | — |
| Aktyubinskaya obl. | 0.17 | — | — | — | 0.20 | 2 | 0.47 | 2.35 | 0.23 | 1 | 0.29 | 1.26 |
| Alma-Atinskaya obl. | 0.85 | 1 | 0.28 | 0.33 | 0.73 | 1 | 0.23 | 0.32 | 0.61 | 2 | 0.58 | 0.95 |
| Dzhambulskaya obl. | 0.23 | — | — | — | 0.28 | 2 | 0.47 | 1.68 | 0.33 | 1 | 0.29 | 0.88 |
| Karagandinskaya obl. | 0.46 | 3 | 0.83 | 1.74 | 0.56 | 4 | 0.94 | 1.68 | 0.66 | 6 | 1.74 | 2.64 |
| Kokchetavskaya obl. | 0.28 | — | — | — | 0.26 | 2 | 0.47 | 1.81 | 0.24 | 2 | 0.58 | 2.42 |
| Kustanaiskaya obl. | 0.45 | — | — | — | 0.41 | 3 | 0.71 | 1.73 | 0.37 | — | — | — |
| Kzylordinskaya obl. | 0.11 | 1 | 0.28 | 2.55 | 0.16 | — | — | — | 0.21 | — | — | — |
| Pavlodarskaya obl. | 0.18 | 2 | 0.56 | 3.11 | 0.24 | 1 | 0.23 | 0.96 | 0.30 | 1 | 0.29 | 0.97 |
| Semipalatinskaya obl. | 0.22 | — | — | — | 0.26 | — | — | — | 0.30 | 2 | 0.58 | 1.93 |

Table 6.3.1 (contd)

| | 1950 | | | | 1960 | | | | 1970 | | | |
|---|---|---|---|---|---|---|---|---|---|---|---|---|
| | Population, % of USSR* | Number of instructions | Instructions in % | Attention coefficient C/A | Population, % of USSR | Number of instructions | Instructions in % | Attention coefficient C/A | Population, % of USSR | Number of instructions | Instructions in % | Attention coefficient C/A |
| | $A$ | $B$ | $C$ | $D$ | $A$ | $B$ | $C$ | $D$ | $A$ | $B$ | $C$ | $D$ |
| Taldy-Kurganskaya obl. | 0.30 | 1 | 0.28 | 0.93 | 0.28 | 2 | 0.47 | 1.68 | 0.26 | 1 | 0.29 | 1.12 |
| Tselinogradskaya obl. | 0.34 | – | – | – | 0.33 | – | – | – | 0.32 | 3 | 0.87 | 2.72 |
| Vostochno-Kazakhstanskaya obl. | 0.39 | – | – | – | 0.37 | 1 | 0.23 | 0.62 | 0.35 | 1 | 0.29 | 0.83 |
| Brestskaya obl. | 0.58 | 1 | 0.28 | 0.48 | 0.56 | – | – | – | 0.54 | – | – | – |
| Grodnenskaya obl. | 0.54 | 1 | 0.28 | 0.52 | 0.50 | – | – | – | 0.46 | – | – | – |
| Minskaya obl. | 0.87 | 3 | 0.83 | 0.95 | 0.95 | 3 | 0.71 | 0.75 | 1.03 | – | – | – |
| Mogilevskaya obl. | 0.59 | 1 | 0.28 | 0.47 | 0.55 | – | – | – | 0.51 | 2 | 0.58 | 1.14 |
| Vitebskaya obl. | 0.63 | 2 | 0.56 | 0.89 | 0.60 | – | – | – | 0.57 | – | – | – |

* Estimated population. The change in 1950–60 has been assumed to be as large as that in 1960–70.

Bashkir ASSR and the Tatar   ASSR. None of these represent blank
spots in the *Pravda* material, but they are not given more than
proportional attention during all three of the years studied. Moscow and
Leningrad, for example, are mentioned only a few times in 1950, and the
figures for Leningrad are low in 1970 as well. It can be seen from the list
of regions in Table 6.3.3 ranked according to total absolute frequencies
for all years that all of the ten most densely populated regions occur
among the 25 most frequently mentioned regions in *Pravda*'s editorials.

TABLE 6.3.2 Problem regions

| | |
|---|---|
| Voronezhskaya oblast' | Sverdlovskaya oblast' |
| Gorkovskaya ,, | Tambovskaya ,, |
| Kuibyshevskaya ,, | Yaroskavskaya ,, |
| Kurskaya ,, | Krasnoyarskii krai |
| Novosibirskaya ,, | Stavropolskii ,, |
| Omskaya ,, | Khabarovskii ,, |
| Orlovskaya ,, | Chelyabinskaya oblast' |
| Penzenskaya ,, | Karagandinskaya ,, |
| Saratovskaya ,, | |

The regions most often exposed to criticism are the Chelyabinsk
region in central Siberia and the Moscow region. Tables 6.3.4 and 6.3.5
present the instructions addressed to the responsible organisations in
these regions. Messages in both cases extend over a broad range of
topics, but those addressed to Moscow deal to a somewhat greater
extent with light sectors such as consumer goods, services, etc. There is
another difference in the specific targets of *Pravda*'s criticism. The
generalised formulations in the remarks directed at Chelyabinsk cast
a shadow on the Party organisations of the region, whereas the deficiencies noted in Moscow are more often connected with individual,
specified units.

In recent years, a few analysts have tried to rank the various Soviet
regions according to political significance. Frank has devised a scale
based on (1) the position of the regions in their sovnarkhozes and
(2) the presence or absence of permanent or candidate members from a
given region in the Central Committee.[3] McAuley has used additional
socio-economic factors to try to explain which regions attain representation in the Central Committee.[4] Frank has also ranked the regions
according to the significance of their respective Party organizations
based on the size of the delegations from the regions to the XXIII Party
Congress.[5] This rating is included in Table 6.3.3 above together with a
ranking (also borrowed from Frank) of the regions according to their
population in 1966.

TABLE 6.3.3 Regions in the RSFSR ranked according to political significance and frequency in the *Pravda* instructions

| Region | Number of delegates to XXIII Party Congress | Rank according to (1) | Population 1966 ('000) | Rank according to (3) | Representation in Central Committee* | Number of editorial instructions | | | Total | Rank according to (9) |
|---|---|---|---|---|---|---|---|---|---|---|
| | | | | | | 1950 | 1960 | 1970 | | |
| | *1* | *2* | *3* | *4* | *5* | *6* | *7* | *8* | *9* | *10* |
| Leningrad | 187 | 1 | 4363 | 2 | M | 4 | 11 | 4 | 19 | 14.5 |
| Moscow | 154 | 2 | 5336 | 1 | M | 3 | 13 | 12 | 28 | 1.5 |
| Rostov | 91 | 3 | 3730 | 5 | M | 4 | 10 | 4 | 18 | 16 |
| Gorkii | 83 | 4.5 | 3668 | 7 | M | 10 | 8 | 4 | 22 | 10 |
| Krasnodar | 83 | 4.5 | 4218 | 4 | M | 3 | 10 | 2 | 15 | 22 |
| Sverdlovsk | 81 | 6 | 4349 | 3 | M | 8 | 9 | 7 | 24 | 4.5 |
| Kemerovo | 67 | 7 | 3033 | 11 | M | 5 | 8 | 3 | 16 | 20 |
| Kuibyshev | 66 | 8.5 | 2559 | 14 | M | 7 | 8 | 7 | 23 | 7.5 |
| Saratov | 66 | 8.5 | 2386 | 17 | M | 7 | 6 | 10 | 23 | 7.5 |
| Bashkiriya | 63 | 11.5 | 3719 | 6 | M | 9 | 5 | 2 | 16 | 20 |
| Volgograd | 63 | 11.5 | 2163 | 19 | M | 7 | 1 | 5 | 13 | 24.5 |
| Tatarskaya | 63 | 11.5 | 3082 | 10 | M | 9 | 3 | 2 | 14 | 23 |
| Chelyabinsk | 63 | 11.5 | 3263 | 8 | M | 12 | 9 | 7 | 28 | 1.5 |
| Voronezh | 61 | 14 | 2477 | 15 | M | 9 | 6 | 5 | 20 | 12.5 |
| Altai | 54 | 15 | 2766 | 13 | M | 4 | 12 | 1 | 17 | 17.5 |
| Krasnoyarsk | 51 | 16 | 2919 | 12 | M | 7 | 13 | 6 | 26 | 3 |
| Novosibirsk | 51 | 17.5 | 2468 | 16 | M | 8 | 9 | 4 | 21 | 11 |
| Kalinin | 51 | 17.5 | 1736 | 25 | M | 8 | 2 | 1 | 11 | 28 |
| Perm | 49 | 19 | 3106 | 9 | M | 7 | 8 | 8 | 23 | 7.5 |
| Orenburg | 46 | 21 | 2045 | 21 | M | 8 | 1 | 2 | 11 | 28 |
| Primorskii | 46 | 21 | 1607 | 26 | M | – | 1 | – | 1 | 63.5 |

TABLE 6.3.3 (contd)

| Region | Number of delegates to XXIII Party Congress | Rank according to (1) | Population 1966 ('000) | Rank according to (3) | Representation in Central Committee* | Number of editorial instructions 1950 | 1960 | 1970 | Total | Rank according to (9) |
|---|---|---|---|---|---|---|---|---|---|---|
| | 1 | 2 | 3 | 4 | 5 | 6 | 7 | 8 | 9 | 10 |
| Tula | 46 | 21 | 1964 | 22 | M | 3 | 3 | 1 | 7 | 41 |
| Stavropol | 43 | 23 | 2144 | 20 | M | 11 | 7 | 5 | 23 | 7.5 |
| Irkutsk | 42 | 24 | 2254 | 18 | M | 5 | 7 | 1 | 13 | 24.5 |
| Omsk | 40 | 25 | 1807 | 23 | M | 4 | 11 | 4 | 19 | 14.5 |
| Vladimir | 39 | 26 | 1492 | 31 | C | 4 | — | 1 | 5 | 45.5 |
| Yaroslav | 37 | 27 | 1395 | 34 | C | 3 | 6 | 7 | 16 | 20 |
| Ivanovo | 35 | 29.5 | 1355 | 36 | C | 2 | 2 | 3 | 7 | 41 |
| Penza | 35 | 29.5 | 1543 | 28 | C | 7 | 6 | 4 | 17 | 17.5 |
| Tambov | 35 | 29.5 | 1529 | 29 | Nil | 8 | 7 | 5 | 20 | 12.5 |
| Kirov | 35 | 29.5 | 1775 | 24 | C | 1 | 5 | 1 | 7 | 41 |
| Khabarovsk | 34 | 32 | 1300 | 39 | M | 4 | 2 | 3 | 9 | 33 |
| Arkhangelsk | 33 | 33.5 | 1404 | 33 | C | 2 | 1 | 6 | 9 | 33 |
| Riazan | 33 | 33.5 | 1444 | 32 | M | 7 | 1 | 2 | 10 | 30 |
| Vologda | 30 | 35 | 1308 | 38 | C | 3 | 4 | — | 7 | 41 |
| Bryansk | 29 | 36.5 | 1564 | 27 | M | 6 | 3 | 2 | 11 | 28 |
| Kursk | 29 | 36.5 | 1496 | 30 | M | 12 | 7 | 5 | 24 | 4.5 |
| Ulyanovsk | 28 | 38 | 1175 | 44 | M | 5 | 3 | 1 | 9 | 33 |
| Udmurtsk | 27 | 39 | 1375 | 35 | C | — | 1 | — | 1 | 63.5 |
| Kaluga | 25 | 41 | 964 | 51 | C | 4 | 2 | 3 | 9 | 33 |
| Lipetsk | 25 | 41 | 1241 | 42 | C | — | — | 5 | 5 | 45.5 |
| Smolensk | 25 | 41 | 1098 | 45 | Nil | 3 | 1 | 4 | 8 | 37 |

TABLE 6.3.3 (contd)

| Region | Number of delegates to XXIII Party Congress | Rank according to (1) | Population 1966 ('000) | Rank according to (3) | Representation in Central Committee* | Number of editorial instructions | | | Total | Rank according to (9) |
|---|---|---|---|---|---|---|---|---|---|---|
| | | | | | | 1950 | 1960 | 1970 | | |
| | _1_ | _2_ | _3_ | _4_ | _5_ | _6_ | _7_ | _8_ | _9_ | _10_ |
| Belgorod | 24 | 44.5 | 1249 | 41 | M | — | 4 | 3 | 7 | 41 |
| Dagestan | 24 | 44.5 | 1325 | 37 | M | — | 2 | 2 | 4 | 51 |
| Kurgan | 24 | 44.5 | 1081 | 47 | C | 1 | 2 | 1 | 4 | 51 |
| Murmansk | 24 | 44.5 | 714 | 60 | C | 1 | — | 1 | 2 | 58 |
| Kostroma | 23 | 47.5 | 870 | 54 | C | 7 | 1 | — | 8 | 37 |
| Mordovsk | 23 | 47.5 | 1009 | 48 | C | — | — | 2 | 2 | 58 |
| Tiumen | 22 | 49.5 | 1292 | 40 | C | 1 | 2 | 1 | 4 | 51 |
| Chita | 22 | 49.5 | 1095 | 46 | C | 1 | 4 | 3 | 8 | 37 |
| Orel | 20 | 51.5 | 942 | 52 | M | 7 | 3 | 2 | 12 | 26 |
| Pskov | 20 | 51.5 | 875 | 53 | C | 4 | 3 | 2 | 9 | 33 |
| Amursk | 19 | 54.5 | 781 | 57 | C | 3 | — | 1 | 4 | 51 |
| Astrakhan | 19 | 54.5 | 801 | 55 | C | — | 4 | — | 4 | 51 |
| Novgorod | 19 | 54.5 | 724 | 59 | C | 2 | 1 | 3 | 6 | 44 |
| Chuvashsk | 19 | 54.5 | 1177 | 43 | C | 2 | — | 2 | 4 | 51 |
| Komi | 17 | 57 | 996 | 50 | Nil | — | — | — | — | 68 |
| Kareliya | 16 | 59.5 | 700 | 61 | C | 3 | — | 1 | 4 | 51 |
| Sakhalin | 16 | 59.5 | 640 | 63 | C | — | — | 3 | 3 | 56 |
| Tomsk | 16 | 59.5 | 782 | 56 | C | — | 2 | — | 2 | 58 |
| Checheno-Ing. | 16 | 59.5 | 1008 | 49 | Nil | 1 | 1 | 2 | 4 | 51 |
| Buryatsk | 15 | 62 | 771 | 58 | C | — | — | 1 | 1 | 63.5 |
| Mariisk | 12 | 64 | 652 | 62 | C | 1 | — | — | 1 | 63.5 |

TABLE 6.3.3 (contd)

| Region | Number of delegates to XXIII Party Congress | Rank according to (1) | Population 1966 ('000) | Rank according to (3) | Representation in Central Committee* | Number of editorial instructions | | | Total | Rank according to (9) |
|---|---|---|---|---|---|---|---|---|---|---|
| | | | | | | 1950 | 1960 | 1970 | | |
| | *1* | *2* | *3* | *4* | *5* | *6* | *7* | *8* | *9* | *10* |
| **Severo-Osetinsk** | 12 | 64 | 510 | 66 | C | — | 1 | — | 1 | 63.5 |
| **Yakutsk** | 12 | 64 | 631 | 64 | C | — | 1 | — | 1 | 63.5 |
| **Kabardino-Balk.** | 12 | 66 | 518 | 65 | C | 2 | 2 | — | 4 | 51 |
| **Kamchatka** | 10 | 67.5 | 261 | 68 | Nil | 1 | — | — | 1 | 63.5 |
| **Magadan** | 10 | 67.5 | 318 | 67 | C | — | — | — | — | 69.5 |
| **Tuvinsk** | 5 | 69 | 213 | 70 | C | — | — | — | — | 69.5 |
| **Kalmytsk** | 3 | 70 | 241 | 69 | C | — | 1 | — | 1 | 63.5 |

* M = member   C = candidate   Nil = no representation.
Columns 1–5 according to Frank, op. cit., pp. 229f.
The Rho coefficient for the relation 'No. of delegates' to 'No. of editorial instructions' is 0.83.
The Rho coefficient for the relation 'Population 1966' to 'No. of editorial instructions' is also 0.83.

TABLE 6.3.4 Criticism of the Moscow region

*1950*

| | |
|---|---|
| May | Moscow theatre repertories are too narrow. The Drama Theatre features only 'Ladies and Gentlemen' and the Mossoviet Theatre only 'Dangerous Crossing'. |
| August | Although it features some good plays, the Drama Theatre also runs superficial and unimportant ones such as 'The Sampans of the Yellow River'. The Mossoviet Theatre was careless with the text of the play 'The Goblet of Joy' by the talented young author N. Vinnikov. |

*1960*

| | |
|---|---|
| February | Moscow is one area where the establishment of people's kitchens for semi-prepared foods is behind schedule. |
| July | Not even in Moscow, with its huge construction organisations, has a single school dormitory been completed during the first half of the year. |
| August | Sewing machines manufactured by the 'Kalinin' factory do not satisfy consumer demands. |
| September | Factories in the Moscow region (and elsewhere) have failed to achieve their production goals with respect to new types of equipment for light industry. |
| September | The Committee for Automation and Machine Construction and the Moscow City Sovnarkhoz still display an incorrect attitude toward scientific organisations. |
| September | The foundry machine factory 'Krasnaya Presnya' in Moscow has delivered a shipment of automatic machinery which lacks certain essential components. |
| October | The textile workers in Moscow have ignored the production of children's toys. |
| November | A series of lectures on important problems of Marxist-Leninist theory and the history of the Party delivered at the Moscow Pedagogical Institute for Foreign Languages failed to relate them to the present or to current communist construction. |
| December | Not a single school or school dormitory has been completed in (among other regions) the Moscow region. |

*1970*

| | |
|---|---|
| February | Only one skiing competition was held during the whole academic year at the Moscow Textile Institute. |
| April | The Voskresensk Chemical Complex should use inland waterways for its shipments rather than burden the Moscow-Riazan railway line. |
| August | Attempts to stifle criticism, such as those that have occurred at the 'Khimreaktivkomplekt' in the Noginsk district of the Moscow region, will naturally not be tolerated. |
| September | It is particularly alarming that the construction of school buildings and student housing at the Moscow Technological Institute and other institutions is progressing so slowly. |
| November | It was noted at the latest plenary session of the Moscow Party Committee that certain new interpretations of the classics are merely attempts to distort the ideological and artistic content of the works. |

TABLE 6.3.5 Criticism of the Chelyabinsk region

*1950*

| | |
|---|---|
| January | Party training at the Soviet and Machine-Tractor district in the city of Chelyabinsk is poorly organised. |
| February | Only 76.3 per cent of the 1949 construction plan in the Chelyabinsk region has been fulfilled. |
| March | Tractor and trailer repairs are too slow. |
| March | Attendance at Party Seminars is too low. |
| April | Failure to observe certain elementary technical rules at the Zlatoustovsk factory results in a great deal of waste. |
| June | The construction of new hospitals managed by the Chelyabinsk Sanatorium Board is proceeding too slowly. |
| June | The *gorkom* (Party Committee) in Miassk does not have enough contact with its officials. |
| August | The newspaper *Chelyabinskii Rabochii* writes nothing about new books and pamphlets printed by the publishers of the region. |
| December | The *gorkom* in Kopeisk is guilty of bureaucratic methods of management. Instead of providing firm and continuous leadership, it tries to govern by means of sporadic inspections and telephone calls, ignoring political work at the factories. |

*1960*

| | |
|---|---|
| March | The January work of the construction organisations in the Chelyabinsk Sovnarkhoz was unsatisfactory. The housing plan for the year has not been fulfilled. |
| March | Almost no seed grain has been cleaned in the sovkhozes of the Chelyabinsk region. |
| May | The Chelyabinsk region is among the areas which are behind in the manufacture of building materials. |
| August | Chelyabinsk farmers are wasting time. Instead of harvesting fields that are already ripe, they wait for the crops to ripen in all fields. |
| September | Large quantities of grain that should be in the silos are still lying in the barns of the Chelyabinsk sovkhozes and kolkhozes. |
| November | Builders in the Chelyabinsk region have neglected iron ore mining and the steel industry. |
| December | Chelyabinsk is among the regions behind in housing construction. |

*1970*

| | |
|---|---|
| May | Construction is slow in the consumer goods and service sectors in the Chelyabinsk region. |
| May | The vacation resorts in the Chelyabinsk region have still not received doctors. |
| June | Specialists at the Central Laboratory of the Zlatoustovsk Metallurgical Factory have not accomplished much in recent years. Most of their proposals have been little better than the contents of the 'suggestions box' at the factory. |
| June | Repairs of agricultural machinery on the Chelyabinsk kolkhozes and sovkhozes are slow, even slower than last year. |
| September | Stores of machinery and equipment in the depots of the iron and steel industry have increased by 33 per cent in the last two years; their value is an estimated several hundred million roubles. Many products are lying in the warehouses of ball-bearing factories nos. 18 and 15 at the Chelyabinsk automobile plants. |

October          The transport sections at the iron and steel plants in the Chelyabinsk region
                 are unable to cope with rail shipments of ore, metals, coal and fluorite that
                 have been left on sidings. Unloading techniques are inadequate.

## 6.4 MOSCOW LOOKS TO THE SOUTHEAST

Our geographical analysis strongly confirms *Pravda*'s rank of national
newspaper. Its criticism is distributed quite evenly throughout the
country, and in all three years there are very few 'blank spots' which are
not noticed at all. Each republic and practically all regions occasionally
have their knuckles rapped; this is among the most prominent impressions one gets from the material.

Nor is Moscow's survey of the empire restricted to certain branches or
problems. When individual regions are criticised, discussion includes
not only their external achievements – that part of production which is
exported to other areas of the country – but also internal regional
conditions which have no immediate bearing on that export. Delays in
school construction, inadequate political training, deficiencies in public
communications, underdeveloped recreational activities, bureaucratic
red tape in the treatment of local issues – such matters are not too small
for consideration by the leading Party organ in Moscow. *Pravda* seeks to
combine a national perspective and nationwide coverage with a
penetrating and detailed analysis of shortcomings at the regional and
local level.

What is the purpose of such an inquisitive coverage of individual failures
throughout the country? A first, 'naïve' answer is that the paper wants to
correct the specific faults being criticised. This is surely true, but there
must be more to the matter than that. If the leadership were only
concerned about the situation at any one place, it would seem both
simpler and more effective to use other channels of communication than
a daily newspaper with a circulation of over ten million copies. Criticism
must be aimed at broader targets. When *Pravda* reproaches a region for
delays in repairing tractors or for failures to meet plan quotas, its
intention is surely to criticise a problem of more universal dimensions,
using the negative examples to exhort others guilty of the same faults to
mend their ways. A leader in the Sverdlovsk region, therefore, can find
little consolation in the fact that it is his colleagues in a neighbouring
region rather than his own Party organisation that receive a blow, for
the question of concern to him is whether he is also vulnerable to
criticism by the Central Committee. The 'general prophylactic' intent of
this form of publicistic sanction is very important: sentence is publicly
passed as a punishment to the culprit and a warning to others.

The central question then becomes how *Pravda* selects its examples.
We cannot exclude the assumption that the even distribution of criticism
throughout the country may to some extent be influenced by the Party's

'nation-building' ambitions. The patriotism that the Soviet mass media seek to inculcate in the people has historical and revolutionary but also spatial dimensions – citizens are to have a sense of belonging to a nation of gigantic proportions. With this purpose in mind, the enormous expanse of the country is romanticised by means of a well-balanced mixture of near and far in the news. Reports flow in not only from the large metropolises but also from remote border regions at all points of the compass. The fact that criticism is similarly spread out in broad circles may derive from the same desire to emphasise the immensity of the Soviet Union. *Pravda*'s choice of examples may also to some degree depend on chance, but considering the importance that criticised parties attach to the newspaper and the consequences criticism can have, it does not appear likely that its depth of intention is normally so shallow. The systematic differences in attention that have actually been observed are another argument against the hypothesis of random selection. Keeping the reservations mentioned well in mind, we may nevertheless assume that *Pravda* takes rather careful aim before opening fire.

A check of *Pravda*'s frequencies against the population of the various republics, economic areas and regions indicates that certain parts of the country attract little editorial attention. This is especially true of the western areas of European Russia. The industrial regions south of Moscow, in the Volga-Ural area and in the Kuznetsk Basin, on the other hand, arouse more interest, as do the Central Asian republics and – increasingly during the period – the three Caucasian republics. Over-simplifying somewhat, it might be said that Moscow tends to look to the south and east rather than to the north and west.

Differences in the economic structure of the different areas probably account for some of these distinctions. The regions with high attention coefficients are generally industrial areas. Criticism of the industrial regions, however, is not aimed exclusively or directly at industrial production, but also treats more or less distantly related aspects such as services, agriculture, education, etc. Yet even such interest may be a by-product of the leadership's concern for the industrial potential of the region.

That the Ukraine and Belorussia receive relatively little criticism may – in line with the various interpretations discussed in 5.12 – be explained in several different ways. According to the 'power politics' interpretation, representatives for these republics might have been strong enough to block criticism. This hypothesis is supported to some degree by what we know about the position of Ukrainian politicians in post-war Soviet politics. The surprisingly low frequency for Georgia in 1950 is another argument in favour of the interpretation.

The 'objective' interpretation represents another approach. It proceeds from the assumption that variations in *Pravda*'s attention reflect differences in actual performance and goal-attainment. This hypothesis also seems plausible on several points. The western parts of the Soviet Union have the highest cultural level measured by means of such indicators as mass media consumption per capita, number of university graduates, etc.[6] It is not unreasonable to assume that this circumstance is also reflected in a higher culture of production and administration, and that the social apparatuses in the Ukraine, Belorussia, the Baltic republics and the western RSFSR are 'objectively' easier to manage than the corresponding machinery in areas such as Central Asia, southern Russia and Siberia.

A third approach, the 'informational' interpretation, regards the observed differences in attention as derivable from distinctions in the supply of information available to the leadership. According to this view, the leaders know more about the most frequently criticised areas than about other parts of the country. Both the 'power politics' and 'objective' hypotheses offer possible explanations of the origin of such an imbalance of information, but reasons may also be sought in the informational system at the disposal of the top Party leadership. Unfortunately, we lack the data necessary for testing such a hypothesis, but it does not seem particularly plausible on purely logical grounds. To the extent that information on shortcomings in Soviet society is mainly extracted, as is presumed by the totalitarian model, it appears reasonable to assume that the Party leaders would not content themselves indefinitely with an unbalanced system of surveillance unless they were very keenly intent on following developments in those parts of the country that just such a system of surveillance was capable of photographing in great detail. And if the flow of information – in line with a pluralist or bureaucratic model – originated to a significant extent from autonomous sources at a low level, such an unbalanced informational system would not remain intact unless that imbalance corresponded to differences in the degree of activity of the senders.

If the attention patterns observable in *Pravda*'s editorials are determined by an uneven supply of information, therefore, there is reason to take into account the causes of that unevenness. However the alternative or complementary explanations presented here are to be weighed against one another, it seems clear that the Soviet Party leadership subjectively regards the western parts of the country as less troublesome than the eastern areas, and that Central Asia and the industrial areas in southern Russia and western Siberia attract particular attention.

# 7 Political Problems: The Institutional Dimension

The Soviet Union is sometimes described as a command economy. This military analogy, however, is not an adequate one, for the Soviet chain of command is anything but clear. Most of the economic and administrative organs of the country are under what may at least be said to be a dual command – they are formally subordinate to one or more governmental organs, but are in reality responsible to the organisations of the Party. If we broaden our field of vision, we can discern other institutions, such as trade unions, banks, planning agencies, the security service, procurement agencies, etc., which are also capable of exerting a certain influence on individual enterprises and authorities. The hierarchical pyramids interlock with one another, creating an institutional pattern that is asymmetrical, difficult to survey, and in constant flux. During the twenty years between 1950 and 1970, ministries and civil service departments have continuously been founded, abolished or have changed name and functions, jurisdictions have been combined or divided, the structure of individual enterprises has been altered, and the boundaries between governmental and public organisations has been adjusted. Significant changes include the drastic cut in the number of ministries and the establishment of regional economic councils (*sovnarkhozy*) in 1957, the merger of these councils into larger units in 1962, and the return in 1965 to an order resembling the situation before 1957. The regional Party organisations were divided into special units for industry and agriculture during Khrushchev's last year in power, but this was a temporary development which was terminated after his fall. Other shifts in the system were caused by the economic reforms begun in 1965, which to some degree extended enterprise autonomy.

*Pravda* tells us very little about how this institutional network functions in practice, but it does provide a picture of normative role distribution, i.e. how the leadership feels the system ought to operate. Critical comments indicate which organs the leaders hold responsible for noted deficiencies, and remedial directives similarly reveal the people and institutions on which they set their hopes. The instructions in *Pravda* thus tells us something about the political strategy of the

151

leadership. By comparing all the items dealing with or addressed to Party agencies, soviets, unions, Komsomol, etc., we can consequently form an opinion as to the agendas or orders of the day that are issued to different hierarchies and levels. Shifts in this total picture of the tasks of the organisations can provide information about the changes that may have occurred in the leadership's evaluation of the various components of the system; an institution that seems on one occasion to be the best lever to pull to advance social or economic development in a given area may gradually lose its appeal as another appears in a more promising light. The treatment of different institutions in *Pravda*, therefore, can indicate how the problems of society are diagnosed at various times and how the agents of change capable of contributing to their solution are evaluated.

When *Pravda* addresses political, administrative or economic institutions, they usually appear in one of the following five roles:

(*a*) In certain cases they are *senders* of a message which *Pravda* wants to pass on or develop. The object of certain editorials, for example, is to explain a Central Committee decision which all Party organisations are obliged to implement.

(*b*) More commonly, institutions function as *targets* of *Pravda*'s criticism: a steelworks that has failed to fulfil its quota, an academy of sciences working in isolation from the sectors or branches which apply the results of its research. The target is often obvious even when institutions are not mentioned by name; Party organisations are thus always implicitly accused when *Pravda* criticises deficiencies in various republics, regions or districts. Such criticism is normally meant to be noted by an entire category of institutions – the specified scapegoat is pointed out as a warning example.

(*c*) Thirdly, institutions are often the *receivers* of more or less specific directives. When a certain step is recommended it is usually clear where the responsibility for implementing the measure rests, whether on a single specified organisation, a whole institutional category (e.g. the trade unions or local Party organs), or even all workers and employees in a particular branch ('kolkhoz farmers', 'Soviet railwaymen') or all members of the Communist Party.

(*d*) A fourth variant regards institutions as arenas of activity or '*objects of mobilization*', as when a Party agency is directed to stimulate the activities of an organisation or to keep a closer watch on the units for which it is already responsible.

(*e*) Finally, institutions sometimes occur as the *beneficiaries* of the measure *Pravda* prescribes. This is the case, for example, when schools are exhorted to give more support to the Komsomol or when one ministry is urged to give another ministry better goods or more punctual deliveries. From the viewpoint of the 'bureaucratic model' (cf. Chapter 2) it seems reasonable to suspect that such beneficiaries have also in some way actively sought *Pravda*'s support, but such initiatives are very rarely suggested in the text of the editorials. A 'totalitarian' interpretation would instead regard this type of demand as emanating from the leadership's observations of shortcomings at lower levels.

## 7.1 THE PARTY

Superior Party organs are mentioned in *Pravda*'s editorials exclusively as senders of messages. Criticism of the Central Committee, the Central Control Commission, the Politburo, the Secretariat or its sections does not occur. These agencies may be said to lie in a free zone outside the critical field of vision of the newspaper.

The central committees in the larger of the fifteen republics appear to be included in the free zone, whereas those of the smaller ones are sometimes subjected to criticism. Thus deficiencies in relations with the Komsomol in the Karelian SSR are attacked in 1950, as is formalism in the ideological work of the Lithuanian Central Committee in 1960. The Armenian Central Committee is reproved in the same year for inefficient control of the publishing houses of the republic. Certain messages dealing with the Party's role in moulding public opinion are also often directed to all republican central committees. For example:

> The republican central committees and the regional committees must provide the publishing houses with daily leadership, making them active participants in the effort to strengthen the ties between science and production and ensure the broad dissemination of progressive experiences and scientific achievements. (50.237)
> The republican central committees and the regional committees do not devote sufficient attention to the content of TV programmes and the recruitment and training of television personnel. (60.073)

The regional Party agencies (*obkoms* in the regions, *kraikoms* in territories, central committees in autonomous republics and *gorkoms* in the largest cities) often function both as the targets of *Pravda*'s criticism and the receivers of its exhortations. The fire is especially intense in 1950, when Party officials in a number of specified regions are reprimanded for their failures. The frequencies for both criticism and directives decrease during the following years, as attention is turned instead to the 'internal' activities of the regional agencies, that is, to their contributions to organisational and propaganda work and their relations with Party organs at lower levels. In addition, there are complaints about inadequate supervision of other organisations (for example, the soviets, youth organisations, kolkhozes and – in 1950 – the MTSs). The chain of command is occasionally lengthened – regional Party agencies are criticised for failing to mobilise their own local institutions for the control of other social organs.

The following are some typical messages, either in the form of criticism or as generally formulated recommendations, addressed to the regional level:

> *obkoms* devote too little attention to educating their officials.
> *obkoms* are guilty of bureaucratic methods. They try to govern from their offices instead of going out into the field.
> *obkoms* spend more time criticising the mistakes of lower organisations than helping them to correct their errors.
> *obkoms* have too little control over the implementation of their own decisions.
> *obkoms* do not pay enough attention to the Komsomol.
> *obkoms* do not listen to criticism from below, show too little interest in the primary organisations.
> *obkoms* neglect the use of modern educational and mass propaganda aids.
> *obkoms* neglect Party discipline, violate established Party work rules, supress criticism.
> *obkoms* ignore recruitment questions, selection and training of cadres.

Some of the same themes appear in the messages sent to institutions at the district level (the *raikoms* in regions and major cities and the *gorkoms* in medium-sized and smaller cities). Here, however, there is more emphasis on the lowest organisations and supervision of the different units of production. The district agencies are reminded of their important roles as organisers of socialist competition and supervisors of industrial and agricultural enterprises. On one occasion a local organ is urged to dismiss the managers of an enterprise, but such items are not common. Internal Party matters, on the other hand, are discussed a great deal. Reminders not to neglect elections and meetings recur regularly, as do remarks on the responsibility of the district committees for Party education. Many instructions are directed to regional and district institutions simultaneously:

> The most important task of the Party *obkoms*, *gorkoms* and *raikoms* is to strengthen the primary organisations, increase their effectiveness and stimulate initiative and independent enterprise on the part of the Party masses (50.105).
> Certain *obkoms* and *gorkoms* have not checked to see that their decisions concerning libraries have been implemented (60.206).

Frequencies for both the district and regional organs decrease considerably after 1950. Criticism of individual institutions is less extensive and less severe, and there are fewer general directives. It is above all *Pravda*'s interest in agitprop activities and internal Party matters that diminishes. In 1960 and 1970, however, many admonitions are issued to 'the local Party organs' (*mestnye partiinye organy*) as a group, an expression that includes institutions at the regional and district level but not the primary organisations in agriculture, industry and offices.[1] *Pravda* sends relatively few messages to the latter category. The primary organisations are addressed a total of only nineteen times in all three years, and criticism is usually directed at deficiencies in internal activities. On eight occasions, however, the newspaper complains of inadequate supervision of the production units with which these organisations are connected. Indirect requests for better surveillance are also made in messages to the regional and district organs. The primary organisations figure in *Pravda*'s editorials not mainly as targets of criticism or receivers of messages, but rather as 'objects of mobilisation' for superior agencies.

At the same time as the number of instructions to regional and local Party organisations decreases during the period, the content of the messages becomes more generalised and impersonal. In 1950, named regional, city and district committee secretaries were often pilloried in *Pravda*'s editorials, sometimes after their dismissal ('. . . the former secretary of the Kostroma *obkom*, Comrade I. Kuznetsov . . . has committed grave errors in the selection, promotion and placement of personnel and has neglected to encourage criticism and self-criticism', 50.281). Such warning examples seem to have been abandoned in 1960 and 1970. Leading Party officials are no longer subjected to criticism.

## 7.2 THE GOVERNMENTAL APPARATUS

Within the governmental apparatus as well there is a free zone which appears to be safe from *Pravda*'s criticism, but it is not a large one. The Supreme Soviet, its Presidium and Council of Ministers, and certain departments lie within the free zone. No criticism occurs of the Ministry of Foreign Affairs, the armed forces or the security agencies. Individual union ministers are never criticised, but ministers at lower levels are. A charge of insubordination is levelled in 1970 against certain leaders, including republican ministers, who attempted to create the impression that their dismissal of 'persons unworthy of confidence' was based on orders from above rather than on their own initiative. RSFSR Vice-Minister of Agriculture Ryndin is reproached in the same year for introducing a system of reporting for kolkhozes and sovkhozes containing no fewer than 820 indicators, and it is noted that Nikonov, the Vice-Minister of the building materials industry of the same republic, has failed to correct a stoppage at a factory for the

TABLE 7.2.1 Instructions to national ministries in 1950 and 1970 ranked according to frequency (frequencies in parentheses)

| Ministries 1950 | Ministries 1970 |
|---|---|
| 1. Agriculture (12) | 1. Agriculture (10) |
| 2. Pulp and paper industry (8) | 1. Commerce (10) |
| 3. Petroleum industry (5) | 3. Timber and wood processing industry (8) |
| 3. Sovkhozes (5) | 4. Chemical industry (7) |
| 3. Metallurgical industry (5) | 4. Iron and steel industry (7) |
| 6. Health (4) | 6. Agricultural machine-building industry (5) |
| 6. Machine-building for heavy industry (4) | 6. Construction materials industry (5) |
| 6. Communications (4) | 6. Rural construction (5) |
| 6. Machine-tool building industry (4) | 9. Higher and professional education (4) |
| 10. Fish industry (3) | 10. Machine tool and tool building industry (3) |
| 10. Construction materials industry (3) | 10. Purchase of agricultural produce (3) |
| 10. Education (3) | 10. Light industry (3) |
| 10. Electric power and the electric industry (3) | 10. Soil improvement and Water (3) |
| 10. Telecommunications industry (3) | 10. Food industry (3) |
| 10. Agricultural machine-building Industry (3) | 10. Communal services (3) |
| 10. Coal (3) | 10. 'Soiuzseltekhnika' (3) |
| 17. Labour reserves (2) | 10. Construction (3) |
| 17. Post Office and telecommunications (2) | 18. Automotive industry (2) |
| 17. Heavy industry construction (2) | 18. Machine-building for light and food industries (2) |
| 17. Machine-building for the transport sector (2) | 18. Instrument-making, automation equipment and control systems (2) |
| 17. Chemical industry (2) | 18. Paper and cellulose industry (2) |
| 17. Machine and tool engineering (2) | 18. Electrotechnical industry (2) |
| 23. Higher education (1) | 18. Culture (2) |
| 23. Machine-building for the building industry (1) | 18. Meat and dairy industry (2) |
| 23. Machine-building industry (1) | |

TABLE 7.2.1 (contd)

| Ministries | 1950 | Ministries | 1970 |
|---|---|---|---|
| 23. | Commerce (1) | 18. | Justice (2) |
| 23. | Automobile and tractor industry (1) | 18. | Industrial construction (2) |
| 23. | Cotton-growing (1) | 18. | Education (2) |
| | | 18. | Coal mining (2) |
| | | 18. | Energy and electrification (2) |
| | | 18. | Consumer co-operatives (2) |
| | | 18. | The State Committee for Construction Affairs (2) |
| | | 18. | The State Committee of People's Control (2) |
| | | 33. | Construction, road and municipal machine building (1) |
| | | 33. | Machine-building for heavy industry, power supply and the transport sector (1) |
| | | 33. | Installations and special construction projects (1) |
| | | 33. | Petroleum and petroleum refining industries (1) |
| | | 33. | Fish industry (1) |
| | | 33. | Post Office and telecommunications (1) |
| | | 33. | Finances (1) |
| | | 33. | The State Television Committee (1) |
| | | 33. | The State Film Committee (1) |
| | | 33. | The State Press Committee (1) |
| | | 33. | The State Standardisation Committee (1) |

manufacture of much needed insulating materials, although he has been aware that the unit has stood idle for some time.

The free zone for such middle-level politicians seems to contract in the later years. The same is true of Gosplan, which appears to be out of the range of criticism in the earlier years but is attacked by *Pravda* on several occasions in 1970. The only unit of the planning organ to be criticised in 1950 is its publishing division, Gosplanizdat, the products of which are said to be technically inferior. The Gosplan institutions of the various republics are assailed ten years later, but the national planning agency escapes unscathed. Gosplan RSFSR, for example, is said to have neglected the development of electric machines for the textile industry, Gosplan Ukraina has ignored the steel industry in Dnepropetrovsk, and several republican planning organs have failed to ensure an adequate production of school furniture. In 1970 the shafts strike higher. Now branch divisions of Gosplan SSSR are occasionally attacked together with the appropriate sectoral departments, and both are accused of weak supervision and neglect of sectors such as the consumer goods industry. In two cases criticism is levelled not against sections of Gosplan but directly at Gosplan itself, even though the remarks concern discernible branch questions. The supreme planning agency seems, then, to have fallen outside the free zone. Other co-ordinating institutions at the national level such as the supply agency Gossnab and the construction agency Gosstroi also receive pungently worded reminders from *Pravda* in 1970.

The great majority of ministries – unlike the ministers – lie quite obviously outside the free zone. Criticism and instructions are relatively sparse in 1950, but they become increasingly abundant in the later years, particularly in 1970, and are addressed to the ministries for various sectors at both the republican and national level.

Table 7.2.1 represents a list ranked according to frequency of the national ministries that receive instructions or are subjected to criticism by *Pravda* in 1950 and 1970. In this context, 1960 is of less interest, since most national ministries had been 'liquidated' by the 1957 administrative reforms and replaced by state committees with considerably diminished authority. There are relatively few items dealing with such committees. Most of the 1960 instructions to departments or state committees address agencies in the culture and education sector. Communications to industry and commerce are transmitted in that year through other channels.

The samples of instructions in Table 7.2.2 offer a picture of the substance of *Pravda*'s messages to the ministries. Most of the complaints in the paper concern the lack of respect for established plans and other directives from superior organs, weak management of subordinate units, leniency toward incompetence out in the field, poor co-ordination and insufficient aid to other organisations, and bureaucracy and red tape within the ministries themselves. Several organisations are often addressed at the same time; for example, 'the ministries for machine building', 'the national ministry of communications and its department *Soiuzpechat'* (the press distribution agency)', or ministries and civil service departments more generally, with or without Soviet political jargon's pregnant attribute 'certain':

TABLE 7.2.2 Instructions to the Ministry of Agriculture in 1950 and 1970

*1950*

*The Ministry of Agriculture* and its local agencies have not attempted to trace missing stocks of annual and perennial seed grains (50.027).
*The Ministry of Agriculture* must better organise Selkhozstroiproekt (50.101).
*The Ministry of Agriculture* and the MTSs are not devoting enough attention to the improvement of meadows and pasturelands. The MTSs must raise the level of stock-breeding (50.109).
*The Ministry of Agriculture* must take note of the criticism expressed by deputies to the soviets and eliminate the faults observed in the management of the MTSs (50.170).
In connection with the above, increased demands are made on the MTS employees and *the Ministry of Agriculture*, which must improve the everyday functioning of the MTSs (50.170).
*The Ministry of Agriculture*, the Ministry of Sovkhozes and its local agencies must organise and implement a broad mass study of agricultural and stock-raising techniques (50.174).
*The Ministry of Agriculture* and the Ministry of Sovkhozes have failed to organise a systematic study of the dissemination and practical implementation of scientific advances and progressive discoveries on all kolkhozes, sovkhozes and MTSs. Valuable innovations, new methods and approaches are not being applied on a broad scale (50.174).
Local Party and soviet agencies, *the Ministry of Agriculture*, the Ministry of Sovkhozes and its local organs must provide considerably better leadership in the area of fodder production, and see to it that all kolkhoz and sovkhoz plans are fulfilled on schedule (50.194).
It is the urgent responsibility of Party and soviet organs, *the Ministry of Agriculture* and the Ministry of Cotton Growing to employ professionally competent, well-educated and politically reliable persons (50.208).
Civil servants in *the Ministry of Agriculture* and the Department for Sovkhozes have uncritically approved and recommended crop rotation plans, which has resulted in the cultivation of summer wheat in areas where fall and winter wheat give the best harvests (50.215).
*The Ministry of Agriculture*, especially, and the Ministry for Forests and the paper industry pay too little attention to their periodical publications (50.347).
Responsibility for the mass education of kolkhoz workers rests largely on *the Ministry of Agriculture* and its section for agricultural propaganda. The propaganda section must speed up its efforts to provide the kolkhozes with all necessary professional literature (50.357).

*1970*

*The Ministry of Agriculture* and the Ministry for Rural Construction, aided by local Party and soviet agencies, are to organise studies in construction techniques for workers in rural areas (70.063).
*The Ministry of Agriculture* and the All-Union Association of Agricultural Technology must redistribute technical resources and see to it that machinery is sent where it is most needed (70.138).

The Committee of People's Control has established that the paper and wood-processing industry and *the Ministry of Agriculture* in the RSFSR have circumvented the law and obtained a number of accounts and certificates in a manner contrary to regulations (70.209).

The production of fine-fibred flax must be increased to satisfy consumer demands for various types of linen. This is the responsibility of *the Ministry of Agriculture* and the centres for textile research (70.219).

It is very important that the All-Union Academy of Agronomy and *the Ministry of Agriculture* better co-ordinate the activities of the scientific institutes to avoid an unnecessary splitting of resources (70.251).

*The Ministry of Agriculture* and Gosplan must ensure that economists are more rapidly supplied with all necessary information (70.278).

Certain *Ministries* and civil service departments evidently underestimate the problem of educating and retraining leaders of production (70.072).

*Ministry* officials visit production units entirely too rarely, they have little contact with the pioneers of production, and are not energetic enough in propagating the valuable new approaches of these innovators (50.192).

*Ministries* and agencies together with the Party committees must review the situation at these construction projects at the very beginning of the year and take the necessary measures to ensure their punctual completion (70.011).

The republican councils of ministers do not lie within the free zone, but criticism of them is relatively rare. There is a certain rise in directives to this level in 1960, when the number of national ministries that can be addressed decreases due to the administrative reform. In this year *Pravda* also calls upon the regional economic councils (*sovnarkhozy*), which are noticed an average of about once a week. Approximately half of these items criticise one or more named sovnarkhozes, while the remainder deal with the faults of 'some' or 'certain' economic councils.

Individual authorities immediately under the ministry level – which in the Soviet Union are called departments (*vedomstvo*), central boards (*glavnoe upravlenie*), central committees (*glavnyi komitet* or *glavk*), associations (*ob"edinenie*), trusts (*trest*), and the like – are seldom mentioned in *Pravda*'s editorials in 1950 and 1960, but they receive more attention in the last year of the period. The main principle seems to be that the paper addresses either the appropriate ministry or the ministry and its agency together. Particularly large and significant authorities such as the strategic *Selkhoztekhnika* (which is responsible for agricultural machinery), important industrial concerns or regional giants in the building sector, however, are sometimes put into a pillory of their own. The same applies to certain independent public organisations which perform the same functions as ministries or departments – *Tsentrosoyuz*, for example, which resembles a ministry for kolkhozes. In addition, authorities often occur in the editorials as targets or collective receivers of messages, alone or together with other agencies ('ministries, authorities, Party organisations and soviets must . . .'). The authorities also function as objects of mobilisation – ministries and Party agencies are urged to tighten their control of subordinate organisations.

|  | *1950* | *1960* | *1970* |  |
|---|---|---|---|---|
| DEPARTMENTS |  |  |  |  |
| CENTRAL BOARDS | 30 | 15 | 82 | absolute figures |
| CENTRAL COMMITTEES | 0.62 | 0.53 | 1.40 | frequency per mille |

The regional economic councils, which during the time of Khrushchev's administrative reform (1957–65) were responsible for regional production, naturally occur in the material only in 1960. Most of *Pravda*'s 67 instructions to the sovnarkhozes criticise deficiencies in different branches of industry – unfulfilled plans, undelivered shipments, uncompleted construction projects, poor utilisation of production capacity, etc. In some cases the councils are singled out as exclusively responsible for such shortcomings, but often they are merely parts of larger complexes ('sovnarkhozes and enterprises', 'sovnarkhozes and civil service departments', 'planning organs, sovnarkhozes, Party and soviet agencies, trade unions and the Komsomol') which are urged to make joint efforts. What is often demanded is better control over the enterprises within the domain of the various economic councils.

The regional and local soviets (*sovet deputatov trudyashchikhsya*) and their executive organs (*oblispolkom, gorispolkom, raiispolkom*) at first play an obscure role in the material. Several editorials in 1950 deal with elections to the soviets, but *Pravda* has little to say about their everyday activities. The paper sponsors a crusade against various manifestations of 'bureaucracy' in local administrations, criticising bosses who have screened themselves off from the people. There are three almost identical calls to the Party organisations to stimulate 'sound criticism' of the soviets, but it is not specified what the regional and local organs are to accomplish. The infrequent directives to the soviets during the Stalin year are generally abstract.

In 1960 the number of signals to the soviets increases at the same time as they become more precise, and this tendency continues and is strengthened in 1970. Construction is the primary area of concern under Khrushchev. The soviets are called upon to devote more energy to urban development and housing construction and maintenance. Public eating facilities and other consumer services are also emphasised areas. Another and somewhat unusual task concerns the stimulation of technical innovations in agriculture. Generally, however, the soviets are expected to perform typically municipal functions.

In 1970 *Pravda*'s list of demands becomes noticeably longer. Calls to the soviets and their executive organs now occur several times a month, and the functional register is considerably broader than before. Besides street construction and maintenance, city planning, housing construction and aid to new tenants, the soviets are now expected to perform a variety of other functions. Hygiene is one new area. The soviets are required to check sanitary standards in the retail branch, but they must also combat water pollution and other dangers to the environment. They should also see to it that the public transportation system functions properly and that consumer services are shipshape. Several editorials take up the soviets' responsibility for the school system and for channelling graduates into jobs. Furthermore, the soviets are expected to concern themselves with the professional and ideological development of employees in the retail trades. Recreational activities and tourism also lie within their jurisdiction; one editorial complains that there is a lack of eating facilities for vacationers. Other tasks assigned to the soviets include winter fuel supplies, the maintenance of public order, the taking of the 1970 census; and the supervision of agricultural production plans. The culmination of this trend toward increasingly broader functions is reached in an editorial of December 1970, where the soviets are given general responsibility for the development of the economy:

> It is the duty of the soviets to show a never-failing concern for the development of the economy, for the effective management of every kolkhoz, sovkhoz, and enterprise under their jurisdiction, and for continued socialist competition. Without interfering in production, they can and must effectively check that kolkhozes, sovkhozes and enterprises fulfil their plans and obligations, rationally use land, technology, and fertilisers, and are careful and economical with their resources. (70.335)

When the regions are criticised for poor production results, however, fire is seldom trained on the soviets. Only on one occasion – when the Voronezh region is attacked for its failures – is there also mention of 'serious deficiencies in the style and method of work' of both the Party and state regional organs (*obkom* and *oblispolkom*).

## 7.3 THE PUBLIC ORGANISATIONS

One of the campaigns during the Khrushchev era sought to broaden the functions of the public organisations. The trade unions and the Komsomol were given a new boost, and certain state agencies were transformed into independent public organisations. Mobilising citizens to make voluntary contributions to society was presented as an important component in the 'intensified construction of communism'.

The *Pravda* editorials send appeals to the public organisations in a fairly steady stream during the three years, but a slight rise can be noted in 1960. Messages consist mainly of positive exhortations. The paper seldom criticises – individually or *in corpore* – the public organisations for failures, but it often points out to them their 'most important task', 'first obligation' or 'principal role'. An article on construction, for example, might say that many construction workers are young, so that it is the duty of the Komsomol to further labour discipline and make sure that plans are followed. Or an editorial dealing with goods distribution might point out that the trade unions are expected to check on the retail branch. The total number of editorials mentioning trade unions or the Komsomol during the three years is given in Table 7.3.1.

TABLE 7.3.1 Editorials containing instructions to the trade unions and the Komsomol

|  | No. of editorials | | | Percentage of editorials of the year | | |
|---|---|---|---|---|---|---|
|  | 1950 | 1960 | 1970 | 1950 | 1960 | 1970 |
| Trade unions | 42 | 45 | 44 | 19.4 | 31.7 | 17.3 |
| Komsomol | 44 | 50 | 44 | 20.4 | 35.2 | 17.3 |

Aside from the weak rise in 1960, the frequencies suggest that interest in these two organisations is both equally strong between them and evenly distributed throughout the three years. Another search for instructions addressed exclusively to either the Komsomol or the trade unions, and not mentioning any other organisation, however, provides a different picture of their respective ranks (Table 7.3.2). While the Komsomol asserts itself fairly well as an independent actor with its own functions, the trade unions appear more and more as belonging to an ensemble of actors. When the editorial writers specify the address of their directives, the unions are increasingly often included as one receiver among many, an auxiliary agency expected to participate in joint efforts.

TABLE 7.3.2 Editorials containing instructions directed exclusively to the trade unions or the Komsomol

|  | No. of editorials | | | Percentage of editorials of the year | | |
|---|---|---|---|---|---|---|
|  | 1950 | 1960 | 1970 | 1950 | 1960 | 1970 |
| Trade unions | 31 | 11 | 5 | 14.4 | 7.8 | 2.0 |
| Komsomol | 28 | 20 | 22 | 13.0 | 14.1 | 8.7 |

Both the trade unions and the Komsomol are generally called upon as collective categories. When messages are included in editorials dealing with a specific branch such as the steel industry, it is of course implicitly understood that the matter concerns the union organisation of that branch, but there is no explicit specification of branch unions. Specific references to levels are also rare, but on isolated occasions *Pravda* addresses the Komsomol of a particular region or republic.

The content of the 131 directives to the trade unions provides an idea of how the Party leadership regards their functions in society. Only a dozen or two are concerned with the tasks that are sometimes described as the primary arena of the Soviet trade unions – recreational activities, rest homes, nurseries, summer camps, vacations, etc. Most messages deal instead with the workers' contributions to production. The trade unions are urged to stimulate innovations, further rationalisation and support 'the initiative of the masses'. The advancement of 'socialist competition' between enterprises is one duty which receives increasing emphasis during the period. The fulfilment and overfulfilment of production plans is presented as an important union function. Most of the 'production-boosting' messages refer to quantitative plan goals, but there is also a small group of items which stress qualitative aspects. Shouldering responsibility for production results is at any rate regarded as the chief obligation of the trade unions.

*Pravda*'s messages to the Komsomol are more varied than those to the trade unions. In 1950 there is a certain emphasis on various types of youth activities. Requests include more camps for children and young people and more varied programmes of activities. It is noted that sports are an important part of the physical upbringing of Soviet youth. The Komsomol is also urged to activate young people for the soviet elections and see to it that everyone votes. The political education of youth is a central task of the organisation.

Ten years later instructions rather tend to deal with active participation in the economic development of the country. Production and productivity must be raised. The seven-year plan must be fulfilled. The Komsomol is responsible for ensuring that young people are energetically involved in these efforts and for keeping the wheels of production turning. The organisation can also contribute to labour recruitment – on one occasion it is noted that it should stimulate the interest of young people in employment in the retail sector. The Komsomol's educational role is stressed at the same time, and its officials are urged to co-operate closely with teachers and school authorities. It must also guide 'parasitic elements' among young people on to better paths.

This educational role is emphasised even more in 1970. 'Parasitic elements' are no longer mentioned, but there is greater stress on the importance of ideological training. Will to defend the country must also be strengthened; the youth organisation must do its share in preparing its members for military service, infusing them with patriotism and combating alien attitudes ('scepticism, apoliticism, unwillingness to fulfil one's civic obligations'). The Komsomol should also help young people to choose a profession and activate them in various types of summer work. Demands for ideological purity and the effective cultivation of a Marxist-Leninist spirit among youth seem to be stronger now than in either of the two earlier years.

## 7.4 FROM MOBILISATION TO PROFESSIONALISM

The *Pravda* instructions provide a picture of normative role distribution in the Soviet political system. That is, they say something about the leaders' understanding of the function of various institutions. This role distribution changes dramatically during the period studied here, but because of the special conditions in 1960 – a year marked by Khrushchev's short-lived structural reforms – the shift is not linear. Each of the three years, therefore, has its own institutional profile.

The diminishing significance of the Party is one striking tendency. The *Pravda* editorials of the Stalin year present the regional and local Party organs as the key levers of social and economic development. Both internal and external Party activities attract a great deal of interest. On the one hand, the Party apparatus has to be consolidated and an effective organisation is needed at the base level; on the other, the Party is urged to utilise all available resources to spur the people on to increased efforts. Instructions to Party agencies at the regional and local level are frequent and forceful but seldom precise. The standard remedies are seldom varied recommendations for propaganda, agitation, and supervision. Week after week *Pravda* grinds out its monotonous demands for mobilisation, mobilisation and yet more mobilisation.

Interest in the Party cools during the last two years. The Party as organiser and supervisor of the economy is now a less prominent theme in *Pravda*'s editorials. Attention in 1960 tends instead to be directed to lower governmental organs, particularly those at the republican level. Although it is not clearly reflected in the frequencies in Table 7.4.1, specialised governmental authorities are in 1970 a more important category of address than Party organisations. Particular agencies now appear to be the prime movers in many areas, and the leaders attempt to direct the activities of these organisations by means of specific instructions. The degree of precision in such directives is considerably greater than in the vague decrees issued under Stalin. *Pravda*'s exhortations in 1970 no longer simply urge the rectification of all errors, but specify more exactly both faults and remedies. The range of recommended measures also becomes broader as problem-solving strategies are refined.

TABLE 7.4.1 Distribution of instructions among the Party, governmental agencies, and public organisations

|  | Instructions in % of total instructions per year | | |
| --- | --- | --- | --- |
|  | 1950 | 1960 | 1970 |
| Soviets | 10.5 | 10.4 | 5.3 |
| Executive governmental organisations | 10.7 | 10.1 | 14.2 |
| Party | 39.9 | 23.3 | 26.4 |
| Komsomol | 4.5 | 6.3 | 2.8 |
| Trade unions | 4.7 | 5.1 | 2.5 |

Accompanying this 'horizontal' functional shift from the Party to the governmental apparatus, there also occurs between 1950 and 1970 a 'vertical' adjustment toward higher organs. Most signals in 1950 are aimed at regional and local Party agencies, while ministries and central agencies seldom come under fire. By 1970 the free zone around the political leadership has shrunk considerably, and even high-ranking agencies in the governmental apparatus now are the targets or receivers of *Pravda*'s criticism. *Pravda* becomes more and more a 'local paper' for the political elite in Moscow; an increasing number of proposals in the newspaper are addressed to the central administration. At the same time, more pressure is exerted on the co-ordinating regional and local governmental organs, the soviets.

The development of the institutional problem map from 1950 to 1970 suggests radical shifts in the functioning of the Soviet system. The leadership under Stalin still regarded the Party as the dominant instrument of change. Political strategy prescribed a mobilisation of human resources that was primitive in the sense that the goals and means of activities were not subjected to any profound analysis. Moscow governed by coarse commands. Twenty years later instructions were more permeated by goal-rationality. Now they went out to a large number of specialised elites, seeking to use them as instruments to influence society. In 1970 the leaders no longer relied on the generalists in the Party, but turned instead to trained specialists.

The extent to which this new normative role distribution corresponds to an empirical change in roles can only be established by empirical investigation. As far as the normative picture is concerned, the approaches tested earlier (5.11 and 6.4) offer different explanations of the results obtained here. According to the 'power politics' interpretation, the decreasing number of instructions to the Party could be due to the fact that Party organisations are now better able to defend themselves against orders from above, while the position of the departments has been correspondingly weakened. The 'informational' interpretation would suggest that our observations reflect the leadership's improved supply of information on the activities of the specialised governmental organs. Neither of these approaches seems very likely. The 'objective' interpretation, according to which higher frequencies result from an increase in the number or extent of 'real' difficulties appears more plausible. Yet in analysing these objective difficulties, the leaders are forced to 'attribute' the trouble to the responsibility of a given agency, and this 'attribution' has obviously changed in the course of time. If the leadership was earlier inclined to place the guilt for an inefficient steelworks on regional Party organs, now the appropriate ministry tends to receive the blame. But behind this shift in responsibilities and expectations there is of course an increased professionalisation of social and economic processes. Functionally differentiated organisations have consequently acquired a more important role in both the 'objective' life of society and in the leaders' strategies for influence and change.

According to a fourth interpretation related to the 'informational' approach, *Pravda*'s increased interest in national departments may be related to increasing difficulties of communication within the central bureaucracy. While it was possible before to maintain contacts by means of closed channels, the growth of the administrative apparatus would make it increasingly necessary to use *Pravda* as a megaphone to reach the many officials in leadership positions. The growing complexity of the administrative network would cause the leaders difficulties of control which they might attempt to counteract by means of broader information to the administrative agencies. Such a hypothesis cannot be tested on the basis of the present materials, but it corresponds well to both the findings of modern organisational research and the 'bureaucratic model' of the Soviet political system.

# 8 Conclusions

What is Soviet politics about? How has the Soviet political agenda changed? How do the leaders try to solve their problems? How does the Soviet polity function?

In this chapter we shall draw some conclusions based on comparisons on three levels. First of all, there is a comparison in time. Between 1950 and 1970 the Soviet Union underwent more than just a series of dramatic changes of regime; it also experienced rapid economic growth, considerable urbanisation, an educational revolution, and a political consolidation. It is impossible to determine the relative influence of each of these processes on the political agenda, but the instructions in *Pravda* provide an interesting illustration of their total effects. The still snapshots at our disposal, of course, do not allow us to follow the process of change through all its convolutions, but by paralleling the three years we can still get an idea of its course. We can see which problems have been regarded as urgent at different points in time, how these problems have been formulated and diagnosed, the strategies the leaders have chosen, the agents of change they have tried to mobilise. In the social analysis that looms behind the instructions, we can discern shifts in both general outlook and scale of values. The two main tendencies are summarised in Section 8.1 as differentiation and rationalisation.

Secondly, the analyses provide a basis for further consideration of the three models introduced in Chapter 2 – the totalitarian, the pluralist and the bureaucratic. The present materials do not permit a thorough examination of these models, but the hypotheses about how political problems are registered, inherent in the interpretations, can be subjected to a weak test. The conclusion of this section is that it is possible to trace elements from all three models in the Soviet system, but that the totalitarian and bureaucratic models should be given a certain preference. The social order that has emerged in the Soviet Union is certainly a command economy in the sense that central government is very important in economic and social development, but it is also a petition economy in which a great many impulses are transmitted from the bottom upwards.

This reasoning is developed in the third section through a comparison of Soviet and Western politics. According to the convergence theory fashionable in the 1950s and 1960s, the advanced industrialised countries would increasingly be confronted by similar problems and drawn toward similar solutions. It was thought that a uniform post-industrial social order would emerge out of the two different systems. How correct was this hypothesis? Many symptoms of overdevelopment obviously appear in the Soviet Union during the period studied here, but there is also evidence of lasting distinctions and divergences. The essence of politics in the Soviet Union – that is, what Soviet politicians are occupied with – still differs radically from the essence of politics in Western industrialised countries. One important reason for this lies in *the complementary nature of politics* – problems that cannot be solved in any other way are passed on to the political sphere. Politicians deal with such questions as individuals and organisations are incapable of solving themselves, and in the Soviet Union this means consumer questions at various levels. Soviet politics deals with consumer problems not because the consumers are strong, but because they are weak.

## 8.1 THE MODERNISATION OF THE POLITICAL AGENDA

Change has been the persistent theme of this study. In our analysis of economic sectors, geographical areas and political institutions, we have constantly noted shifts in *Pravda*'s problem perception, diagnoses and prescriptions. Questions have appeared on the political agenda, moved up or down, or disappeared. It may be that the study has even had a certain methodological bias in favour of the registration of such changes; computerised techniques make it exceedingly easy to note rises and falls in frequencies, and this may tend to distract attention from that which is constantly present or constantly absent.

Before proceeding to summarise the changes themselves, therefore, it may be appropriate to emphasise the *stability* in the relationship of the Soviet leaders to the problem they try to tackle. One of the strongest impressions produced by this study is that there appears to be a fairly uniform Soviet approach to political problems. This impression is reinforced by the many points of similarity between the agendas of the Stalin year and the Brezhnev year, while the Khrushchev year represents a deviation. Thus the changes of the first decade are to a great extent neutralised in the second, and this lends the total picture a considerable measure of continuity. We shall return to the constant features in the following two sections.

Besides such characteristics, there are also many signs of an irreversible development. To summarise the many individual shifts discussed in the three preceding chapters, we shall here indicate thirteen general tendencies. The first six refer to the leadership's problem selection, while the other seven are related to its diagnoses and choice of strategy.

## 1. The range of problems is broadened and modernised

The list of questions repeatedly considered by *Pravda*'s editorials in 1950 was limited. The energy supply had to be guaranteed, primarily by increased coal production. Rapidly increased harvests were needed in agriculture. The printing industry had to be expanded and given ample supplies of ink and paper to be able to spread the Party line effectively. Scientific heresies had to be countered. People were urged to give as much attention as possible to agitprop activities. *Pravada* beat fiercely on just a few drums, leaving large areas of society in peace. Most branches of industry were seldom or never mentioned in its editorials.

The scope of its interests becomes considerably broader in the later two years, particularly in 1970. Now there is a wide range of worries where primary, secondary and tertiary branches are represented. We no longer have to do with a few questions which occupy an undisputed top position in the leadership's priorities; instead, a large variety of deficiencies compete for the attention of the active political stratum. Rather than intense campaigns to attain limited goals, it is now preferred to attack problems on a broader front.

This differentiation results in part from the modernisation of the economy. New products and means of production have appeared on the scene. The chemical industry is a case in point – in contrast to isolated remarks in 1950, a wide range of demands are expressed twenty years later. The increasing attention devoted to radio and television broadens perspectives within the mass media. Demands on scientific research and industrial development now concern many different areas of application. A broad political agenda has replaced the previously narrow one.

## 2. Problems of co-ordination increase

Many demands in *Pravda* have to do with the co-ordination of various organisational units. They deal with co-ordination in the areas of investments, the equipping of new projects, the supply of raw materials, machinery maintenance, co-operation between enterprises and distributors and between different distributors, the Party and the Komsomol or the soviets and the kolkhozes. Such co-ordination problems abound in all three years, but they seem to increase with time. A very large part of *Pravda*'s instructions in 1970 concern measures needed to ensure a better harmonisation of individual units. Within the branches as well the paper often urges broader contacts between advanced and lagging enterprises and divisions. The diffusion of innovation appears to be a lasting worry.

Transportation is often the weak link in the production chain. The railways are a serious bottleneck in both 1950 and 1970, while there are no complaints or directives dealing with rail traffic in the Khrushchev year. The range of problems of co-ordination between production and distribution units becomes broader during the period. By 1970 the difficulties the retail sector experiences in obtaining an even supply of goods have come into the picture differently than before. The quality of the distributional network attracts increased attention.

### 3. Problems shift forward in the chain of production

There are a number of examples of how problems move within the different branches. *Pravda*'s instructions on petroleum in 1950 deal mainly with winning it. Prospecting must be intensified and new, effective drilling methods must be applied. Other questions stand in the foreground twenty years later. Distribution is one headache. For example, there is a shortage of pipes for the pipelines. Dock facilities are inadequate. Refining is another worry. Petroleum policy now concerns bottlenecks which are closer to the users.

The same pattern can be observed with respect to natural gas. Distribution to industry and households is criticised in 1970. The textile and clothing industry is a third branch in which production and consumer aspects acquire increased significance as time goes by. *Pravda*'s many demands on institutes of research and development suggest a similar shift from the problems of the primary sectors to those of the secondary and tertiary branches, but the picture is not clear-cut in all cases. In the steel industry, for example, raw material problems are accentuated in 1970. Transport capacity cannot meet the needs of the industry, which results in serious imbalances in ore and fuel supplies.

### 4. Interest in 'superior goods' increases

A shift of interest toward 'superior goods' is one reflection of economic growth and increased prosperity. In the area of textiles and clothing, *Pravda* discusses more frequently as the period progresses the need for more modern models and colours, a better balanced assortment, and more attention to consumer demands. Another field where aesthetic and functional quality aspects gradually emerge is the housing sector. There is a corresponding shift in the paper's comments on agriculture towards produce that a prosperous society can afford, such as fruit, vegetables, meat and poultry.

### 5. Increased infrastructural investments

Investments in the infrastructure become increasingly more important in *Pravda*'s instructions. It is especially clear in 1960 that education and culture are high-priority sectors. Interest in transport grows during the period, particularly with respect to freight but also to some extent in passenger traffic. Urban planning and construction slowly slide on to the political agenda. The 1970 editorials give the impression that land apportionment has at long last become a political issue; the shortcomings pointed out there suggest that this type of planning has been very underdeveloped in many parts of the country.

### 6. A growing interest in environmental questions

Environmental problems are late arrivals on the political scene, in the Soviet Union as in other industrialised countries. When questions relating to the work environment are brought up in the earlier years, they are usually connected with the needs of production. *Pravda* points to risks in the mines and poor services (cf. Section 5.8) as inhibiting increased productivity. Not until 1970 is nature discussed as a limited resource. Now the newspaper is concerned about the damage to the environment caused by new gas-lines and the water pollution tolerated in certain industrial areas. Questions of health and hygiene are also given more attention, and it is emphasised that various dangers to the environment must be warded off in time. The standard of living now begins to attract notice, and long-range considerations compete to some extent with short-range production goals. This, however, is a feeble tendency; environmental problems occupy a very modest position on the political agenda even in 1970.

### 7. More profound diagnoses

*Pravda*'s evaluations of the circumstances and causes connected with observed deficiencies are differentiated and refined during the period. The explanations of criticised faults given in 1950 are narrow in scope, extending from bureaucratic leadership and a 'boss' mentality to inadequate ideological consciousness on the part of the workers. In 1960 and 1970 the editorials seem prepared for more ambitious discussions of causal factors. Comments no longer merely state that there are difficulties of co-ordination, but also point occasionally to structural factors behind such problems. Organisation theory begins to appear in diagnoses; in comments on waste and long delays in the construction sector, for example, it is noted that enterprises often lack economic incentive to co-ordinate their efforts. Corruption and theft are now admitted, and the reasons for such phenomena are openly discussed. Bottlenecks in the transport sector are also analysed more penetratingly. It seems that diagnostic depth increases in discussions of branches which are 'contact-intensive' in the sense that they are connected with many other branches. Faults within more independent areas of the economy receive less thorough analysis in *Pravda*'s editorials.

## 8. Criticism is generalised and depersonalised

In 1950 *Pravda*'s lash stings many individual scapegoats – negligent Party officials, heretical academicians, dismissed steelworks managers. They, of course, are held up merely as negative examples, the messages being intended for much broader audiences. In 1960 and 1970 such pilloried individuals have for the most part disappeared from the editorials, and criticism is now aimed primarily at various agencies. There is also an increase of addresses to entire professional groups and their organisations. In one sense, then, *Pravda* becomes less differentiated, as broader groups are invoked. At the same time, however, its messages become more diverse, in that concrete instructions become more specific. In 1970, for example, the Soviet Union of Writers is told more precisely what should be written than in either of the earlier years. On the other hand, individualised criticism of erring leaders decreases. *Pravda* concentrates more on constructive directives.

## 9. Strategies are differentiated

Just as *Pravda*'s diagnostic range was narrow under Stalin, its variety of remedies for noted deficiencies was also limited. The standard recommendation was for 'better political work' – by intensifying their educational and stimulative activities and checking more carefully to see that directives were followed and obligations fulfilled, it was felt that Party agencies would succeed in mobilising the population. Although Party work is still regarded as an important lever in 1970, by then there are considerably broader variations. The Party organisations seem to have a better grip on their areas of responsibility, which means that general mobilising efforts become less important. Instead, much is said about scientific organisation and the guidance of specific units and activities. Optimum results can only be attained if available instruments of control are carefully adapted to particular goals and problems. *Pravda*'s 1970 directives are characterised by a rational outlook – leading production is now less a matter of enthusiastic Party work and more a question of skilful management. Awareness of the causal connections between measures and results and of the interdependence of different sectors seems to have been sharpened. One editorial in which it is emphasised that city planning and urban transport must be co-ordinated can serve as a typical expression of this consciousness.

## 10. Greater emphasis on all types of incentive

Increased interest in various kinds of stimulation is another manifestation of *Pravda*'s more differentiated strategy. The 'scientific' approach advocated in the later years includes a more sophisticated analysis of the motivation to work. Especially in 1970 it is often mentioned that enterprises have to learn to handle material incentives correctly, and the paper is open to the thought that the behaviour of the enterprises themselves may be influenced by the economic incentive structure within which they operate. Changes in this structure are demanded in certain cases; for example, it is noted that the construction branch requires stronger economic stimulation to complete its projects on time.

One might have expected that increased pressure on economic rewards would be accompanied by a diminishing interest in moral incentives. Such, however, is not the case. The mobilisation pursued by the Party in its agitprop activities and general education of the working population does indeed decrease in *Pravda*'s editorials, but on the other hand the paper demands more and more specially adapted actions to strengthen social and production morals. Interest in public opinion remains high.

## 11. No decline of ideology

It is commonly assumed that ideology and rationalism are opposed to one another. No such tension, however, can be discerned in *Pravda*'s editorials. In 1970 as well, ideological training appears to have an important position in the leaders' overall strategy. Instructions to the opinion-forming organs become increasingly specific at the same time as they more frequently than before deal with questions with no direct bearing on production. Among the exhortation in the Brezhnev year, for example, there is an entire group urging the cultural intelligentsia and agitprop officials to stimulate an attitude of increased respect for the family. Patriotic themes also become more widespread.

## 12. Greater emphasis on specialists as agents of change

The instructions in 1950 were founded to a considerable extent on the assumption that necessary efforts would be produced through mobilisation and supervision by regional and local Party officials. This was a strategy based on generalists. In the following years, problem diagnoses are deepened at the same time as the range of demands is broadened, and this development necessitates increased reliance on specialists in various areas – scientists, managers, organisational experts and better-educated officials. The leaders' strategy of change is consequently professionalised – the experts are given a new role in social and economic development.

## 13. Instructions are issued to higher institutions

There is a general expansion between 1950 and 1970 in *Pravda*'s messages to various levels of the governmental apparatus. In the final year they go both lower (more instructions to the local soviets) and higher (more instructions to ministries and civil service departments). The latter tendency, however, is of particular interest, in that it implies a broadening of the paper's signals to include a level that was earlier seldom pressured through public channels. The leaders' use of *Pravda* both to criticise and instruct ministries at the national level may be interpreted in several ways. One explanation is that the ministries have to some extent taken over the Party's leadership and supervisory functions and thus increased their role as executive organs; another is that the institutional network has become so complex that the internal signal system no longer functions. According to the latter view, *Pravda* is used more because other communications are clogged. The instructions in 1970 urging film-makers to produce informational films on the approaching census are an example of a potentially internal message that was nevertheless transmitted through *Pravda*. This appeal, of course, is addressed to organisations in several republics, but they can hardly be so many that it would be difficult to reach them by means of a circular letter. The appearance of such a message in the Party's central mouthpiece must be intended to place the matter high on the agenda of the propaganda institutions. *Pravda* is used to give questions high priority, even though there may be very few people involved. One possible explanation of the increased frequency of such messages is that the communications system is so overloaded that even central decision-makers are now difficult to reach. But it is also likely that many functionally specialised central institutions are competing for the attention of general institutions at the regional and local levels.

The tendencies discussed above can generally be summarised in the notions *differentiation* and *rationalisation*. First of all, the Soviet leadership's view over society and approach to political instruments have broadened. Problems, diagnoses, solutions and agents of change range over a wider field in 1970 than in 1950. Soviet politics has become more complex. Secondly, attitudes toward political problems have become more rational and flexible. The leaders are increasingly prepared to allow that different problems have different solutions, that each individual situation demands careful analysis and a broad review of available strategies. Goal-rational thinking has made its appearance in Soviet politics, bringing with it an inclination to reject the instruments of yester-year as too crude. The watchword of the day is 'scientific'.

This intellectual development contains the contours of a new view of human nature. Perhaps it might be said that the leaders of 1950 paid tribute to McGregor's 'theory X', while the leaders of 1970 have shifted somewhat toward 'theory Y'.[1] The notion that producers must be trained and stimulated with all manner of external incentives has of course not at all been abandoned, but the portrait of the object of influence has changed. The Soviet citizen as he appears in official doctrine in 1970 is a more complicated being whose behaviour cannot be programmed through simple learning processes. The ambition to influence him, however, is not any weaker in the instructions of the Brezhnev year. Differentiation and rationalisation seem to have driven the system in two conflicting directions – toward a more effective control of society, on the one hand, and toward an aspiration to channel this control to a broader set of goals, on the other.

## 8.2 COMMAND ECONOMY OR PETITION ECONOMY?

All instructions in *Pravda* express a desire that something be done. They may contain implicit critical remarks ('sovkhozes and kolkhozes in certain southern regions have not yet repaired their combines') or explicit directives ('the Party organisations must now check to see that all combines are in operating order before summer'), but in both cases they include a specific exhortation. Whose requests does *Pravda* express?

Ultimately, of course, the desires of the Party leadership. As has been shown in Chapter 3, *Pravda* is an official mouthpiece that is very firmly bound to the Politburo and the Secretariat of the Central Committee. The observations made in the present study on no point contradict the assumptions which served as its point of departure, but they can in one respect provide a speculative amplification. A conspicuously large number of instructions, especially in the beginning of the period, are addressed to the mass media. This may reflect the high priority given the media by the supreme leadership, but it is also conceivable that it derives from a preference for its own area of jurisdiction, on the part of the section in the Secretariat responsible for both *Pravda* and the other media. It is not unnatural to presume that the chief mouthpiece devotes particular attention to the affairs of that section. However this may be, *Pravda* can generally be assumed to render a faithful and balanced picture of the demands the Party summit as a whole wants to make. The first answer to the question 'whose demands', therefore, is 'the supreme leadership's'.

Such an answer, however, is not very satisfying. That it is the leaders who lead may be said of any society. The most important authoritative decisions are always made by certain organs which, with or without constitutional sanction, are regarded as the highest decision-making institutions in the political system. Power according to the Soviet constitution belongs to certain governmental organs, but apart from a few short succession interludes, there has never been any doubt that the Party's top leaders have the last word in central political questions. It is similarly easy to determine the participants in important decisions in

Stockholm, Washington or New Haven. What has nevertheless prompted political scientists to devote a great deal of interest to the division of power in various societies is the insight that real and formal decisions are not always made in the same room. Behind the people who confirm by an official gesture that an agreement has been reached there are often others who have played more important roles in creating it and piloting it through various preliminary institutions. The question that naturally follows the one answered above, therefore, is how the desires of the Party leadership are formed. Who 'ultimately' has control of the Soviet political agenda?

This is a tougher nut to crack. The three ideal models discussed above – the totalitarian, the pluralist and the bureaucratic – crack it in different ways. According to the totalitarian approach, the leaders possess a good deal of autonomy in their choice of problems and instruments. Their control of society is fairly effective, and they extract the information needed to support their decisions. The totalitarian model presumes that the leaders themselves determine which problems they want to tackle. According to the pluralist point of view, however, the leadership gains support from various groups in society by articulating their opinions and demands. This means that the political agenda reflects different interests. The pluralist model postulates competition between various groups trying to get their own particular affairs recognised as political problems, and competition between élites vying for supremacy. The bureaucratic model also presumes such competition, but emphasises instead the split between various formal units of the system. According to this approach, it is the interests of the 'bureaux', rather than aggregated private interests, which constitute the foundation of the demands that are advanced. The latter two models are based on the assumption that the leaders do not have exclusive control over the social mechanism, but are influenced considerably by pressure from below.

The question then becomes whether the instructions of the Party leadership in *Pravda* are of its own concoction. In only a few exceptional cases is it possible to state conclusively that such has or has not been the case. The great majority of directives and critical comments have no indications of origin. Sometimes, however, the messages contain clues which, carefully interpreted, may be said to point toward one or the other model. The answers to such questions as

— where can the Party leadership have obtained this information?
— in whose interest might the leadership issue such instructions?
— who might the form of the instructions tend to benefit?

at least make it possible to formulate certain hypotheses about the origin of the instructions and the routes they have travelled.

The examples of unrepaired combines given by way of introduction above can serve as a convenient first test. With regard to their form and type of content, these instructions are typical of a large category of signals dealing with hindrances to production that must be removed. They are specific with respect to their subject (the repair of combines), geographical area, apportionment of responsibility, and the appropriate measures to be taken by the Party (supervision). It is difficult to believe that the impulse behind an exhortation of this sort could have come from a 'pluralist' interest group. Nor does it appear likely that initiative was taken by an authority in any other branch than agriculture, an agricultural agency or a governmental organ with general jurisdiction such as a soviet. Finally, it hardly seems plausible to assume that information about the damaged machines could have been furnished voluntarily by the immediately responsible sovkhozes, kolkhozes or Party organisations. It was more probably 'dragged out' of the guilty parties by obligatory reports or gathered by other supervisory agencies. Most evidence indicates that *Pravda*'s exhortations are based on extracted information, which in this case would point toward a 'totalitarian' interpretation.

The summary of the instructions issued to the Chelyabinsk regions (Table 6.3.5) and the Ministry of Agriculture (Table 7.2.2) provide further examples of this type of summons. When *Pravda* notes that Party training is poor in certain districts of Chelyabinsk, that the Party committee in Miassk has insufficient contact with its officials, that the Party committee in Kopeisk is guilty of bureaucratic methods, that seed grain has not yet been cleaned in the Chelyabinsk region, that the Ministry of Agriculture must pay more attention to its publications or mobilise its local organs to trace seed types that have disappeared, the most probable assumption is that the Party leadership has obtained such information without the aid of any institutions with a positive interest in the instructions. A large part of these items may derive from a supervisory study of the republican, regional and local press; information may have also been obtained through internal media such as Party reports, reports from the secret police, the Committee of People's Control, the procurators (a type of public prosecutors), special auditors or *Pravda* correspondents.

In certain cases the newspaper indicates its sources in a way that confirms such assumptions. *Pravda*'s correspondents are occasionally referred to, and in one of the items in Table 7.2.2 it is noted that the Committee of Popular Inspection has studied the forest and wood products industry and the RSFSR Ministry of Agriculture and revealed deviations from established accounting norms. The great majority of such instructions, however, can be categorised only by a process of elimination. If no group in society, no Party organisation and no governmental organ seems to draw demonstrable benefit from a given measure, if none of these may be assumed to have furnished the supreme leadership with the information upon which the instructions are based, and if none of them appears to profit by the way in which the instructions are formulated, then it seems reasonable to prefer the totalitarian hypothesis to the other two models.

Other indications of source point instead to a pluralist interpretation. There are some references to the opinions of readers in 1950 and 1960, and in 1970 this becomes an increasingly common practice. In that year *Pravda* bases fifteen instructions on 'signals', 'complaints' or 'letters' from the public, which are generally said to be 'many' or 'quite a few'. But organised thrusts are never referred to. Mention is occasionally made of criticism levelled by one institution against another or of decisions made by a particular organisation, but appeals from associations or authorities are never quoted as the basis for *Pravda*'s criticism or decrees.

No legitimate pressure groups can be glimpsed in *Pravda*'s editorials; their presence can only be suspected to lie behind the paper's demands. Some examples:

1.  That the Ukraine and Belorussia generally escape criticism in *Pravda*'s review of deficiencies in society may be due to the strong position of 'west Soviet' politicians in the Politburo. A group with certain regional loyalties, that is, may be able to block criticism aimed in a certain direction.

2.  The mildness of the signals to the cultural intelligentsia in 1960 may have to do with the fact that liberal groups were then influential in the Party leadership. The comparatively hard and specific messages in 1950 would analogously derive from the influence of conservative elements.

3.  The increased interest in consumer demands and the tendency to consider service needs and environmental questions that have no direct bearing on production may indicate an increased influence on the part of broad masses in the latter part of the period.

4.  Words such as 'Fatherland', 'patriotic', 'patriot', etc., have high frequencies in 1950, low frequencies in 1960 and become again very frequent in 1970. Patriotic appeals in the final year are on several occasions connected with defence needs; they are aimed at imbuing young people with love of country, stimulating their enthusiasm for military

|  | *1950* | *1960* | *1970* |  |
|---|---|---|---|---|
| PATRIOTISM | 31 | 11 | 32 | absolute figures |
|  | 0.64 | 0.39 | 0.55 | frequency per mille |
| FATHERLAND | 22 | 3 | 13 | absolute figures |
|  | 0.45 | 0.11 | 0.22 | frequency per mille |

service, etc. One possible explanation is that military interests have regained their strong position in the Politburo.

5. Analogously, variations in the occurrence of other components of ideological doctrine may be connected with the interests of other professional or opinion groups. Marxism-Leninism, for example, might be the banner of a conservative grouping or the agitprop apparatus, internationalism might function as a symbol for those who favour an offensive foreign policy demanding conformity to the Soviet line in other socialist countries and communist parties, etc.

6. On a number of instances *Pravda* sympathises with narrow professional groups or groups of decision-makers (agronomists, researchers, urban architects, etc.) which have not received the recognition or support they need for the successful completion of their work. It is conceivable that some sort of trade union pressure may have figured in such reminders.

7. Among consumer demands there are examples of failures to satisfy the needs of particular groups, whether these be skiers, parents with small children or tourists at vacation resorts. Representatives of these citizen categories may have taken the initiative in suggesting the topics of such instructions.

All of the above constructions rest on shaky foundations. We can assume, guess and suspect, but nothing more. No interest groups which would satisfy Meisel's three criteria – consciousness, cohesion and conspiracy – can be detected in *Pravda*.[2] Actors that are representative of different categories sympathetic with the aspirations of those categories have undoubtedly often been able to influence the political agenda, but it cannot be proved that this has happened in exchange for support, as is presumed by classic pluralist theory. That investments in, say, housing construction might have as one of their aims the strengthening of the regime's position among those who benefit from the policy is in itself highly probable. No concrete indications of such considerations, however, can be found in the *Pravda* materials. We cannot show that the Soviet leaders seek to reinforce their popularity among the masses when they compile their goal-catalogues in the same way as the American President undoubtedly does when he plans his State of the Union Address. The notion of politicians as contractors or brokers for various citizen groups as developed by Schumpeter, Downs and others, therefore, is not confirmed by our analyses.[3]

Hough's portrait of the politician as a broker serving bureaucratic interests fares somewhat better. A large and growing number of *Pravda*'s instructions deal with the relations between various branches or categories of instructions: the miners should provide the steel industry with more coal, the steel industry must manufacture more pipe for the petroleum distributors, the petroleum distributors must be careful not to destroy land that can be used for agriculture, etc. Many of these 'cross-demands' have to do with deliveries that never arrive, are late or of inferior quality. Others concern support among different organisations – the Party's support of the Komsomol, the Party's aid to the kolkhozes, the responsibilities of the soviets for the health service, etc. The 'bureaux' called upon in such directives are sometimes named specifically (a particular ministry, civil service agency, enterprise, republic or region), but it is more often a case of entire branches, hierarchies or professions (the wood products industry, the trade unions, Soviet teachers). The same applies to the beneficiaries intended to be helped by the recommended measures.

The role of the beneficiaries in the genesis of 'cross-demands' is not entirely clear. According to a totalitarian interpretation, what may happen is that the leadership observes deficiencies and then makes a diagnosis that traces failures to other branches or hierarchies. Suppliers would consequently come under fire as shortages of necessary items and materials are noted in various sectors of the economy. This explanation, then, would have it that *Pravda*'s exhortations are based on 'extracted' information.

According to a bureaucratic model, 'cross-demands' would instead take form in offended or frustrated bureaux that have not succeeded in gaining sympathy for their demands from organs in other hierarchies. Blocked in their aspirations to fulfil their plan goals or meet the success indicators established by superior organs, these bureaux would then try and manage to get their desires on to the political agenda. Information on the faulty horizontal co-ordination noted by *Pravda*, then, would have penetrated in toward the centre from senders in the periphery that have wanted to gain the support of the top leadership.

Only rarely do 'cross-demands' contain indications of source that firmly support one or other of these interpretations. From what the research of recent decades has told us both about large organisations in general and about Soviet regional and local politics in particular, however, it seems most reasonable to fit the 'cross-demands' in a bureaucratic model. The growing number of demands among various economic sectors corresponds well to the tendencies toward greater differentiation and specialisation that we have noted in *Pravda*'s editorials. The difficulties that arise in co-ordinating more and more units are first noticeable at low levels, so that it seems likely that signals from the bottom upward increase in extent and strength. Just how these signals are transmitted cannot be established with certainty, but both regional Party agencies and ministries and planning authorities may be assumed to function as two-way information channels.

The totalitarian and bureaucratic ideal models have both received certain support from the weak test of the present study. It can hardly be doubted that the Soviet Union is still a state in which a very strong and dominant central power has extensive and profound control over the whole of society. True, ambitions to control appear to diminish between 1950 and 1960, but there is a return to the former level during the following decade. The similarities between the political agendas in 1950 and 1970 are in many respects so great as to justify speaking of a neo-Stalinist polity on a higher organisational and technical level – a more rational dictatorship that attacks a broader range of problems with a broader battery of political and administrative measures.

At the same time, there are fragmentation tendencies that appear to result from increased economic prosperity and an accompanying differentiation of the national economy. Peripheral forces in the system have gained more influence on the political agenda. Many of the decisions made by the top leadership seem to be examples of reactive rather than active government. The problems brought up for consideration are to a great extent those of the bureaucracy. The Soviet Union is no longer only a 'command economy', but also a 'petition economy' in which organisations with difficulties constantly bombard the leaders with demands.

## 8.3 POLITICS IN A SOCIETY OF WEAK CONSUMERS

A comparison of the political agenda in the Soviet Union with its counterpart in an advanced industrialised Western country gives little support to the convergence theory. The substance of politics in the Soviet Union does not correspond at all to the substance of politics in Western Europe or North America. One searches in vain through *Pravda*'s editorials for comments on employment problems, questions relating to pensioners, women, regional politics, drug addiction, prices, safety on the streets, abortions, labour disputes, and much more. Instead, one finds a great variety of subjects which seldom or never concern Western politicians: delays in ore shipments, the repair and maintenance of tractors, the mobilisation of harvest workers, the utilisation of fertilisers, shortages of children's wear in the stores, etc. Certain questions, of course, are discussed by both groups, but the differences are still striking. Why does the Soviet political agenda deviate from our conceptions of 'normal' politics?

Certain answers to that question have already been suggested. One important reason why the political agenda in one society at a given time differs from that of a neighbouring country or of the same society at another time may of course be that socio-economic conditions differ. Industrial policy is naturally connected with industry, questions concerning automobile traffic cannot arise without automobiles, etc. Differences in economic structure, educational system, social benefits and the like may explain some of the distinctions between Soviet and Western politics – the 'objective' foundations of their respective problems are quite simply different. The power politics interpretation offers another explanation. A certain amount of political strength is needed to get a question on to the political agenda, and not all groups in society have that strength. *Pravda*'s silence on the problems of the aged is a case in point. In a multiparty system pensioners are a power factor by virtue of their share of the electorate, but in a society in which the leaders need not worry about the votes of old people, the influence of such groups is understandably much weaker. In other instances the reason is not so much the weakness of those concerned as resistance on the part of the leaders. The gatekeepers of the political system are in a good position to block uncomfortable demands.

Both of these interpretations have a certain validity. The Soviet political agenda reflects in many respects the typical frictions of economic growth and social adjustment. The new elements that appear during the decades after 1950 are closely connected with technological development and industrial expansion. There is also a great deal in the diagnoses of the political leaders which suggests that they view society through the eyeglasses of managers and high civil servants. No scrupulous watch on the interests of various strata of the population can be detected; the managerial perspective appears to be firmly rooted in *Pravda*'s analyses.

Differences in level of economic development and the distribution of power among various groups in society, however, cannot explain the strong emphasis on production in Soviet politics. Alec Nove writes at one point that procurements were all that really interested Stalin, and the *Pravda* editorials of the Khrushchev and Brezhnev years often give the same impression of the leadership's ambitions.[4] Day after day the paper calls for more, better and quicker results from different branches and professions. The leaders seem to be almost possessed by the urge to produce.

That such a materialistic enthusiasm for production should permeate Soviet society may agree with many Western conceptions of the country. Upon closer consideration, however, it seems unlikely that that zeal is so much greater in the Soviet Union than in industrialised Western countries. Enthusiasm for production must somehow be connected with production results, and it does not appear very probable that any society that has attained a considerable measure of economic growth can have done so without strong social motivation. McClelland has shown that the emergence of a spirit of achievement was very important in the modernisation of the developed countries.[5]

Nor are the types of transactions considered by *Pravda* unique to the Soviet Union. Even in Western countries steelworks must have their fuel, agriculture its rail cars and the schools their textbooks and teaching aids. The farther the division of labour is pushed in a society, the greater the degree of social dependence and the more numerous become the human activities which must in one way or another be co-ordinated.

That the type of co-ordination problems discussed here so seldom occur on Western political agendas must be largely due to the fact that they are solved in other ways. Enterprises and authorities by and large manage their contacts without the interference of politicians. What is placed on the political agenda is a *residue* of questions which people and organisations have for some reason failed to solve. Economists tell us that public sector takes care of 'market failures'. Politics, however, is made of more than just economic setbacks – it has to do with all types of failure in a human society. *The political agenda consists of problems which (1) influential persons (2) consider important, (3) have not been able to solve by extra-political means, and (4) hope to solve by political means.*

According to this definition, the political zone is affected by, among other factors, two types of social 'solution capacity' – the extra-political and the political.[6] In states where the extra-political 'solution capacity' is great, demands for political measures are fairly limited; difficulties can be overcome in other ways. Such demands may also diminish if there is little confidence in the capability of political institutions to cope with problems. A strong demand for political measures, however, arises if the extra-political solution capacity is low and the political capacity is judged to be high.

From this point of view, the problem-solving methods of the political system appear as a complement to the methods used in other parts of society, and the demand for public assistance that can be discerned on the political agenda thus reveals lacunas in the 'solution capacity' of the other social sub-systems. The growth of the public sector in Western countries may consequently be regarded as an indication of a decreasing extra-political solution capacity in relation to the problems confronting society. Growing demands for public action reflect the opinion of various groups that their problems can only be solved politically. The total political agenda manifested in state and communal activities thus becomes a résumé of economic and other failures in society. It shows on which points the capitalist system and the prevailing system of norms have fallen short of expectations. Analogously, the current political agenda, i.e. what the politicians are busy with at any given time, summarises the acute deficiencies which influential persons find impossible to solve through extra-political means. Thus the capitalist state supplements capitalist society. The socialist state correspondingly supplements socialist society. Here as well the vast majority of all individual and collective problems must be solved extra-politically, in the sense that they are not brought up for consideration by the central political authorities; otherwise these institutions would long ago have been swamped with work. A characteristic feature of the socialist systems in Eastern Europe, however, is that the central political organs are none the less involved in a great many of the economic problems of society. The political sphere there is in this respect considerably broader than in capitalist states.

It seems natural to derive this feature from the ideological and programmatic foundations of socialist society. A planned economy and a centralised government were from the outset important elements of Bolshevik political doctrine. But none of the pioneers imagined that central decision-making would attain the proportions it has today. In classic socialist and communist writings the 'ministry of production' (Barone), 'the statistical bureau' (Stalin), or the 'central bank' (Lenin) were always institutions of fairly modest dimensions.[7] It hardly seems likely, therefore, that the Soviet leadership would consciously strive to enlarge the central administrative apparatus. A more probable explanation of the expansion that has taken place is that the leaders have been burdened with so many and so serious problems that administrative resources have never proved sufficient. Soviet rulers were soon squarely confronted by the 'government overload' that has recently begun to be discussed in industrialised Western countries.[8]

Viewed in this light the Soviet political agenda reflects in significant respects the weaknesses in the extra-political 'solution capacity' of the system. That production problems (of a sort that Western observers do not recognise as typically political questions in their own societies) play such a prominent role in Soviet politics would then not necessarily be due to a stronger emphasis on production in Soviet society, but would instead mean that this emphasis has registered politically more strongly. Transactions which in a market economy are conducted at the enterprise level occur on the political agenda in a planned economy precisely because in the latter system they are not affected on the initiative of the enterprise.

The pathological feature in the social system to which the *Pravda* editorials bear especially clear witness is the difficulty of obtaining a satisfactory horizontal co-ordination between the organs of various branches and hierarchies. The fact that the paper day after day, week after week, advances demands for more, quicker and better production in individual sectors of the economy must reflect inadequate goal-fulfilment on the part of enterprises and authorities. As the various units seem to lack the incentives or prerequisites to be able to meet their engagements independently, political resources must be applied to penalise, supervise, and stimulate. A large part of *Pravda*'s messages to the Party organisations concern measures needed to stir up the producers. Regardless of whether requests are addressed directly to the workers or indirectly to their organisations and supervisors, the theme is one and the same: more, better, quicker! Such appeals suggest that the users of the products of the enterprises do not command sufficiently strong positive or negative sanctions to stimulate their collaborators to achieve the desired results. Instead, the political leadership is forced to intervene with its authority.

The essential weakness of the consumer's position, in other words, appears to be an important determinant of the presence of many problems on the political agenda. *Pravda*'s editorials resound with constant exhortations to negligent suppliers – the textile industry needs more linen, the steel industry more coal, the automobile industry more durable paints and enamels, the shoe industry more leather, the film studios better equipment, the printing industry more ink and better colours, the clothing industry more electric machinery, agriculture more fertiliser, inland navigation better ports, etc. Such demands would of course be superfluous if the consumers were able to exert the necessary influence on their suppliers. That they occur so frequently and intensely, therefore, is evidence of institutional inferiority. The political support given to many branches suggests that they themselves cannot obtain the products they need for their activity.

In addition to goods, consumer demands also include services. The building industry calls for blueprints and the kolkhozes ask for soil analyses. Research and development organisations are often summoned by branches in need of new methods and machinery. The railways and the inland navigation system are the target of many complaints and directives. Another production factor that enterprises sometimes have difficulty in obtaining is manpower, especially trained workers. *Pravda* returns regularly to the problems of specialist recruitment, in some cases appealing to schools, youth organisations and the mass media to stimulate young people's interest in professions with personnel shortages.

Even more difficult than recruiting new manpower is getting the existing labour force to work. A great deal of attention is devoted during all three years to mobilisation by means of political influence, organisational measures, socialist competition, and all manner of other stimuli. Many of these appeals concern the kolkhoz farmers, who have an alternative place of employment in their own private garden-plots.[9] Organizations in need of labour frequently appear to be as bad off as organisations in need of other inputs.

One common message deals with better co-operation among different units. It is often urged that one type of agency should help another type or that more advanced divisions aid those which have fallen behind. *Pravda* might point out, for example, that the local Komsomol organisations need the help of teachers or that the Party organisations and the soviets must assume responsibility for some neglected area of activity. Here we seemingly have to do with 'immaterial' consumers, but the aid demanded can very well be material in nature. Once again it is horizontal co-operation that is at fault.

It is commonly pointed out in works on socialist systems that the consumer has a weak position in a planned economy. *Pravda*'s extensive intervention in favour of consumers may be said to confirm that assumption. It is of interest to note, however, that the groups about which the paper is particularly concerned are not those which usually come to mind when one speaks of consumers. Much less is heard in Pravda from final consumers, i.e. the citizen at large, than from intermediate consumers demanding raw materials, machines, transport services, semi-manufactured goods, etc. A majority of the consumer demands articulated in the chief organ of the Central Committee have to do with the difficulties of authorities and enterprises and refer, therefore, not to final consumer goods but to inputs into the production process. The weak consumers for which *Pravda* feels the most sympathy are producers that lack the resources to fulfil their plan goals.

*Pravda*'s efforts to improve horizontal co-ordination are not the only confirmation of the consumer's weak position in the social system. Two types of action, one of which is official and legal and the other more or less illegal, point in the same direction and deserve mention. The first consists of the structural reforms implemented since 1965, which have sought to increase the economic responsibility of individual enterprises by means of decentralised book-keeping, market-oriented success indicators and broader authority to conclude contracts with business partners without central intervention. The other type is an activity independently developed by enterprises in order to obtain, within or outside their plans, the materials and services they need for production. It is conducted to a great extent professionally by so called *tolkachi* ('pushers' or 'fixers'), who keep in touch with producers and distributors and see to it that necessary articles arrive on time. Large units employ full-time fixers. Berliner describes their activity as follows:

> They literally live on wheels, apparently spending most of their time out in the 'market', frequenting the supply depots, purchasing organizations and supplying enterprises, seeking to expedite the shipment of commodities to their enterprises and coping with emergency needs for materials as they arise . . . They are used not only when trouble arises, but 'in order to see that the materials will come through without any trouble. When we expect trouble in the future the *tolkach* will be sent out earlier.'[10]

*Tolkach* activities are very extensive. The sovnarkhoz in Dnepropetrovsk, for example, reports that its metal works and chemical factories were visited by 4000 'fixers' in a single year, while an additional 3000 descended upon its machine plants and 1000 beleaguered the sovnarkhoz's own supply agencies – a total, that is, of 8000.[11] They apply a broad assortment of methods – from entreaties to persuasion to promises of return favours, pressures, and downright bribes.

The occurrence of such activities to ensure the supply of commodities to the enterprises must be due to an uneven interest in horizontal contacts on the part of contractors. The consumers are for their part strongly motivated to obtain certain goods and services, but the sellers often lack the incentives or ability to satisfy their demands. This gives rise to a seller's market with competition among different buyers. Since there are strong negative and positive sanctions connected with the fulfilment of plans, the enterprises cannot afford to wait their turn, but attempt by various means to gain the favour of the contracting parties on which they depend. The autarkic tendencies often observed in the Soviet administrative system – territorial 'localism' (*mestnichestvo*) or functional imperialism (*vedomstvennost'*) – represent an institutional-isation of such ambitions. Activities are diversified to ensure a steady supply of strategic production factors, which implies a diffusion of responsibility and resources that from the point of view of the whole is sub-optimal.

Judging by the *Pravda* editorials, neither the structural reforms nor the independent operations on the part of the enterprises seem to have remedied the problems of horizontal co-ordination. Extra-political 'solution capacity' is quite simply inadequate, and the weak consumers' dilemma is consequently transmitted upward to the political level. In many of its messages *Pravda* functions as a kind of super-*tolkach* for different branches – a 'fixer' which tries to mobilise the appropriate agencies to make energetic efforts to guarantee supplies or results. If the political agenda as it appears in *Pravda* reflects the worries of the top Soviet politicians their *tolkach* functions seem to demand a great deal of their energy. Supplying enterprises and authorities with necessary production resources, in other words, would appear to be a political question of the first rank.

Planning is theoretically the instrument used to organise this supply. Our observations, however, suggest that neither planning in itself nor the sanctions developed to make it effective suffice to push enterprises and institutions in the right direction. In the terminology of Wildavsky, who in his book on budgeting in various countries introduced the notions of 'repetitive budgeting' and 'repetitive planning' for the repeated trails of appropriations and plan-goals that occur in poor states, we might say that the leaders are constantly forced to renew their plan decisions.[12] Not even in a consolidated one-party society does 'action under planning' arise without persistent efforts on the part of the leaders.[13]

As the public sector grows, it appears likely that industrialised Western countries will also be increasingly confronted by the problems of weak consumers. There is no lack of indications pointing in that direction. Organisational research long ago observed that the co-ordination of administrative units presents serious difficulties. The ability of clients to influence the results they receive is also limited when they command neither positive nor negative sanctions. Both authorities and clients are consequently forced to 'politicise' their demands, that is, they must appeal to political organs that can exert pressure from above on negligent producers or suppliers.

Here, then, is certain support for the convergence theory. An interesting distinction, however, must also be noted. We have seen that Soviet politicians spend a considerable amount of energy on 'fixing' or 'speeding up' the production of goods and services needed to fulfil plan quotas. Their function in this context is to ensure that the unsatisfied demands of intermediate and to some extent final consumers are met. Recent economic policy in Western Europe has largely had the opposite goal. There are a number of branches which can supply more than is demanded, and the usual requests are for intervention by the state in order to guarantee employment. In the one case the politicians are struggling to increase production, whereas in the other they are trying to market it. While the zero or low prices of the administrative system create weak consumers and an insatiable demand, the high prices of the market economy make consumers so fastidious that political measures are needed to bring them to their knees. The pressure to guarantee employment is so strong in the West that governments aspiring to stimulate demand must resort to greater public financing of so-called merit goods, the merits of which are sometimes appreciated more by the leaders and the employed than by those whose taxes pay the bill. In the East the demand for goods and services is instead so great and the supply so uneven that politicians must continually worry about the efficiency of production. While the politicians of industrialised Western countries attempt to defend the interest of threatened producer groups in an economic system where the consumers have the advantage, the Soviet leaders work to advance the interest of the consumers in a society of sluggish and obstinate producers.

The paradoxical conclusion then is that it is not the strongest members of society who dominate in politics. The strongest have other instruments at their disposal; they are capable of looking after their interests in the economic system. Nor can the weakest get their problems on to the political agenda, for they cannot put enough force into their desires or forge them into effective demands. Politics is instead an arena for the semi-strong and the semi-weak, those who are not powerful enough to assert themselves in everyday economic and social transactions but have access to the commanding heights of the political system. It is in this intermediate group that the political agenda is formed.

# Notes

CHAPTER 1

1 Herbert J. Spiro, 'Comparative Politics: A Comprehensive Approach', *American Political Science Review*, LVI (1962) p. 577.
2 Donald M. Johnson, *Psychology of Thought and Judgement* (New York: Harper & Brothers, 1955) p. 63.
3 Spiro, *loc. cit.*
4 For a different opinion, see Karl Popper, *Unended Quest: An Intellectual Autobiography* (Glasgow: Fontana/Collins, 1976) pp. 138–40.
5 Peter Bachrach and Morton S. Baratz, *Power and Poverty: Theory and Practice* (New York: Oxford University Press, 1970).
6 Matthew A. Crenson, *The Un-politics of Air Pollution: A Study of Non-Decisionmaking in the Cities* (Baltimore and London: The Johns Hopkins Press, 1971).
7 Cynthia H. Enloe, *The Politics of Pollution in a Comparative Perspective: Ecology and Power in Four Nations* (New York: David McKay Company, Inc., 1975).
8 Roger W. Cobb and Charles D. Elder, *Participation in American Politics: The Dynamics of Agenda-Building* (Boston: Allyn & Bacon, Inc., 1972).
9 A short study of the agenda in the mass media has been made by G. Ray Funkhouser, 'The Issues of the Sixties: An Exploratory Study in the Dynamics of Public Opinion', *Public Opinion Quarterly*, XXXVII (1973) pp. 62–75.
10 Albert D. Biderman, 'Social Indicators and Goals' in Raymond A. Bauer (ed.), *Social Indicators* (Cambridge, Mass.: The MIT Press, 1966) pp. 68–153; President's Commission on National Goals, *Goals for Americans* (Englewood Cliffs, N.J.: Prentice-Hall, Inc., 1960).
11 Carl Böhret, *Entscheidungshilfen für die Regierung: Modelle, Instrumente, Probleme* (Opladen: Westdeutscher Verlag, 1970) pp. 90–9.
12 Sergius Yakobson and Harold D. Lasswell, 'Trend: May Day Slogans in Soviet Russia, 1918–1943', in Harold D. Lasswell, Nathan Leites and Associates, *Language of Politics: Studies in Quantitative Semantics* (Cambridge, Mass.: The MIT Press, 1968 (1949)) pp. 233–97. The graph is at p. 244.
13 For references to these studies, see Frederic L. Pryor, *Public Expenditures in Communist and Capitalist Nations* (London: Allen & Unwin, 1968) pp. 497–531; Thomas R. Dye: 'Political Science and Public Policy: Challenge to a Discipline', in Robert N. Spadaro *et al.*, *The Policy Vacuum* (Lexington, Mass.: Lexington Books, 1975) pp. 31–60; Daniel Tarschys, 'The Growth

of Public Expenditures: Nine Modes of Explanation', *Scandinavian Political Studies*, x (1975) 9–31.

14 R. W. Crowley, 'Long Swings in the Role of Government: An Analysis of Wars and Government Expenditures in Western Europe since the Eleventh Century', *Public Finance/Finances Publiques*, IV (1971) 25–43.

15 Richard Rose, 'On the Priorities of Government: A Developmental Analysis of Public Policies', *European Journal of Political Research*, IV (1976).

16 Paul A. Baran, *The Political Economy of Growth* (New York: Marzani & Munsell, 1962); A. F. K. Organski, *The Stages of Political Development* (New York: Knopf, 1966); W. W. Rostow, *Politics and the Stages of Growth* (London: Cambridge University Press, 1971).

CHAPTER 2

1 V. I. Lenin, *Sochineniya* (4 uppl) XXVII, pp. 77, 259.

2 Margaret Masterman, 'The Nature of a Paradigm', Imre Lakatos and Alan Musgrave (eds.), *Criticism and the Growth of Knowledge* (Cambridge: Cambridge University Press, 1970) pp. 59–89.

3 For a more detailed discussion of this question, see William Welch, *American Images of Soviet Foreign Policy* (New Haven and London: Yale University Press, 1970).

4 Leonard Schapiro, *Totalitarianism* (London: Macmillan, 1972), pp. 13–15.

5 Carl J. Friedrich and Zbigniew K. Brzezinski, *Totalitarian Dictatorship and Autocracy*, rev. ed. (New York: Fredrick A. Praeger, 1967).

6 For surveys, see Schapiro, *op. cit.*; Benjamin R. Barber, 'Conceptual Foundations of Totalitarianism'; Carl J. Friedrich, Michael Curtis and Hans Buchheim, *Totalitarian Rule: Its Nature and Characteristics* (Middletown, Conn: Wesleyan University Press 1972); Benjamin R. Barber (ed.), *Totalitarianism in Perspectives: Three Views*, (New York: Praeger Publishers, 1969) pp. 3–52.

7 For a critique of this viewpoint, see Jerry F. Hough, 'The Soviet System: Petrification or Pluralism', *Problems of Communism*, XXI: 2 (1972) pp. 25–45.

8 Nathan Leites, *The Operational Code of the Politburo* (Westport Conn.: Greenwood Press, 1972).

9 Allen Kassof, 'The Administered Society: Totalitarianism Without Terror', *World Politics*, XVI (1964) pp. 558–75.

10 Robert C. Tucker, 'Towards a Comparative Study of Movement-Regimes', *American Political Science Review*, LV (1961) p. 281–9.

11 Jerry F. Hough, *op. cit.*, 1972.

12 Franz Borkenau, *European Communism* (London: Hammersmith, 1953); id., 'Getting at the Facts Behind the Soviet Facade', *Commentary*, XVII (1954) pp. 393–400; Boris Nikolaevsky, *Power and the Soviet Elite* (New York: Praeger, 1965).

13 Myron Rush, 'The Khrushchev Succession Crisis', *World Politics*, XIV (1962) pp. 259–82; Thomas H. Rigby, 'Crypto-Politics', *Survey* (1964) pp. 183–94.

14 David Easton, *A Systems Analysis of Political Life* (New York, London and

Sydney: Wiley, 1965); Gabriel A. Almond and James S. Coleman (eds), *The Politics of the Developing Areas* (Princeton: Princeton University Press, 1960).

15 Michael P. Gehlen, *The Communist Party of the Soviet Union: A Functional Analysis* (Bloomington and London: Indiana University Press, 1969).

16 For references to Polish and Czech authors, see H. Gordon Skilling and Franklyn Griffiths, *Interest Groups in Soviet Politics* (Princeton: Princeton University Press, 1971), pp. 13–17.

17 The article in *World Politics*, xviii (1966), has also been published in Skilling and Griffiths, op. cit. Quoted passage, pp. 28f.

18 James H. Meisel, *The Myth of the Ruling Class: Gaetano Mosca and the Elite* (Ann Arbor: University of Michigan Press, 1958).

19 Ghita Ionescu, *Comparative Communist Politics* (London: Macmillan 1972).

20 Ibid., p. 23.

21 Quoted in D. S. Pugh, D. J. Hickson and C. R. Hinings, *Writers on Organizations* (Harmondsworth: Penguin, 1973) p. 22.

22 H. A. Simon, D. W. Smithburg and V. A. Thompson, *Public Administration* (New York: Knopf, 1950).

23 For example, 'A Behavioral Model of Rational Choice', *Quarterly Journal of Economics*, lxix (1955) pp. 99–118.

24 Anthony Downs, *Inside Bureaucracy* (Boston: Little, Brown, 1967); Aaron Wildavsky, *The Politics of the Budgetary Process* (Boston: Little, Brown, 1964); William A. Niskanen, Jr., *Bureaucracy and Representative Government* (Chicago and New York: Aldine, Atherton, 1971); Francis E. Rourke, *Bureaucracy, Politics, and Public Policy,* (Boston: Little, Brown, 1969); Graham T. Allison, *Essence of Decision: Explaining the Cuban Missile Crisis* (Boston: Little, Brown, 1971).

25 Leonard Merewitz and Stephen J. H. Sosnick, *The Budget's New Clothes: A Critique of Planning – Programming – Budgeting and Benefit-Cost Analysis* (Chicago: Markham Publishing Company, 1971); Robert A. Levine, *Public Planning: Failure and Redirection,* (New York: Basic Books, 1972); Ida R. Hoos, *System and Analysis in Public Policy: A Critique,* (Berkeley: University of California Press, 1972); Jean-Claude Thoenig, 'La rationalité', Michel Crozier *et al, Où va l'administration française?* (Paris: Les éditions d'organisation, 1974) pp. 141–62

26 C. Alphandéry *et al., Pour nationaliser l'Etat* (Paris: Editions du Seuil, 1968) p. 27.

27 Jean-Pierre Worms, 'La découverte du politique' in Michel Crozier *et al.,* op. cit., pp. 187–206, quoted passage, p. 197.

28 Harold Seidman, *Politics, Position, and Power: The Dynamics of Federal Organization* (New York: Oxford University Press, 1970) p. 20.

29 V. I. Lenin, *Selected Works,* ii (Moscow: Progress Publishers, 1967), pp. 397f.

30 Joseph S. Berliner, *Factory and Manager in the USSR* (Cambridge, Mass.: Harvard University Press, 1957); David Granick, *Management of the Industrial Firm in the USSR,* (New York: Columbia University Press, 1954); id., *The Red Executive: A Study of the Organization Man in Russian Industry* (Garden City, New York: Doubleday, 1961); John A. Armstrong, *The Soviet*

*Bureaucratic Elite: A Case Study of the Ukrainian Apparatus* (New York: Praeger, 1959).

31 Karl Deutsch, 'Cracks in the Monolith', in Carl J. Friedrich (ed.), *Totalitarianism* (Cambridge: Harvard University Press, 1954) p. 321.

32 Alfred G. Meyer, 'USSR, Incorporated', *Slavic Review* (1961) pp. 369–76; Alfred G. Meyer, *The Soviet Political System: An Interpretation* (New York: Random House, 1965), p. 3.

33 Ibid. (1965) pp. 467f.

34 Robert V. Daniels, 'Soviet Politics Since Khrushchev', John W. Strong (ed.). *The Soviet Union under Brezhnev and Kosygin* (New York: Van Nostrand Reinhold Co., 1971) pp. 22f.

35 E.g. David D. Cattell, *Leningrad: A Case Study of Soviet Urban Government* (New York: Praeger, 1968); Philip D. Stewart, *Political Power in the Soviet Union: A Study of Decision-Making in Stalingrad* (Indianapolis: Bobbs-Merrill, 1968).

36 Philip D. Stewart, 'Diversity and Adaptation in Soviet Political Culture: The Attitudes of the Soviet Political Elite', Paper at the First International Slavic Conference, Banff, 1974; William Taubman, *Governing Soviet Cities: Bureaucratic Politics and Urban Development in the USSR* (New York: Praeger, 1973).

37 Jerry F. Hough, 'The Soviet System: Petrification or Pluralism?', *Problems of Communism* (1972) pp. 25–45, especially p. 29; id', 'The Bureaucratic Model and the Nature of the Soviet System', *Journal of Comparative Administration* (1973) pp. 134–68.

38 Gaetano Mosca, *The Ruling Class* (New York: McGraw-Hill Book Company, 1939) ch. xv.

39 For a more detailed treatment of this point, see Daniel Tarschys and Maud Eduards, *Petita: Hur svenska myndigheter argumenterar för högre anslag* (Uddevalla: Liber, 1975) chs 1, 2, 5, and the studies listed there.

40 For a definition of 'bureau', see Downs, op. cit., pp. 24f.

CHAPTER 3

1 P. J. Stone *et al.*, *The General Inquirer: A Computer Approach to Content Analysis* (Cambridge, Mass.: The MIT Press, 1966).

2 For a discussion of Soviet press ideology, see, for example, Afanas'ev, *Sotsial'naya informatsiya i upravlenie obshestvom*, (Moskva, 1975); E. I. Bugaev *et al.*, *Kommunisticheskaya propaganda: voprosy teorii i metodiki* (Moskva, 1974); *O partiinoi i sovetskoi pechati: sbornik dokumentov* (Moskva, 1957).

3 *Pechat' SSSR v 1970 godu* (Moskva, 1971) p. 67.

4 On Party control of the Soviet press, see Alex Inkeles, *Public Opinion in Soviet Russia: A Study in Mass Persuasion* (Cambridge, Mass: Harvard University Press, 1950); Bruno Kalnins, *Der sowjetische Propagandastaat: Das System und die Mittel der Massenbeeinflussung in der Sowjetunion* (Stockholm: Tiden, 1956); A. Gaev, 'Soviet Press Control', *Bulletin of the Institute for the Study of the History and Culture of the USSR* (München), vol. II, no. 5 (May 1955); *The Press in Authoritarian Countries* (International

Press Institute, Zurich, 1959); Mark Hopkins, *Mass Media in the Soviet Union* (New York: Pegasus, 1970); Gayle Durham Hollander, *Soviet Political Indoctrination: Developments in Mass Media and Propaganda Since Stalin* (New York: Praeger, 1972).
Pertinent Soviet sources include V. Dvorianov and G. Siunkov, *Partijnyi Komitet i gazeta* (Sverdlovsk, 1973); V. I. Vlasov *et al.* (ed.), *Gazeta – organ partijnogo komiteta* (Moskva 1972); V. Kuzin, *Gazeta – organ partiinogo komiteta* (Leningrad 1971); D. S. Emel'janov, *Partijnoe rukovodstvo pechat' yu v sovremennykh usloviyakh (1966–1971 gg)*, Avtoref. diss. kand. ist. nauk (Moskva 1973); V. A. Ovchinnikov, *Rol'pechati v upravlenii sostsia'nymi protsessami* Avtoref. diss. kand. fil. nauk (Sverdlovsk, 1971); V. P. Smirnov, *Leninskie printsipy partiinogo rukovodstva pechat'yu i ikh osushchestvlenie na sovremennom etape*, Avtoref. diss. kand. ist. nauk (Moskva, 1971); T. I. Kharlamova, *Partiinoe rukovodstvo-glavnyi faktor povysheniya effektivnosti pechati (1964–1969 gg)* Avtoref. diss. kand. ist. nauk. (Moskva, 1970); On cadre policy, cf B. D. Levin and M. N. Perfil'ev, *Kadry apparata upravleniya SSSR* (Leningrad 1970).

5 Rosemarie Rogers, 'Soviet Mass Media in the Sixties: Patterns of Access and Consumption', *Journal of Broadcasting,* 1971 : 2, pp. 127–46, esp. p. 131.

6 Hollander, op. cit., pp. 48f. Hollander's source may be Leonid Vladimirov, who in *Rossiya bez prikras i umolchenii* (Frankfurt a. M.: Posev, 1968) pp. 219–61, presents a similar picture of Soviet press control.

7 According to G. M. Kondratenko, division head and member of *Pravda*'s editorial board, 26 June 1975.

8 Dvoryanov and Siunkov, op. cit., p. 41.

9 A. Kotlyar, 'Newspapers in the USSR: Recollections and Observations of a Soviet Journalist', *Research Program on the USSR* (New York) no. 71 (1955) pp. 66f.

10 Ark. Gaev, 'Kak delaetsya 'Pravda'?', *Vestnik instituta po izucheniyu istorii i kul'tury SSSR* (München) 1953 : 4, s. 96. Cf. id., 'Pravda and the Soviet Press', *Studies on the Soviet Union* (München) 1957 : 1.

11 Gaev (1953), op. cit., Hollander, op. cit., Vladimirov, op. cit. These and Kondratenko are also the main sources for the following description of work at *Pravda*.

12 Kondratenko, 26 June 1975.

13 A Soviet journalist in exile tells of a case where a night editor on a Soviet paper was dismissed and demoted from Party member to candidate for leaving out a comma in a Lenin quotation. A. Finn, 'Experiences of a Soviet Journalist', *Research Program on the USSR* (New York) no. 66 (1954) pp. 17f.

14 N. Bogdanov and B. Vyazemskii, *Spravochnik zhurnalista* (Leningrad, 1961) p. 79; B. Evladov, A. Pokrovskii and V. Shliapentokh, 'Chetyre tysiachi i odno interviu', *Zhurnalist* 1969 : 10, report that *Pravda* receives over 1000 letters daily. Kondratenko estimates the total number of letters received in 1974 to be 460,000. On *Pravda*'s own efforts to stimulate reader initiative, see Gaev (1963), op. cit.

15 Dvorianov and Siunkov, op. cit., p. 61.

16 V. T. Davydchenkov, *Nekotorye problemy sotsiologicheskogo issledovaniya kanalov svyazi*, Avtoref. diss. kand. fil. nauk (Moskva, 1971), p. 21.

17 Ibid., p. 24. Cf. also E. I. Pronin, *Sredstva i metody vozdeistviya gazety na formirovanie obshestvennogo mneniya*, Avtoref. diss. kand. fil. nauk (Moscow, 1968). Attempts to extract politically relevant information from letters to the editor are an old tradition in the Soviet Union. Lenin once wrote a letter to the editor of *Bednota*, V. A. Karpinskii, requesting regular reports on (1) the average number of letters received, (2) the mood of the people, and (3) the most important questions of the day. V. I. Lenin, *Polnoe sobranie sochinenii*, vol. LIV, pp. 143f. Regularly recurring recommendations urging that letters be given better consideration, however, suggest that this reporting has not been conducted methodically, especially in the local and regional press.

18 On the editing of *Pravda's* foreign news page, see S.P. Glushko, 'Nekotorye osobennosti informatsionnoi sluzhby v "Pravda". Mezhdunarodnaya informatsionnaja polosa', *Vestnik Moskovskogo Universiteta*, Seriya XI (Zhurnalistika), 1973: 4, pp. 20–9.

19 Kondratenko, 26 June 1975.

20 A. Finn, loc. cit.

21 Ju. A. Boldyrev, *Rukovodstvo TsK VKP (b) Severo-Kavkazskoi kraevoi partorganizatsiei v gody sozdaniia fundamenta sotsializma v SSSR (1926–1932 gg)*, Avtoref. diss. kand. ist. nauk (Rostov-na-Donu, 1974), p. 20.

22 M. Argynbaev, *"Pravda" i poslevoennyi Kazakhstan (1945–1958 gg)*, (Alma-Ata, 1972), pp. 33f.

23 *Pechat' SSSR v. 1970 godu*, p. xix, says 9,000,000. In June 1975 it was claimed at *Pravda's* editorial office that circulation had reached 10,400,000 copies. On the advance of the central press at the expense of the republican, regional, and local press (from 23 per cent in 1940 to 46 per cent in 1967), see Rogers, op. cit., p. 132

24 Bogdanov and Vyazemskii, loc. cit.

25 Hollander, op. cit., pp. 59ff.

26 V. Piramidin, 'Na osnove tochnykh znanii' *Rasprostranenie pechati* 1967 : 1, pp. 13–15.

27 Hollander, loc. cit.

28 Piramidin, op. cit.

29 Hollander, loc. cit.

30 Rosemarie Rogers, 'Education and Political Involvement in USSR Elite Newspaper Reading', *Journalism Quarterly* XXXXVII (1970) pp. 735–45; id., *How Russians Read Their Press: Patterns of Selection in Pravda and Izvestija* (Cambridge, Mass.: MIT Center for International Studies, 1968) p. 33.

31 See e.g. G. T. Zhuravlev, *Sotsial'naya informatsiya i upravlenie ideologicheskim protsessom* (Moscow, 1973).

32 Ovchinnikov, op. cit., p. 15f.

33 M. Kitaeff, 'Communist Party Officials: A Group of Portraits', *Research Program on the USSR* (New York) no. 67 (1954) pp. 77ff.

34 Cf. Wolfgang Leonhard, *The Kremlin Since Stalin* (New York: Praeger, 1962) pp. 19ff.; id., *Kreml Ohne Stalin* (Cologne: Verlag Für Politik Und Wirtschaft, 1959) pp. 41ff.

35 A. Iu. Gorcheva, *Sovremennaya gazetnaya polemika kak forma partiinoi propagandy*, Avtoref. diss. kand. fil. nauk (Moscow, 1974). Chapter 2, which is entitled 'The Control of Polemics and Polemics as a Means of Control',

describes the 'polemics cycle' as consisting of four stages: establishment of goals, development of a plan of the debate, implementation, goal-fulfilment. The author reports that the much noticed Soviet press debate between 'physicists' and 'lyricists' was initiated for a pedagogical purpose. On how press debates can none the less be used for articulating interests, see Jerry F. Hough, 'The Mass Media and the Policy Making Process in the Soviet Union and the United States: Implications for Comparative Studies', paper at the 1967 Annual Meeting of APSA, section II.

36 Leonhard, op. cit. p. 44.
37 *O partiinoi i sovetskoi pechati. Sbornik dokumentov* (Moscow, 1954) p. 255.
38 *Spravdchnik zhurnalista*, op. cit., p. 235.
39 N. Klinkov, 'Peredovye na urovne', *Sovetskaya Pechat'* 1958 : 7.
40 M. N. Gurenkov, 'Flag nomera dolzhen byt' yarkim', P. Ya Khavin (ed.), *Problemy gazetnykh zhanrov* (Leningrad, 1972)
41 S. Balbekov, 'Napishite peredovuyu o reforme!', *Zhurnalist* 1967; 10, pp. 24–6.
42 Chapter "Statja" in M. S. Cherepakhov, ed., *Zhanry sovetskoi gazety* (Moscow, 1959).
43 Ibid., pp. 91f.
44 Ibid., p. 98.
45 According to a Soviet survey conducted by sociologists at the Siberian division of the Soviet Academy of Sciences, 68 per cent of *Pravda*'s readers thought that the paper had improved during the past two years (1966–8), while 2 per cent considered that it had become worse, 9 per cent that quality was unchanged, and 23 per cent refused to answer. Hollander, op. cit., p. 64; cf. Evladov *et al.*, op. cit.
46 Kondratenko, 26 June 1975.
47 Philip D. Stewart, 'Diversity and Adaptation in Soviet Political Culture: The Attitudes of the Soviet Political Elite', paper at the First International Slavic Conference, Banff, 1974.
48 Zbigniew Brzezinski, *Between Two Ages: America's Role in the Technetronic Era* (New York: Viking Press, 1970) p. 153.
49 Stewart, op. cit., p. 35.
50 Heinrich Lausberg, *Handbuch der literarischen Rhetorik* (München: Max Heuber Verlag, 1960).
51 Albert D. Biderman, 'Social Indicators and Goals', Raymond A. Bauer (ed.), *Social Indicators* (Cambridge, Mass.: The MIT Press, 1966) p. 95.
52 Ghita Ionescu, *Comparative Communist Politics* (London: Macmillan, 1972), pp. 18ff. The other view is expressed in Milton G. Lodge, *Soviet Elite Attitudes Since Stalin* (Columbus, Ohio: Charles E. Merrill Co., 1969).
53 On the notions of political investment and political consumption, cf. Warren F. Ilchman and Norman Thomas Uphoff, *The Political Economy of Change* (Berkeley and Los Angeles: University of California Press, 1969) p. 199ff.
54 Merle Fainsod, *Smolensk Under Soviet Rule* (New York: Vintage Books, 1963).
55 A. A. Beljakov and I. A. Shvets, *Partiinaya informatisiya* (Moscow, 1970). Cf. Erik P. Hoffmann, 'Soviet Metapolicy: Information-Processing in the Communist Party of of the Soviet Union', *Journal of Comparative Administration*, vol. V, 1973, pp. 200—32.

56 Cf. M. A. Varshavchik, *Istochnikovedenie istorii KPSS* (Moscow, 1973).
57 Robert H. McNeal's collection is valuable, even if it is not quite complete. *Guide of the Decisions of the Communist Party of the Soviet Union 1917–1967* (Toronto: University of Toronto Press, 1972).
58 Klas Törnudd, *Soviet Attitudes Towards Non-Military Regional Cooperation* (Helsingfors: Societas Scientiarum Fennica, 1963) pp. 8–13.
59 Cf. Rogers, 'Soviet Mass Media . . .' in Kotlyar, op. cit.
60 Sergius Yakobson and Harold Lasswell, 'May Day Slogans in Soviet Russia', in Harold D. Lasswell, Nathan Leites *et al.*, *Language of Politics* (Cambridge, Mass.: The MIT Press, 1965).
61 Cf. Bertram M. Gross, 'Activating National Plans', Bertram M. Gross (ed.), *Action under Planning: The Guidance of Economic Development* (New York: McGraw-Hill, 1967).
62 Leonhard, loc. cit.
63 For a short résumé, cf. Ionescu op. cit. and Daniel Bell, 'Ten Theories in Search of Reality: The Prediction of Soviet Behavior', in Vernon V. Aspaturian (ed.), *Process and Power in Soviet Foreign Policy*, (Boston: Little, Brown, 1971).
64 Cf. Leonhard, loc. cit.; Franz Borkenau, 'Getting at the Facts Behind the Soviet Facade', *Commentary*, vol. xvii, 1954, pp. 393–400; William E. Griffith, 'Communist Esoteric Communications: Explication de Texte', *Handbook of Communication* (Chicago: Rand McNally College Publishing, 1973), pp. 512–20.
65 Charles Gati, 'Soviet Elite Perception of International Regions: A Research Note', in Roger Kane (ed.), *The Behavioral Revolution and Communist Studies* (New York: The Free Press, 1971); Lodge, op. cit.; Alfred Evans, Jr., 'Trends in Soviet Secondary School Histories of the USSR', *Soviet Studies* vol. xxviii (1976) pp. 224–43.
66 For a general introduction, see Kenneth Janda, *Information Retrieval: Applications to Political Science* (Indianapolis: Bobbs-Merrill, 1968) especially ch. 7. Cf. also Howard P. Iker and Norman I. Harway, 'A Computer System Approach Toward the Recognition and Analysis of Content', in George Gerbner *et al.* (ed.), *The Analysis of Communication Content: Development in Scientific Theories and Computer Techniques* (New York: Wiley, 1969), the point of departure of which is that the analytical categories are not known before processing of the text: 'The key question we have been exploring for almost six years . . . is whether there exists a method for content analysis that will allow the user to discover what his data are about without having to furnish a priori categorizations within which to classify these data.'
67. References to editorials are given as five-figure numbers, where the first two figures denote the year and the following three indicate the number of the issue, e.g. 50.312.

CHAPTER 4

1 On the consequences of the war, see *Soyuz Sovetskikh Sotsialisticheskikh Respublik 1917–1967* (Moscow, 1967) p. 211, and the article 'SSSR' in

198     *The Soviet Political Agenda*

*Bolshaya Sovetskaya Entsiklopediya* (Moscow, 1957).

Other sources used here and in the next chapter include the statistical year books, *Ezhegodnik Bolshoi Sovetskoi Entsiklopedii* (various years), *Pravda, Kommunist* and Ellen Mickiewicz, *Handbook of Soviet Social Science Data* (Toronto: The Free Press, 1973); Roger A. Clarke, *Soviet Economic Facts 1917–1970*, (London: Macmillan, 1972); the description of 1950 is also based on Isaac Deutscher, *Stalin: A Political Biography*, 2nd ed. (Oxford: Oxford University Press, 1967) ch. xv.

2  G. Warren Nutter, *Growth of the Industrial Production in the Soviet Union* (Princeton: Princeton University Press, 1962) pp. 213–16.

3  Robert Conquest, *The Great Terror*, 2nd ed., (Harmondsworth: Penguin, 1971) Appendix A.

4  'Pretvorim v zhizn' resheniya iiul'skogo plenuma Tsk KPSS', *Kommunist* 1960:11, pp. 3–10, esp. p. 3.

CHAPTER 5

1  Mickiewicz, op. cit. (Chapter 5, n.1 above), p. 94.

2. Ibid., p. 120.

3  J. Wilczynski, *Technology in Comecon: Acceleration of Technological Progress through Economic Planning and the Market* (London: Macmillan, 1974), pp. 196–99.

4  Janet Chapman, *Real Wages in Russia since 1928* (Cambridge, Mass: Harvard University Press, 1963) p. 166.

5  Reckoned according to Clarke, op. cit. (Chapter 4, n. 1 above), pp. 4, 82.

6  Reckoned according to ibid., p. 9.

7  The Soviet terms are nitron and lavsan. On Soviet textile terminology, see Imogene Erro, 'Textiles, Clothing, Footwear, and Selected Consumer Durables in the Soviet Union and the United States: A Comparison of Quantity and Quality', Harry G. Schaffer (ed.), *The Soviet Economy: A Collection of Western and Soviet Views* (London: Methuen, 1964) pp. 261–70.

8  Holland Hunter, *Soviet Transport Experience: Its Lessons for Other Countries* (Washington: The Brookings Institution, 1968).

9  Karl-Eugen Wädekin, *The Private Sector in Soviet Agriculture* (Berkeley: University of California Press, 1973).

10  Ibid., pp. 156ff.

11  Werner G. Hahn, *The Politics of Soviet Agriculture, 1960–1970* (Baltimore: Johns Hopkins University Press, 1972); Sidney I. Ploss, *Conflict and Decision-Making in Soviet Russia: A Case Study of Agricultural Policy* (Princeton: Princeton University Press, 1965).

12  Current prices. The price level sank below that of the first half of the 1950s and has since been fairly stable, according to official statistics. On the hidden inflation that may still have occurred, see Getrud Schroeder, 'An Appraisal of Soviet Wage and Income Statistics', in Vladimir G. Treml and John P. Hardt (eds.), *Soviet Economic Statistics* (Durham, North Carolina: Duke University Press, 1972).

13 *Narodnoe Khoziaistvo SSSR v 1970 g. Statisticheskii Ezhegodnik* (Moscow, 1971) p. 634.
14 *Obsluzhivanie* also covers the maintenance of agricultural machines and the like.
15 *Pechat' SSSR v 1970 godu* (Moscow, 1971) pp. 65f.
16 Mickiewicz, op. cit., p. 183. Cf. Section 3.1.1 above.

CHAPTER 6

1 Robert N. Taaffe and Robert C. Kingsbury, *An Atlas of Soviet Affairs* (London: Methuen, 1965) p. 28.
2 With the exception of the Leningrad area, also included in the GOELRO plan. Cf. *Atlas razvitiya khozyaistva i kul' tury SSSR*, p. 20.
3 Peter Frank, 'Constructing a Classified Ranking of CPSU Provincial Committees', *British Journal of Political Science*, 4 (1974) pp. 217—30.
4 Mary McAuley, 'The Hunting of the Hierarchy: RSFSR Obkom First Secretaries and the Central Committee', *Soviet Studies*, xxvi (1974) pp. 473—501.
5 Frank, loc. cit.
6 Jan-Åke Dellenbrandt, 'Massmedias regionala utbredning i Sovjetunionen', *Uppsats vid symposiet Massmedia i Sovjetunionen*, Avdelningen för öststatskunskap vid Uppsala universitet, 26 March 1976; *Narodnoe Khozyaistvo SSSR v 1970 godu* (Moscow, 1971) p. 649.

CHAPTER 7

1 Cf. Hough, op. cit. (1969) p. 2.

CHAPTER 8

1 Douglas McGregor, *The Human Side of Enterprise* (New York: McGraw-Hill, 1960) pp. 33—57.
2 Cf. Chapter 2, note 17.
3 Joseph A. Schumpeter, *Capitalism, Socialism, and Democracy*, (London: Allen & Unwin, 1950 (first published 1943)) pp. 269—83; Anthony Downs, *An Economic Theory of Democracy* (New York: Harper & Row, 1957).
4 Nove, op. cit. (1969) p. 367.
5 David McClelland, *The Achieving Society* (Princeton: Princeton University Press, 1961).
6 The notion of 'solution capacity' ('Lösungskapazität') is borrowed from modern West German organisation research. Cf. Fritz W. Scharpf, *Planung als politischer Prozess: Aufsätze zur Theorie der planenden Demokratie* (Frankfurt am Main: Suhrkamp, 1973).
7 Tarschys, op. cit. (1972) pp. 122—5, 216.

8 Cf. Richard Rose, 'Overloaded Government: The Problem Outlined', *European Studies Newsletter*, vol. v, 1975 : 3, pp. 13–18; Anthony King (ed.), *Why is Britain Becoming Harder to Govern?* (London: BBC, 1976).

9 Cf. Robert C. Stuart, *The Collective Farm in Soviet Agriculture* (Lexington, Mass.: Lexington Books, 1972) pp. 115–28.

10 J. S. Berliner, *Factory and Manager in the USSR* (Cambridge, Mass.: Harvard University Press, 1957) s. 210f., quoting Abram Bergson, *The Economics of Soviet Planning* (New Haven: Yale University Press, 1964) pp. 152f.

11 Alec Nove, *The Soviet Economy: An Introduction*, 2nd ed. (London: Allen & Unwin, 1965) pp. 210f.

12 Aaron Wildavsky, *Budgeting: A Comparative Theory of the Budgeting Process* (Boston: Little, Brown, 1975) pp. 144f.; Naomi Caiden and Aaron Wildavsky, *Planning and Budgeting in Poor Countries* (New York: Wiley, 1974) pp. 72–8.

13 Bertram M. Gross (ed.), *Action Under Planning: The Guidance of Economic Development* (New York: McGraw-Hill, 1967) pp. 186–232.

# Bibliography

1  SOVIET BOOKS

Afanas'ev, V. G., *Sotsial'naya informatsiya i upravlenie obshestvom* (Moskva, 1975).
Argynbaev, M., *"Pravda" i poslevoennyi Kazakhstan (1945–1958)* (Alma – Ata, 1972).
*Atlas razvitiya khozyaistva i kul'tury SSSR* (Moskva, 1967).
Beljakov, A. A., and Shvets, I. A., *Partiinaya informatsiya* (Moskva, 1970).
Bogdanov, N., and Vyazemskij, B., *Spravochnik zhurnalista* (Leningrad, 1961).
Boldyrev, Ju. A., *Rukovodstvo TsVKP (b) Severo-Kavkazskoi kraevoi partorganizatsiei v gody sozdaniya fundamenta sotsializma v SSSR (1926–1932 gg)*, Avtoref. diss. kand. ist. nauk. (Rostov-na-Donu, 1974).
*Bol' shaya Sovetskaya Entsiklopediya* (Moskva, 1949–1958, 1969–1975).
Bugaev, E. I., *et al.*, *Kommunisticheskaya propaganda: voprosy teorii i metodiki* (Moskva, 1974).
Cherepakhov, M. S. (ed.), *Zhanry sovetskoi gazety* (Moskva, 1959).
Davydchenkov, V. T., *Nekotorye problemy sotsiologicheskogo issledovaniya kanalov svyazi*, Avtoref. diss. kand, fil. nauk. (Moskva, (1971).
Dvoriakov, V., and Siunkov, G., *Partiinyi komitet i gazeta* (Sverdlovsk, 1973).
Emel'janov, D. S., *Partiinoe rukovodstvo pechat' yu v sovremennykh usloviyakh (1966–1971 gg)*, Avtoref. diss. kand. ist. nauk. (Moskva, 1973).
*Ezhegodnik Bol'shoi Sovetskoi Entsiklopedii* (Moskva, 1957–75).
Gorcheva, A. Ju., *Sovremennaya gazetnaya polemika kak forma partiinoi propagandy*, Avtoref. diss. kand. fil. nauk. (Moskva, 1974).
Kharlamova, T. I., *Partiinoe rukovodstvo – glavnyi faktor povysheniya effektivnosti pechati (1964–1969 gg)*, Avtoref. diss. kand. ist. nauk. (Moskva, 1970).
Kuzin, V., *Gazeta – organ partiinogo komiteta* (Leningrad, 1971).
Lenin, V. I., *Polnoe sobranie sochinenii* (Moskva, 1958–65).
Lenin, V. I., *Selected Works* (Moskva, 1967).
Levin, B. D., and Perfil'ev, M. N., *Kadry apparata upravleniya SSSR* (Leningrad, 1970).

*Narodnoe Khozjajstvo SSSR v 1960 g. Statisticheskii Ezhegodnik* (Moskva, 1961).

*Narodnoe Khozjajstvo SSSR v 1970 g. Statisticheskii Ezhegodnik* (Moskva, 1971).

*O partiinoi i sovetskoi pechati: sbornik dokumentov* (Moskva, 1954).

Ovchinnikov, V. A., *Rol' pechati v upravlenii sotsialinymi protsessami*, Avtoref. diss. kand. fil. nauk. (Sverdlovsk, 1971).

*Pechat' SSSR v 1970 godu* (Moskva, 1971).

Pronin, E. I., *Sredstva i metody vozdeistviya gazet na formirovanie obshchestvennogo sozdaniya* Avtoref. diss. kand. fil. nauk. (Moskva, 1968).

Smirnov, V. P., *Leninskie printsipy partiinogo rukovodstva pechat' yu i ikh osushchestvlenie na sovremennom etape*, Avtoref. diss. kand. ist. nauk. (Moskva, 1971).

*Soyuz Sovetskikh Sotsialisticheskikh Respublik 1917–1967* (Moskva, 1967).

Varshavchik, M. A., *Istochnikovedenie istorii KPSS* (Moskva,1973).

Vladimirov, Leonid, *Rossiya bez prikras i umolchanii* (Frankfurt a. M.: Posev-Verlag, 1969).

Vlasov, V. I., *et al.* (ed.), *Gazeta – organ partiinogo komiteta* (Moskva, 1972).

Zhuravlev, G. T., *Sotsial'naya informatsiya i upravlenie ideologicheskim protsessom* (Moskva, 1973).

## 2 SOVIET ARTICLES

Balbekov, S., 'Napishite peredovuyu o reforme!', *Zhurnalist*, 1967 : 10, s. 24–6.

Evladov, B., Pokrovskii, A. and Shljapentokh, V., 'Chetyre tysyachi i odno intervyu', *Zhurnalist*, 1969 : 10, s. 34–7.

Glushko, S. P., 'Nekotorye osobennosti informatsionnoj sluzhby v "Pravda", Mezhdunarodnaya informatsionnaya polosa 21', *Vestnik Moskovskogo Universiteta,* Seriya xi, Zhurnalistika, 1973:4, s. 20–9.

Gurenkov, M. N., 'Flag nomera dolzhen byt' yarkim', P. Ja. Khavin (ed.), *Problemy gazetnykh zhanrov* (Leningrad, 1972).

Klinkov, N., 'Peredovye na urovne', *Sovetskaya pechat'*, 1958 : 7.

Piramidin, V., 'Na osnove tochnykh znanii', *Rasprostranenie pechati*, 1967 : 1, s. 13–15.

'Pretvorim v zhizn' resheniya iyul'skogo plenuma Ts KPSS', *Kommunist*, 1960: 11, s. 3–10.

## 3 WESTERN BOOKS

Adorno, Theodor W., *et al.*, *The Authoritarian Personality* (New York: Knopf, 1950).

Allison, Graham T., *Essence of Decision: Explaining the Cuban Missile Crisis* (Boston: Little, Brown, 1971).

Almond, Gabriel A., and Coleman, James S. (eds), *The Politics of the Developing Areas* (Princeton: Princeton University Press, 1960).

Alphandéry, C., *et al.*, *Pour nationaliser l' Etat* (Paris: Editions du Seuil, 1968).

Appleby, Paul, *Policy and Administration* (University, Ala.: University of Alabama Press, 1949).

Arendt, Hannah, *The Origins of Totalitarianism* (New York: Harcourt, Brace, 1951).

Armstrong, John A. *The Soviet Bureaucratic Elite: A Case Study of the Ukrainian Apparatus* (New York: Praeger,1959).

Avtorkhanov, Abdurakhman, *The Communist Party Apparatus* (Chicago: Henry Regnery Company, 1966).

Bachrach, Peter, and Baratz, Morton S., *Power and Poverty: Theory and Practice* (New York: Oxford University Press, 1970).

Baran, Paul A., *The Political Economy of Growth* (New York: Marzani and Munsell, 1962).

Barghoorn, Frederick C., *Politics in the USSR* (Boston: Little,Brown, 1966).

Bentley, Arthur F., *The Process of Government* (London: Unwin, 1908).

Bergson, Abram, *The Economics of Soviet Planning* (New Haven: Yale University Press, 1964).

Berliner, Joseph S., *Factory and Manager in the USSR* (Cambridge, Mass.: Harvard University Press, 1957).

Borkenau, Franz, *European Communism* (London: Hammersmith, 1953).

Brown, A. H., *Soviet Politics and Political Science* (London: Macmillan, 1974).

Brzezinski, Zbigniew, *Between Two Ages: America's Role in the Technetronic Era* (New York: Viking Press, 1970)

Brzezinski, Zbigniew K., and Huntington, Samuel P., *Political Power USA/USSR* (New York: Viking Press, 1964).

Buchheim, Hans, *Totalitarian Rule: Its Nature and Characteristics* (Middletown, Conn.: Wesleyan University Press, 1972).

Burnham, James, *The Managerial Revolution* (New York: John Day, 1941).

Böhret, Carl, *Entscheidungshilfen für die Regierung: Modelle, Instrumente, Probleme* (Opladen: Westdeutscher Verlag, 1970).

Caiden, Naomi, and Wildavsky, Aaron, *Planning and Budgeting in Poor Countries* (New York: Wiley, 1974).

Cattell, David D., *Leningrad: A Case Study of Soviet Urban Government* (New York: Praeger, 1968).

Chapman, Janet, *Real Wages in Russia Since 1928* (Cambridge, Mass.: Harvard University Press, 1963).

Chenery, Hollis, and Syrquin, Moises, *Patterns of Developments, 1950–1970* (London: Oxford University Press, 1975).

Churchward, L. G., *The Soviet Intelligentsia: An Essay on the Social Structure and Roles of Soviet Intellectuals During the 1960's* (London and Boston: Routledge & Kegan Paul, 1973).

Clarke, Roger A., *Soviet Economic Facts 1917–1970* (London: Macmillan, 1972).

Cobb, Roger W., and Elder, Charles D., *Participation in American Politics: The Dynamics of Agenda-Building* (Boston: Allyn Bacon, 1972).

Conquest, Robert, *The Great Terror* (Harmondsworth: Penguin, 1971).

Conquest, Robert (ed.), *Industrial Workers in the USSR* (London: The Bodley Head, 1967).

Conquest, Robert (ed.), *The Politics of Ideas in the USSR* (London: The Bodley Head, 1967).

Crenson, Matthew A., *The Un-Politics of Air Pollution: A Study of Non-Decisionmaking in the Cities* (Baltimore: The Johns Hopkins Press, 1971).

Deutscher, Isaac, *Stalin: A Political Biography* (Oxford: Oxford University Press, 1967).

Douglas, MacGregor, *The Human Side of Enterprise* (New York: McGraw-Hill, 1960).

Downs, Anthony, *Inside Bureaucracy* (Boston: Little, Brown, 1967).

Drucker, Peter, *The End of Economic Man: A Study of the New Totalitarianism* (London: Heinemann, 1939).

Easton, David, *A Systems Analysis of Political Life* (New York: Wiley, 1965).

*Encyclopedia of the Social Sciences* (London: Macmillan, 1931–5).

Enloe, Cynthia H., *The Politics of Pollution in a Comparative Perspective: Ecology and Power in Four Nations* (New York: David McKay Company, 1975).

Fainsod, Merle, *Smolensk Under Soviet Rule* (New York: Vintage Books, 1963).

Friedrich, Carl J., and Brzezinski, Zbigniew K., *Totalitarian Dictatorship and Autocracy*, rev. ed. (New York: Praeger, 1967).

Gehlen, Michael P., *The Communist Party of the Soviet Union: A Functional Analysis* (Bloomington: Indiana University Press, 1969).

Gerber, George, *et al.*, *The Analysis of Communication Content: Developments in Scientific Theories and Computer Techniques* (New York: Wiley, 1969).

Granick, David, *Management of the Industrial Firm in the USSR* (New York: Columbia University Press, 1954).

Granick, David, *The Red Executive: A Study of the Organization Man in Russian Industry* (Garden City, N.Y.: Doubleday, 1961).

Granick, David, *Soviet Metal-Fabricating and Economic Development: Practice Versus Policy* (Madison: University of Wisconsin Press, 1967).

Grant, Nigel, *Soviet Education* (Baltimore: Penguin Books, 1972).

Gross, Bertram M. (ed.), *Action Under Planning: The Guidance of Economic Development* (New York: McGraw-Hill, 1967).

Hahn, Werner G., *The Politics of Soviet Agriculture, 1960–1970* (Baltimore: Johns Hopkins University Press, 1972).

Hammer, Darell P., *USSR: The Politics of Oligarchy* (Hinsdale, Ill.: The Dryden Press, 1974).

Hayek, Friedrich A., *The Road to Serfdom* (London: Routledge & Kegan Paul, 1944).

Hodgins, Jordan A., *Soviet Power: Energy Resources, Production and Potentials* (Englewood Cliffs, N.J.: Prentice-Hall, 1961).

Hollander, Durham G., *Soviet Political Indoctrination: Developments in Mass Media and Propaganda Since Stalin* (New York: Praeger, 1972).

Hoos, Ida R., *Systems and Analysis in Public Policy: A Critique* (Berkeley: University of California Press, 1972).

Hopkins, Mark, *Mass Media in the Soviet Union* (New York: Pegasus, 1970).

Hough, Jerry F., *The Soviet Prefects: The Local Party Organs in Industrial Decision-Making* (Cambridge, Mass.: Harvard University Press, 1969).

Hunter, Holland, *Soviet Transport Experience: Its Lessons for Other Countries* (Washington: The Brookings Institution, 1968).

Ilchman, Warren F., and Uphoff, Thomas N., *The Political Economy of Change* (Berkeley and Los Angeles: University of California Press, 1969).

Inkeles, Alex, *Public Opinion in Soviet Russia: A Study in Mass Persuasion* (Cambridge, Mass.: Harvard University Press, 1950).

Ionescu, Ghita, *Comparative Communist Politics* (London: Macmillan, 1972).

Janda, Kenneth, *Information Retrieval: Applications to Political Science.* (Indianapolis: Bobbs-Merrill, 1968).

Johnson, Chalmers (ed.), *Change in Communist Systems* (Stanford: Stanford University Press, 1970).

Johnson, Donald M., *Psychology of Thought and Judgment* (New York: Harper, 1955).

Kalnins, Bruno, *Der sowjetische Propagandastaat: Das System und die Mittel der Massenbeeinflussung in der Sowjetunion* (Stockholm: Tiden, 1956).

King, Anthony (ed.), *Why is Britain Becoming Harder to Govern?* (London: BBC, 1976).

Kornhauser, William, *The Politics of Mass Society* (Glencoe, Ill.: Free Press, 1969).

Laird, Roy D., and Laird, Betty A., *Soviet Communism and Agrarian Revolution* (Baltimore: Penguin Books, 1970).

Lausberg, Heinrich, *Handbuch der literarischen Rhetorik* (München: Max Hueber Verlag, 1960).

Leites, Nathan, *The Operational Code of the Politburo* (Westport, Conn.: Greenwood Press, 1972).

Leonhard, Wolfgang, *The Kremlin Since Stalin* (New York: Praeger, 1962).

Levine, Robert A., *Public Planning: Failure and Redirection* (New York: Basic Books, 1972).

Linden, Carl A., *Khrushchev and the Soviet Leadership 1957–1964* (Baltimore, Md.: The Johns Hopkins Press, 1966).

Lodge, Milton G., *Soviet Elite Attitudes Since Stalin* (Columbus, Ohio: Charles E. Merrill Co, 1969).

McClelland, David, *The Achieving Society* (Princeton: Princeton University Press, 1961).

McNeal, Robert H., *Guide to the Decisions of the Communist Party of the Soviet Union 1917–1967* (Toronto: University of Toronto Press, 1972).

Meisel, James H., *The Myth of the Ruling Class: Gaetano Mosca and the Elite* (Ann Arbor: University of Michigan Press, 1958).

Merewitz, Leonard and Sosnik, Stephen, J. H., *The Budget's New Clothes: A Critique of Planning-Programming-Budgeting and Benefit-Cost Analysis* (Chicago: Markham Publishing Company, 1971).

Meyer, Alfred G., *The Soviet Political System: An Interpretation* (New York: Random House, 1965).

Mickiewicz, Ellen, *Handbook of Soviet Social Science Data* (Toronto: The Free Press, 1973).

Miller, Margaret, *Rise of the Russian Consumer* (London: Institute of Economic Affairs, 1965).

Milosz, Czeslaw, *The Captive Mind* (New York: Knopf, 1953).

Moore, Barrington, *Terror and Progress USSR: Some Sources of Change and Stability in the Soviet Dictatorship* (Cambridge, Mass.: Harvard University Press, 1954).

Moorsten, Richard and Powell, Raymond P., *The Soviet Stock, 1928–1962* (Homewood, Ill.: Richard D. Irwin, 1966).

Mosca, Gaetano, *The Ruling Class* (New York: McGraw-Hill, 1939).

Nikolaevsky, Boris, *Power and the Soviet Elite* (New York: Praeger, 1965).

Niskanen, William A., *Bureaucracy and Representative Government* (Chicago and New York: Aldine, Atherton, 1971).

Nove, Alec, *The Soviet Economy: An Introduction* 2nd ed. (London: Allen & Unwin, 1965).

Nutter, G. Warren, *Growth of Industrial Production in the Soviet Union* (Princeton, N.J.: Princeton University Press, 1962).

Organski, A. F. K., *The Stages of Political Development* (New York: Knopf, 1966).

*Oxford Regional Economic Atlas: The USSR and Eastern Europe* (London: Oxford University Press, 1956).

Ploss, Sidney I. *Conflict and Decision-Making in Soviet Russia: A Case Study of Agricultural Policy* (Princeton: Princeton University Press, 1965).

Popper, Karl R., *The Open Society and Its Enemies* (Princeton: Princeton University Press, 1950).

Popper, Karl, *Unended Quest: An Intellectual Autobiography* (Glasgow: Fontana/Collins, 1976).

President's Commission on National Goals, *Goals for Americans* (Englewood Cliffs, N.J.: Prentice-Hall, 1960).

*The Press in Authoritarian Countries* (International Press Institute, Zurich, 1959).

Pryor, Frederic L., *Property and Industrial Organization in Communist and Capitalist Nations* (Bloomington and London: Indiana University Press, 1973).

Pryor, Frederic L., *Public Expenditures in Communist and Capitalist Nations* (London: Allen & Unwin, 1968).

Pugh, D. S., Hickson, D. J., and Hinings, C. R., *Writers on Organizations* (Harmondsworth: Penguin, 1973).

Reshetar, John S., *A Concise History of the Communist Party of the Soviet Union* (New York: Praeger, 1960).

Rogers, Rosemarie, *How Russians Read Their Press: Patterns of Selection in Pravda and Izvestiya* (Cambridge, Mass.: MIT Center for International Studies, 1968).

Roggemann, Herwig, *Die Staatsordnung der Sowjetunion* (Berlin: Berlin Verlag, 1971).

Rostow, W. W., *Politics and the Stages of Growth* (London: Cambridge University Press, 1971).

Rourke, Francis E., *Bureaucracy, Politics and Public Policy* (Boston: Little, Brown, 1969).

Schapiro, Leonard, *Totalitarianism* (London: Macmillan, 1972).

Scharpf, Fritz W., *Planung als politischer Prozess: Aufsätze zur Theorie der planenden Demokratie* (Frankfurt a. M.: Suhrkamp, 1973).

Schumpeter, Joseph A., *Capitalism, Socialism and Democracy* (London: Allen & Unwin, 1950 (1943)).

Seidman, Harold, *Politics, Position, and Power: The Dynamics of Federal Organization* (New York: Oxford University Press, 1970).

Shabad, Theodore, *Basic Industrial Resources of the USSR* (New York and London: Columbia University Press, 1969).

Simon, Herbert A., Smithburg, D. W., and Thompson, V. A., *Public Administration* (New York: Knopf, 1950).

Skilling, Gordon H., and Griffiths, Franklyn, *Interest Groups in Soviet*

*Politics* (Princeton: Princeton University Press, 1971).

Skotheim, Robert A., *Totalitarianism and American Social Thought* (New York and Chicago: Holt, Rinehart and Winston, 1971).

Spulber, Nicolas, *The Soviet Economy, Structure, Principles, Problems* (New York: W.W. Norton and Company, 1969).

Stewart, Philip D., *Political Power in the Soviet Union: A Study of Decision-Making in Stalingrad* (Indianapolis: Bobbs-Merrill, 1968).

Stuart, Robert C., *The Collective Farm in Soviet Agriculture* (Lexington, Mass.: Lexington Books, 1972).

Taaffe, Robert N., and Kingsbury, Robert C., *An Atlas of Soviet Affairs* (London: Methuen, 1965).

Talmon, J. P., *The Origins of Totalitarian Democracy* (New York: Praeger, 1960).

Tarschys, Daniel, *Beyond the State: The Future Polity in Classical and Soviet Marxism* (Uddevalla: Läromedelsförlagen, 1972).

Tarschys, Daniel, and Eduards, Maud, *Petita: Hur svenska myndig-heter argumenterar för högre anslag* (Uddevalla: Liber, 1975).

Taubman, William, *Governing Soviet Cities: Bureaucratic Politics and Urban Development in the USSR* (New York: Praeger, 1973).

Trotsky, Leon D., *The Revolution Betrayed. What is the Soviet Union and Where is It Going?* (London: Faber, 1937).

Truman, David B., *The Governmental Process: Political Interest and Public Opinion* (New York: Knopf, 1951).

Törnudd, Klas, *Soviet Attitudes Towards Non-Military Regional Cooperation* (Helsingfors: Societas Scientarium Fennica, 1963).

Ward, Benjamin N., *The Socialist Economy: A Study of Organizational Alternatives* (New York: Random House, 1967).

Welch, William, *American Images of Soviet Foreign Policy* (New Haven: Yale University Press, 1970).

Wilczynski, J., *Technology in Comecon: Acceleration of Technological Progress through Economic Planning and the Market* (London: Macmillan, 1974).

Wildavsky, Aaron, *Budgeting: A Comparative Theory of the Budgetary Process* (Boston: Little, Brown, 1975).

Wildavsky, Aaron, *The Politics of the Budgetary Process* (Boston: Little, Brown, 1964).

Wädekin, Karl–Eugen, *The Private Sector in Soviet Agriculture* (Berkeley: University of California Press, 1973).

4  WESTERN ARTICLES

Barber, Benjamin R., 'Conceptual Foundations of Totalitarianism', Carl J. Friedrich, Michael Curtis and Benjamin R. Barber, *Totalit-*

*arianism in Perspectives: Three Views* (New York: Praeger, 1969) pp. 3–52.

Bauer, Raymond A., and Gleicher, David B., 'Word-of-Mouth Communication in the Soviet Union', Lewis A. Dexter and David M. White (ed.), *People, Society, and Mass Communications* (London: The Free Press of Glencoe, 1964) pp. 413–28.

Bell, Daniel, 'Ten Theories in Search of Reality: The Prediction of Soviet Behavior', Vernon V. Aspaturian, *Process and Power in Soviet Foreign Policy* (Boston: Little, Brown, 1971) pp. 289–323.

Biderman, Albert D., 'Social Indicators and Goals', Raymond A. Bauer (ed.), *Social Indicators* (Cambridge, Mass.: The MIT Press, 1966) pp. 68–153.

Borkenau, Franz, 'Getting at the Facts Behind the Soviet Facade', *Commentary*, vol. xvii, 1954:4, pp. 393–400.

Crowley, R. W., 'Long Swings in the Role of Government: An Analysis of Wars and Government Expenditures in Western Europe since the Eleventh Century', *Public Finance/Finances Publiques*, vol. xxvi, 1971, pp. 25–43.

Daniels, Robert V., 'Soviet Politics Since Khrushchev', John W. Strong (ed.), *The Soviet Union under Brezhnev and Kosygin* (New York: Van Nostrand Reinhold Co., 1971) pp. 16–25.

Dellenbrant, Jan-Åke, 'Massmediernas regionala utbredning i Sovjetunionen', *Uppsats vid symposiet Massmedia i Sovjetunionen*, Avdelningen för öststatskunskap vid Uppsala universitet, 26 March 1976.

Deutsch, Karl W., 'Cracks in the Monolith: Possibilities and Patterns of Disintegration in Totalitarian Systems', Carl J. Friedrich (ed.), *Totalitarianism* (Cambridge; Mass.: Harvard University Press, 1954) pp. 308–33.

Dye, Thomas R., 'Political Science and Public Policy: Challenge to a Discipline', Robert N. Spadaro *et al.*, *The Policy Vacuum* (Lexington, Mass.: Lexington Books, 1975) pp. 31–60.

Erro, Imogene, 'Textiles, Clothing, Footwear, and Selected Consumer Durables in the Soviet Union and the United States: A Comparison of Quantity and Quality', Harry G. Schaffer (ed.) *The Soviet Economy: A Collection of Western and Soviet Views* (London: Methuen, 1964) pp. 261–70.

Finn, A., 'Experience of a Soviet Journalist', *Research Program on the USSR*, no. 66 (New York, 1954).

Frank, Peter, 'Constructing a Classified Ranking of CPSU Provincial Committees', *British Journal of Political Science*, vol. iv (1974) pp. 217–30.

Funkhouser, Ray G., 'The Issues of the Sixties: An Exploratory Study in the Dynamics of Public Opinion', *Public Opinion Quarterly*, vol. xxxvii (1973) pp. 62–75.

Gaev, A., 'Kak delaetsya Pravda?', *Vestnik Instituta po izucheniyu istorii i kul'tury SSSR* (München, No. 4, 1953) pp. 87–96.

Gaev, A., 'Pravda and the Soviet Press', *Studies on the Soviet Union* (Institute for the Study of the USSR, München) vol. I, 1957:1, pp. 86–94.

Gaev, A., 'Soviet Press Control', *Bulletin of the Institute for the Study of the History and Culture of the USSR* (München) vol. II, no. 5 (1955) pp. 3–12.

Gati, Charles, 'Soviet Elite Perception of International Regions: A Research Note', Roger E. Kanet (ed.), *The Behavioral Revolution and Communist Studies* (New York: The Free Press, 1971) pp. 281–99.

Griffith, William L., 'Communist Esoteric Communications: Explication de Texte', *Handbook of Communication* (Chicago: Rand McNally College Publishing, 1973) pp. 512–20.

Hoffman, Erik P., 'Soviet Metapolicy: Information-Processing in the Communist Party of the Soviet Union', *Journal of Comparative Administration*, vol. V (1973) pp. 200–32.

Hough, Jerry F., 'The Mass Media and the Policy-Making Process in the Soviet Union and the United States: Implications for Comparative Studies', paper at 1967 Annual Meeting of APSA.

Hough, Jerry F., 'The Soviet System: Petrification or Pluralism?', *Problems of Communism*, vol. XXI (1972:2) pp. 25–45.

Kassof, Allen, 'The Administered Society: Totalitarianism Without Terror', *World Politics*, vol. XVI (1964) pp. 558–75.

Kitaeff, M., 'Communist Party Officials: A Group of Portraits', *Research Program on the USSR*, no. 67 (New York, 1954).

Kotlyar, A., 'Newspapers in the USSR: Recollections and Observations of a Soviet Journalist', *Research Program on the USSR*, no. 71 (New York, 1955).

McAuley, Mary, 'The Hunting of the Hierarchy: RSFSR Obkom First Secretaries and the Central Committee', *Soviet Studies*, vol. XXVI (1974) pp. 473–501.

Masterman, Margaret, 'The Nature of a Paradigm', Imre Lakatos and Alan Musgrave, *Criticism and the Growth of Knowledge* (Cambridge: Cambridge University Press, 1970) pp. 59–89.

Meyer, Alfred G., 'USSR, Incorporated', *Slavic Review*, (1961) pp. 369–76.

Rigby, Thomas H., 'Crypto-Politics', *Survey*, no. 50 (1964) pp. 183–94.

Rogers, Rosemarie, 'Education and Political Involvement in USSR Elite Newspaper Reading', *Journalism Quarterly*, vol. XXXXVII (1970) pp. 735–45.

Rogers, Rosemarie, 'Soviet Mass Media in the Sixties: Patterns of Access and Consumption', *Journal of Broadcasting*, vol. XV (1971–2) pp. 127–46.

Rose, Richard, 'On the Priorities of Government: A Developmental

Analysis of Public Policies', *European Journal of Political Research*, vol. ɪᴠ (1976) pp. 247–89.

Rose, Richard, 'Overloaded Government: The Problem Outlined', *European Studies Newsletter*, vol. ᴠ (1975) pp. 13–18.

Rush, Myron, 'The Khrushchev Succession Crisis', *World Politics*, vol. xɪᴠ (1962) pp. 259–82.

Schroeder, Gertrude, 'An Appraisal of Soviet Wage and Income Statistics', Vladimir G. Treml and John P. Hardt (eds), *Soviet Economic Statistics* (Durham, North Carolina: Duke University Press, 1972) pp. 287–314.

Simon, Herbert A., 'A Behavioral Model of Rational Choice', *Quarterly Journal of Economics*, vol. ʟxɪx (1955) pp. 99–118.

Spiro, Herbert J., 'Comparative Politics: A Comprehensive Approach', *American Political Science Review*, vol. ᴠɪ (1962) pp. 577–95.

Stewart, Philip D., 'Diversity and Adaptation in Soviet Political Culture: The Attitudes of the Soviet Political Elite', paper at the First International Slavic Conference, Banff, 1974.

Tarschys, Daniel, 'The Growth of Public Expenditures: Nine Modes of Explanation', *Scandinavian Political Studies*, vol. x (1975) pp. 9–31.

Thoenig, Jean-Claude, 'La rationalité', Michel Crozier *et al.*, *Où va l'administration française?* (Paris: Les éditions d'organisation, 1974) pp. 141–62.

Tucker, Robert C., 'Towards a Comparative Study of Movement Regimes', *American Political Science Review*, vol. ʟᴠ (1961) pp. 281–9.

Worms, Jean-Pierre, 'La découverte du politique', Michel Crozier *et al.*, *Ou va l'administration française?* (Paris: Les éditions d'organisation, 1974) pp. 187–206.

Yakobson, Sergius, and Lasswell, Harold D., 'Trend: May Day Slogans in Soviet Russia, 1918–1934', Harold D. Lasswell, Nathan Leites and Associates, *Language of Politics: Studies in Quantitative Semantics* (Cambridge, Mass.: The MIT Press, 1968 (1949)) pp. 233–97.

# Index